Mothers, Mothering and Sex Work

Mothers, Mothering and Sex Work

EDITED BY

REBECCA BROMWICH AND MONIQUE MARIE DEJONG

DEMETER

DEMETER PRESS

Funded by the Government of Canada
Financé par la gouvernement du Canada | Canada

Demeter Press
140 Holland Street West
P. O. Box 13022
Bradford, ON L3Z 2Y5
Tel: (905) 775-9089
Email: info@demeterpress.org
Website: www.demeterpress.org

Demeter Press logo based on the sculpture "Demeter" by
Maria-Luise Bodirsky <www.keramik-atelier.bodirsky.de>

Cover art: Rebecca Bromwich, "All at Once," 2014, acrylic on canvas, 16 x 20 inches.

Printed and Bound in Canada

Library and Archives Canada Cataloguing in Publication

Mothers, mothering and sex work / editors, Rebecca Bromwich and Monique Marie DeJong.

Includes bibliographical references.
ISBN 978-1-926452-12-8 (paperback)

1. Mothers—Canada. 2. Motherhood—Canada. 3. Prostitutes—Canada. I. Bromwich, Rebecca, author, editor II. DeJong, Monique Marie, 1983–, author, editor

HQ759.M9285 2015 306.874'30971 C2015-904278-X

This book is dedicated to all mothers,
wherever and however they work.

Table of Contents

Acknowledgements

We are grateful for the courageous and brilliant women who have shared their stories, creativity, art, and academic acumen within this anthology, all of whom made this book possible. We extend particular acknowledgement to Dr. Andrea O'Reilly, an amazingly energetic, powerful visionary who is a devout supporter of feminist research as well as an advocate for mothering.

Rebecca: I would like to thank my family and especially Matt, my steady and visionary travelling companion, for always being with me on my academic and personal journeys. I would also like to acknowledge my children, who are present always in my work. May they grow to adulthood and undertake motherwork in a better world transformed and filled with new possibilities, and may my work help make that possible.

Monique: I would like to thank Marguerite Rigoglioso, Theresa C. Dintino, Joy Reichard, Claire Sierra, and Renee Jeffus, my mentors who have inspired my personal healing journey. I also thank Shiloh Sophia for introducing me to the art of intentional creativity and for inspiring me to own the artist within myself. I offer a special thanks to Cosi Fabian for sharing with me her story and impressive library. Through our talks, I gained a rich insight into feminine empowerment around sexual expression. A final thanks goes to my beloved Tanja Rademacher for her steadfast, loving support and playful inspiration.

Introduction

REBECCA BROMWICH AND MONIQUE MARIE DEJONG

Sometimes, just by staying alive, you find you have become someone who can live in the world after all.
—Evelyn Lau, Poet Laureate of Vancouver and former teen prostitute (qtd. in Crozier and Lane)

IN A TRANSNATIONAL, INTERSECTIONAL FRAMEWORK, this anthology discusses lived experiences of, legal and governmental frameworks affecting, and theorizations of mothers and sex work. This is the first collaboration of its kind that is specifically focused on the intersection of mothering and sex work with special attention on the legal regime in Canada, and explores not only what is done *to* or *about* sex workers who are mothers under governmental regimes or exploitative traffickers in the context of political and social systems that continue to disempower women in general and mothers in particular, but also explores the agencies of mothers who are sex workers and the mothers of those engaged in sex work. It looks at discourses of sex work and motherhood as complementarily regulating the sexuality of women in a way that re-inscribes and maintains a patriarchal social order.

This anthology is intended to provide a space for a wide range of "talk" about mothers, mothering, and sex work. It is not primarily a venue for the release of new empirical data, although there is rich data within the scholarly articles the volume contains. Equally, this volume limits its focus to the lives of sex workers who are women, and in particular on the experiences of women sex workers who are mothers of children, whether biologically or by adoption or some other care arrangement. We acknowledge that a significant minority of sex workers and prostituted individuals in Canada are males. Further research and writing should be undertaken to address their situations as well, but it is outside the scope of this project. Rather, our intention is to provide new theoretical and experiential lenses on the subjects of mothering, prostitution, and sex work, treated together.

The book does not privilege a single perspective on mothers, mothering, and sex work: no representation of sex work or sex workers is presented as a singular, monolithic paradigmatic definition. We present myriad perspectives without giving primacy to one vision. In opposition to current polarized debates about sex work that articulate "pro" and "con" sides to the issue of legalization, we have deliberately chosen not to make the book into an argument. Instead, we have curated contributions with our purpose being to provide insight into the rich depth of the messy range of perspectives and experiences mothers have about and with prostitution in its many forms, including consensual sex work. In the face of social activism that seeks to articulate the perspectives of sex workers and the perspectives of recanting former sex workers into diametrically opposed debate positions, we have chosen to complicate the discussion to make imaginable and speakable the messiness of divergent perspectives and experiences, which are lost when sex work is articulated as a binary political debate. Also lost in this debate are emotion, nuance, detail, and art, many of the very things that are most valuable in conversations that produce empathy and understanding. This is why this particular collection is timely. Our methodology constitutes an attempt to open up a space for reflection that precedes the deployment by social activism of representations of sex workers in service of one or another social agenda.

This book also seeks to open a space for the study of connections between sex work and mother work. The text provides a venue for telling stories by sex workers who are or were mothers. As such, this collection goes beyond a study of how mothering in the context of sex work is regulated by law and society to look at the agencies and lived experiences of sex workers who are mothers. It looks at the ways in which they reify the understanding and acceptance of their identities and even ways in which they find comfort, healing, and transformation.

Although this anthology centers on Canada, additional contributors hail from a wide variety of geographical and social contexts around the world, and their chapters are, in consequence, focused on a many local contexts. We are particularly delighted that the book is truly an interdisciplinary collaboration composed of academic papers, creative writing, poetry, photography, and artwork. It is uniquely valuable for readers, in this text, to be able to participate in the conversation of all of these writers and artists working together. We are heartened to present a book that contains a breadth of perspectives in a collaboration that is especially unusual in the context of today's highly polarized political and public discourses about sex work.

The chapters in this collection are authored by researchers, lawyers, students, activists, community workers, artists, creative writers, photographers, and women who have been interested in, engaged in, or documented sex work. The chapters contained in this volume explore meanings and experiences of mothering and the sex trade from academic disciplines including motherhood studies, anthropology, history, literature, popular culture, women's studies, women's spirituality, ecofeminism, law, and sociology. Contributions consider the ways motherhood and sex work intersect as ideas, performances, and social practices across a wide range of maternal identities including racial, ethnic, regional, religious, national, social, cultural, political, familial, and sexual. The chapters explore theoretical connections between sexual agency and maternal agencies; common interests between "outlaw" mothers and sex trade workers; legal regimes and their treatment of the sex trade; how the sex trade affects mothers; lived experiences of mothers in the sex trade; and mothers of sex trade workers.

This book stands alone, but it also exists as part of an emerging academic field of study. This text is one in a burgeoning field of feminist studies that foreground consideration of mothers and mothering. Feminist scholarship of this variety relies heavily on "maternal thinking," (Ruddick) a particular strain of feminist theory developed in large part by philosopher Sara Ruddick and more recently expanded upon and clarified by Canadian academic

Andrea O'Reilly. As discussed by O' Reilly, Sara Ruddick, Patricia Hill Collins, and Adrienne Rich are leading thinkers who have thus far developed feminist motherhood theory. Ruddick sees maternal thinking as a discipline analogous to the discourses of religion or science with particular dimensions as a practice. Although traditionally understood as women's work, maternal thinking is not essentially female. It is a philosophical orientation that cognitively and performatively involves a kind of caring labour that is engaged and physical and involves "protection, nurturance and training ... care and respect" (62). Ruddick identifies the "maternal standpoint" as a way of looking at all children and other people as human.

Mothering is, for Ruddick, work, not an identity. Ruddick focuses on the performativity of maternal thinking and not on essential biological traits, thereby disaggregating "maternalism" from any particular embodied subject. She focuses not on static personal attributes but on themes characteristic of maternal thinking. Similarly, O'Reilly draws together Judith Butler's notions about the performativity of gender with Ruddick's maternal thinking to further advance a non-essentialist understanding of maternal activism. She writes that, far from being essentially feminine, "drawing upon Judith Butler's theory of the performativity of gender ... motherhood is similarly performed by maternalist activists" (16). Maternal thinking is performed rather than "biologically inhabited." The overarching project of this book is to open up a space for maternal thinking about sex work and sex workers and to create a venue to explore and appreciate the maternalities of sex workers as subjects.

SEX WORK

In a variety of contexts, for at least the past decade, academics, activists, and sex workers themselves, have been expending a great deal of effort to undertake new empirical research about sex work in Canada.[1] Despite the strong value of this developing scholarship, sex work generally remains poorly understood by social science research in large part because many aspects of the lives of sex workers are difficult to study. Illegality and social stigma associated with the contemporary sex trade render data difficult to collect and make what information is collected questionable as to its reliability.

Further, when sex work is considered, it is not always easy to clearly delineate what is being studied. Definitions of "sex work," "sex trade," "sex trafficking," and "prostitution" are generally taken for granted. While this book understands sex work, as a working definition, to mean the voluntary exchange of sexual services for money and prostitution to refer to the exchange of sexual services for money, whether voluntary or involuntary, one of the purposes of this book is to problematize dominant definitions of what constitutes sex work and prostitution and what material conditions are inevitably associated with this exchange. Static conditions that inevitably produce oppression are not something this text assumes. Rather, without naively moving to the opposite polarity and representing all sex work as somehow emancipatory, it is hoped that the articles in this volume raise questions about what aspects of sex work are inevitable and what aspects are contingent.

Oftentimes referred to as "the oldest profession," sex work has not always been lived in similar material conditions for women generally and mothers specifically. Further, sex work has not been thought about the same way in all places and times, and has not involved precisely the same cluster of tasks. Historically, women who did paid work relating to companionship and sex with paying consumers have had varying degrees of social recognition, legitimacy within the social order, and status. High status was especially afforded, for example, to the Heterae of Ancient Greece and Geisha of Japan. Social categories occupied by people who did work in providing sexual services have not been unitary, closed, or consistent. The tasks typically performed by "courtesans" or companions like Geisha and Heterae, for instance, involved listening to male customers, pouring them tea, entertaining them with drama and music, and generally acting as their companions; these tasks did not always involve sexual contact (Garrison), and one could argue aspects of these roles resemble the modern-day sexual therapy.

Muddiness around the edges of the category of what constitutes sex work and who is a sex worker is not limited to examples from the ancient world. Geisha continue to work in Japan. Furthermore, in nineteenth-century France and contemporary China, "mistresses" are frequently "kept" by wealthy men, occupying a quasi-worker status whereby they perform sexual labour in exchange for wealth, some measure of security, and material comfort (Kushner). Seeking-Arrangement.ca, one of a number of international websites, links young people, including university students, with adult partners (called "Sugar Daddies" and "Sugar Mommies") who will pay for their tuition and debts in exchange for "dates." The site claims to have had 130,000 users in Canada in 2014.

Amsterdam and the U.S. State of Nevada are renowned for their legal sex work industries in which workers are often unionized (Ditmore). Further, while the purchase of sex for money is highly stigmatized and driven underground by the illegality of solicitation in Canada, work that borders or verges on the sex trade is not. To the contrary, "exotic dancing," which includes stripping and the provision of "lap dances" is not only legal but was until 2012 deemed to be a high-needs occupation by Canada's immigration laws. So people, usually women, engaging in this work were fast-tracked to receive "temporary foreign worker" permits. Without adopting a naively utopian vision of any of these contexts, it is clear that the conditions under which sex workers labour and the cluster of activities known as sex work have not always been defined the same way over time and space.

Social science studies of sex work over the past few decades lay contemporary contextual groundwork for this book. Anthropological and sociological studies have shown that most sex workers in Canada and worldwide are relatively young female adults. A recently conducted, but not yet full released, comprehensive study of sex work in Canada found that it is a diverse industry, with most participants being young, Caucasian women (although aboriginal women were over-represented in the most dangerous sector of the industry doing street-level sex work), many who are partnered and have children.[2] Reportedly, the age of sex workers in Canada is between 22 and 25 on average, although researcher Fran Shaver has also documented problems with the recruitment and exploitation of underage girls into prostitution. Although this is especially difficult to track reliably, specifically since this work largely runs "underground" in many countries, sociological and anthropological studies also indicate that many sex workers are mothers (Shaver "Prostitution"). Men and boys are also engaged in sex work, although their numbers are fewer according to available studies. Regardless of their age and gender, sex workers are overwhelmingly servicing a male consumer demand.

Unequal relations on matrices of race, nationality, and social class that intersect with unequal gender relations are linked to statistics about who has generally engaged in sex work and under what sorts of circumstances. Histories of sex work in North America and ongoing processes of human trafficking are linked to sexualized violence against children as well as to colonialism and globalization. In Canada, aboriginal women and children have historically been involved in prostitution in disproportionately large numbers (Frideres qtd. in Kelm 295-296). These same studies also show that Canada's aboriginal population has also been exposed to violence and sexualized violence as children in disproportionately large numbers (Frideres qtd. in Kelm 295-296). US studies tend to link victimization by sexual violence in childhood to later involvement with sex work. Available statistics about street-level sex workers in Canada indicate that they are still statistically disproportionately of aboriginal heritage (Lynne). Other studies of North American sex workers indicate that sex workers in the US are disproportionately of African American descent (West, Williams and Siegel). Unequal representation of people from socioeconomically marginal backgrounds and who hail from marginalized social groups is also found in studies of sex workers from other parts of the world. For example, data from Nairobi indicate that race and the ongoing legacy of colonialism in Africa are similarly linked to women's involvement with sex work (White).

Those who service the demand for sex in exchange for pay are often very vulnerable to violence and exploitation in many forms. Not only do many sex workers often hail from marginal populations, where, as in Canada, they operate in shadowy grey areas of legality, but also they are not easily able to obtain the protection of the law (Krusl et al.). Sex workers have historically been, and in many places continue to be, tremendously vulnerable to violence, torture, and even murder, not to mention poverty. In Canada, marginality, the risk of criminalization and social stigma have made sex workers vulnerable to exploitation, violence, and, most strikingly, predation by serial killers in many instances, especially by Robert Pickton and his associates in British Columbia (Cunningham and Christensen). While in *R v. Pickton*, the accused was found guilty of killing six women involved in the sex trade, the hundred-plus women missing from Vancouver's East Side as well as women missing from or killed on the "highway of tears" indicates that sex workers, and in particular sex workers of First Nations descent, are not adequately protected against violence and murder. It is clear that sex workers in Canada daily face dangers such as diseases, rape, beatings, exploitation, and murder.

DISAGREEMENTS AND DEBATES

In recent decades considerable debate has raged between "abolitionists," who seek to fight what they characterize as "sexual slavery," "sex trafficking," and sexual abuse by abolishing prostitution, and other scholars and activists who would like to see sex work legalized. This latter group isolates the sale of sexual services for money away from contemporary and historical problematic contexts in which sex workers are coerced into, or engage in, sex work under duress. They do not see sex work as inevitably or primarily oppressive. Their primary concern is the safety of and empowerment for sex workers. The proponents of this position seek to reduce harms associated with sex work by providing means to prevent and manage sexually transmitted diseases, safe working conditions, pathways out of sex work for workers, and other support services.

While a movement is growing toward the legalization of sex work in many countries, an oppositional, robust social movement has also developed against what is called "sex trafficking" (Soderlund) that involves diverse groups, including religious institutions as well as some "abolition" feminists. The coalition fighting sex trafficking starts from basic assumptions that prostitution is immoral, threatens marriage and the family, and is oppressive to women. Feminists who identify as abolitionist define prostitution as inherently an institution of male domination that inevitably exploits women (Dworkin, "Prostitution"; Mackinnon). The scholarship and activism of feminists and others fighting sex trafficking is not to be easily dismissed: coercion and deception are not myths, and facilitators of migration to support the sex trade are not uniformly benign agents. However, what the discourse of sex trafficking can miss is the varied complexity of the range of scenarios in which women become involved in sex work: sometimes those recruiting sex workers employ no force or fraud (Weitzer).

CHANGING GOVERNMENTAL REGIMES

Sex work itself has never been formally illegal in Canada, but the work has not been fully legalized or recognized as legitimate activity. In the theoretical framework of governmentality from a post-Foucauldian perspective, legal regimes formally controlling sex work should not be considered separately from governance of sex work by means of other forms of social control through discourses of medicine, mental health, and morality.

It may be that the dominant understandings of sex work and motherhood are about to change or are in the process of changing. The legal regimes in relation to prostitution are in a state of significant change in many developed countries. New Zealand decriminalized prostitution in 2003 by means of the New Zealand Prostitution Reform Act. Sex work was made partially legal in Sweden in 1999; Norway and Iceland followed suit, and this regime has been called the "Nordic Model" (Ekberg). In these countries, sex workers will not be criminalized but those who purchase sex are still subject to criminal sanction. Adoption of this legal model in reference to the sex trade is also being considered in France, and some are advocating adoption of this approach in the UK. The intended normative effect of the Nordic model of laws in relation to prostitution is to continue to stigmatize and socially condemn the sex trade but to shift the social stigma from the sex workers to the consumers. Survey data from Sweden indicate that this may not be effective: persons surveyed were strongly in favour of the continued criminalization of purchasers of sex but also in favour of the re-criminalization of sex worker (Kuosmanen).

In *Canada (Attorney General) v. Bedford*, the Supreme Court of Canada in December 2013 struck down existing laws that pro-

abilities to realize their human rights and their willingness to participate in programs designed to ameliorate their conditions (Sloss and Harper). And stigma and shame have been found to be dominant themes for mothers who are sex workers (Sloss and Harper). Even if sex workers do not experience shame, they do live in a world of social shaming and face pervasive stereotypes either personally or via systemic or legislative stigmatization and moralization of their work.

Structural stigma against sex workers can be found in many sites: police, communications, mainstream media texts, political rhetoric, religious doctrines and sermons, among other kinds of social talk. This stigmatization of sex workers justifies and legitimizes regulations through stereotypes such as a sex worker being a risk to society or at risk to herself.

Some U.S. cities have begun participating in "campaigns of shame," whereby they expose the johns (purchasers of sex) on social media platforms before the system declares them guilty or innocent. Although blame centers on johns in this instance, live-tweeting a prostitution sting can also include photos of sex workers during their arrest.

The social deployment of shame has become a very lucrative industry, and with tools such as social and online media, shaming has a seemingly endless audience reach. Former White House intern and romantic partner of President Clinton Monica Lewinsky recently broke a decade of silence due to deep feelings of shame. At her TED talk in March 2015 she spoke about public shaming:

> This invasion of others is a raw material, efficiently and ruthlessly mined, packaged and sold at a profit. A marketplace has emerged where public humiliation is a commodity and shame is an industry. How is the money made? Clicks. The more shame, the more clicks. The more clicks, the more advertising dollars. We're in a dangerous cycle. The more we click on this kind of gossip, the more numb we get to the human lives behind it, and the more numb we get, the more we click. (Lewinsky, "The Price of Shame")

The more public shaming becomes an acceptable form of expressing opinions in our culture, the more behaviours such as harassment and cyber-bullying are fuelled.

This stigmatization of prostitution silences and veils sex work and pushes sex workers to keep their stories anonymous and private, which severely limits the opportunity for a cohesive, collective, prevailing narrative to originate from these women. As is typical with a stigmatized trait, as discussed by Lewinsky and others, the stigmatized identifier comes to define the person so that this single dimension of what the individual does is read as who she *is*. It is significant that many sex workers feel their work is as legitimate as tasks more typically considered to be work, like employment in an office or factory; however, even when these women do feel comfortable with, or even enjoy, their sex work, they do form their identities within a stigmatized society, and the collective narrative remains flawed when taking into consideration society's behaviour toward and beliefs around sex workers. As author Starhawk says, "What shames us, what we most fear to tell, does not set us apart from others; it binds us together if only we can take the risk to speak it" (27). It is the "speaking," the claiming or redefining of our personal mythologies or narratives, that can offer empowerment, assist in an identity crisis, or help a mother choose whether to enter, to leave, or to remain in sex work. And sometimes, as explored in a few of our contributions, this journey toward healing or re-creation is an inner one that possesses a spiritual, metaphorical, or experiential dimension.

As artist Shiloh Sophia, one of our contributors, stated at the United Nations Commission on the Status of Women 59th Session on March 10, 2015, our experience of trauma and our senses live in story, so to move through and transform trauma, we must work with our story. Similarly, for women who are empowered by their sex work, their empowerment is found and unleashed in story. This is another reason why we have chosen to combine fictional and non-fictional accounts of sex workers experiences: stories are intrinsically malleable and shift for many reasons such as viewpoints or personal preferences. Blurring the lines of storytelling, sex workers' artistic representations are sometimes marketed as fiction for numerous reasons—one being it offers a more empowering venue to express their voices and their stories—

but even though someone tells their story in a "fictional" way, it doesn't make it fiction.

Social stigmatization is all the more complicated by the Madonna-whore complex, and within this construct, "good" and pure mothers can never be sex workers. As Jessica Valenti says in *The Purity Myth*, "People have been talking authoritatively about virginity for thousands of years, yet we don't even have a working medical definition for it!" (20). Internalizing this purity myth—the virgin/whore dichotomy—damages women and also creates a social and political climate that works against women and especially against sex workers and their rights. Clearly, it seems absurd to place value, shame, and blame on an abstraction that cannot even be logically defined, an abstraction that does not even exist in some cultures. Doing so only further separates and obfuscates sex workers from themselves, their maternal roles and society as a whole.

Some women enter into prostitution to finance addictions in an attempt to numb deep-seated childhood wounds; however, as revealed in our contributions, some women proudly "own" and even celebrate their sex work. Not all women have abusive experiences; in fact, numerous women have positive experiences as sex workers. It is important to note that they are not all "victims," because lumping all sex workers into one category dehumanizes them and fuels popular misconceptions and prejudices; however, in one way or another, they all collectively, either directly or indirectly, face the oppression of societal stigma.

In perusing our various contributions, it becomes apparent that tidily defining "sex work" is a complex and perhaps insurmountable task in so far as trying to determine where to place blame and stigma, and, therefore, elicit shame: what is the difference, for example, between a mother accepting payment for sex work out of the need to support her children versus a mother staying in a loveless and perhaps even violent marriage for the same need? Clearly, there is no hard threshold that can be constructed between these identities.

In order for mothers who are sex workers to share their stories or to even privately examine their own personal mythologies, they must become vulnerable. As Brené Brown notes in *The Gifts of Imperfection*, "Owning our story and loving ourselves through that process is the bravest thing that we will ever do" (ix), and we do this through vulnerability, which is never a weakness but in fact a strength. It takes an incredible amount of strength to pursue this level of self-examination, yet it can offer deep healing and transformation needed to ease the suffering and inner discord sex workers experience or to remedy the discord experienced existing within a society that fails to understand their agency, needs, and desires.

We must remember that sex workers' stories are *our* stories. There is no "other." We are all co-creators of the collective story, and as such, we need to assume the responsibility that is ours and find the means necessary to help sex workers heal or own their stories in ways that truly benefit them. As Elizabeth Cunningham says in a paper prepared for The New Seminary, "Until the holy whore archetype is honored, there will be a whore stigma. Women will be divided against each other and themselves, and we will all be at odds with our own human nature." All women are multi-faceted. We are sexual beings, we are mothers, biologically, by adoption, and even, when women do not have children or nurture children, we can exercise maternal thinking when creating for the sake of creating or in nurturing ourselves. Women may find it beneficial to integrate maternal archetypes with which they choose to self-identify.

Among women's spirituality and art communities, a definition for the term "virginity" has been circling: "one-in-herself" (Harding). Although many linguists argue against this definition in terms of it being the *original* definition, what *is* certain is women today are searching for ways of reinvention, re-creation, identity healing, wholeness, and empowerment to reclaim their own sovereignty. This desire for re-envisioning virginity has no bearing on puritanical notions. A similar trend is occurring related to sacred sexual priestesses. Again, heated debates center on the existence of such women who supposedly would, for example, "take the war out of men" when they returned from bloody battles or who would provide their bodies and sexual love in service of healing emotional wounds or to honour the goddess. Whether such women truly existed is still up for discussion, but what cannot be ignored is the fact that many women—including sex workers, some of whom have contributed to this anthology—find great empowerment, spirituality, or healing in embracing sacred sexual archetypes of such goddesses as Aphrodite, Inanna, Isis, Lilith, Mary Magdalene and others.

As do many other women, some sex workers discover a need to identify or connect with a mother figure, icon, or archetype because at some level, there may exist a mother wound, a form of pain that has passed down throughout many generations of women in patriarchal cultures. Bethany Webster, transformational coach and author of the forthcoming book *Healing the Mother Wound: Move Beyond What Your Mother Never Gave You and Become the Woman You're Meant to Be* says:

> Simply put, if a daughter nternalizes her mother's unconscious beliefs (which is some subtle form of "I'm not good enough"), then she has her mother's approval but has in some way betrayed herself and her potential. However, if she doesn't internalize her mother's unconscious beliefs in her own limitations but rather affirms her own power and potential, she is aware that her mother may unconsciously see this as a personal rejection.

Any criticism of one's mother can feel like betrayal and summon feelings of shame. "It may feel dangerous for a woman to actualize her full potential because it may mean risking some form of rejection by her mother. Many of us confuse being loyal to our mothers with being loyal to their wounds, and thus, complicit in our own oppression" (Webster). Because our society doesn't afford mothers a safe space to process and express their rage around such aspects as the innumerable sacrifices society demands of them, the mother wound can exist and persist.

Healing the mother wound and identity conflicts, exploring one's inner landscape, and re-creating one's narrative can occur through a variety of possible pathways. Some of our contributions touch on the power of forgiveness; transpersonal psychology; intentional creativity; expressive movement/dance therapy; a physical or spiritual reconnection with Mother Earth by realizing ways in which our planet has suffered as women have suffered (ecofeminism); reclaiming archetypes, saints, or goddesses as witnessed in The

Magdalene Movement, and more. However sex workers may seek to forge their identities and careers, or heal possible wounds, are personal choices, and the purpose of this volume is to open a space for acknowledgement of a diverse range of lived and felt experiences where sex workers are acknowledged and respected, not degraded or diminished.

THIS BOOK

The contributions in this volume offer a range of perspectives on issues relating to mothering, mothers, and sex work, and they do not line up neatly on one or the other side of binary "abolitionist" and "empowerment" positions that have been the "sides" in Canadian pro-/anti-sex work debates. Taken as a whole, this book neither asserts that sex work is a social good nor a social harm. Rather, the focus of this book is not on grand moralizations. Instead, it is intended to provide a discursive space for consideration of a particular group of sex workers—those who are mothers—and Sara Ruddick's conceptualization of maternal thinking. In reality, the quality of sex work relates to the individual experience of women and mothers. The contributions in this volume inquire how sex work is experienced by mothers, as workers, as mothers of workers, and spouses and mothers of consumers. The book also looks at sex work by mothers governed not only by the law but also in discourse.

OUR CONTRIBUTIONS

The editors of this anthology purposefully chose to curate multidisciplinary contributions; accordingly, the following chapters include scholarly essays and such media as paintings, photography, poetry, creative writing, street art, and fictional pieces. The purpose of our choosing a more eclectic collection of contributions, rather than assembling a purely scholarly anthology, is to offer a larger, more nuanced platform for the voices of and about sex workers and the many ways meanings are made of sex work. To truly hear the voices of others, a variety of expressions must be acknowledged. As such, we have veered away from silencing negativity or perceived stereotypes in perspectives herein articulated. Our anthology is intended to give these sex workers and others a space to be heard alongside much more positive portraits as well as to exhibit a variety of perspectives without criticizing any one approach. Contributions specifically from Canada include the following authors: Alice Munro, Gordana Eldjupovic, Alison Granger Brown, Amanda Staller, Steven Moore, Rebecca Bromwich, and anonymous narrative contributors who are sex-work-identified women.

Cosi Fabian, "The First Compassion"

Known as the Holy Whore, poet Cosi Fabian became a prostitute for seven years at the age of forty-two due to unemployment and a disinterest in the poor labour market for women, yet this profession also guided her along a journey of self-forgiveness and self-respect, which also created a space for her male clients to experience deep nurturing and healing. Inspired by the "qadeshet," or "sacred prostitutes," Cosi reclaimed pre-patriarchal archetypes to embrace the noble and empowering expressions of female sexuality. From a poetry collection titled *The Sacred Whore's Book of Prayer*, "The First Compassion" describes her sacred practice of invoking various Goddesses such as The Great Mother prior to client sessions.

Marie Hald, "Bonnie, A Life in Prostitution"

Over the course of a year, photojournalist Marie Hald recorded intimate details of the life of mother Bonnie Cleo Andersen, a prostitute since the age of eighteen. To separate herself from her work, Bonnie calls herself Patricia. The single most important thing in Bonnie's life is her children. She hopes they will have a better childhood and life than her own. Her childhood was scarred by her dysfunctional family and abuse. The three selected photographs depict Bonnie's personal identity, her motherhood, and her sex work. Her profession is not easy on the children, and they have been bullied and ridiculed by schoolmates.

Alison Granger-Brown, Gordana Eldjupovic, Amanda Staller, and Steven Moore, "The Spectrum of Motherhood"

The authors of this chapter interweave personal narrative writing with expositive academic analysis to identify main themes and factors impacting sex workers, and they unpack ways in which social participants all play a role in constructing the identities of these mothers. This chapter also reminds us that a mother's act of "selling" herself to provide for her children manifests in a variety of ways and doesn't exclude more traditionally accepted forms of motherhood, such as that of a girlfriend or middle-class wife. It also follows the personal evolution of the storyteller's identity, structured roles, and transformation as well as the reconciling of multiple events and the complexity of one's development from hurt through hope to healing.

"Portrait of Maya Angelou as Dancer"

Poet and dancer Maya Angelou poses for a portrait circa 1950. During World War II, Angelou moved to San Francisco, California, where she won a scholarship to study dance and acting at the California Labor School. As she describes in *Gather Together in My Name*, her show business career came to a halt after her dancing partner and lover R. L. Poole reunited with his former partner. Shortly thereafter, Angelou, called Rita, fell in love with, and was seduced into prostitution by, pimp and conman L. D. Tolbrook.

Maya Angelou, "Gather Together in My Name"

Gather Together in My Name, the second volume in Maya Angelou's series of autobiographies, takes place at the end of World War II when teenage Angelou, called Rita, has given birth to her son. She struggles for the next few years with trying to find a job, a man, and a place where she and her son belong in the world. The excerpt, Chapter 27, chronicles her short time serving as a "cherry," a young, inexperienced "virgin," in a whore house. As Angelou states in an interview, the intention of her book's title is to counteract adults' tendencies to veil their pasts by telling their children lies (Tate).

Selena Bateman, "Continuing the Policy Debate: Canadian Prostitution Legislation and the Implications for Sex Workers"

Canada's recent reforms to prostitution legislation, influenced by international and domestic values, lead to negative ramifications for the lives of sex workers. This chapter explores contemporary sex work set within dominant political ideology and critiques The Protection of Communities and Exploited Persons Act of 2014. International social policy and policy debates are investigated to analyze the effects of various approaches and to look ahead to Canada's future.

Alice Munro, "Voices" from Dear Life

Alice Munro's short story "Voices," excerpted from *Dear Life,* offers an autobiographical perspective in the voice of a girl child of a community's response, and specifically a mother's felt and expressed obligation to act, when a known sex worker arrives at a community event she is attending with the narrator-daughter. It provides critical insight into mid-century Canadian values about prostitutes being a contaminant stigmatized in society, social condemnation, and the ongoing existence of sex workers as members of communities.

Monique Marie DeJong, "Cosmic Creatrix" (poem and painting)

Drawing upon her interests in ecofeminism, transpersonal psychology, indigenous shamanic knowledge, Jungian archetypes, embodiment practices, and the sacred feminine as sources of empowerment and healing, Monique Marie DeJong's poem and painting capture the power personal mythology has to heal inner wounds and reclaim one's identity through intentional creativity and expressive movement. The belly dancer represents the legends of ancient temple priestesses who once served as sacred sexual healers. She created these works in *LEGEND: Awaken the Hidden Stories*, one of several online painting and writing programs offered by artist and poet Shiloh Sophia.

Rebecca Bromwich, "Maternal Thinking about Adolescent Mothers Engaged in Sex Work: Towards Alternatives to 'Secure Care'"

Rebecca Bromwich's chapter looks critically at an aspect of legal governance of sex work that has received comparatively little attention in contemporary debates about sex work in Canada. She examines ways in which discourses of protection of adolescents against child sexual abuse have been deployed to impose effectively carceral measures against girls. Bromwich examines juridical measures taken to constrain adolescent girls' sexual agency. She contends these too often fail to support girls' agencies in seeking ways to leave, or simply to be safe within sex work. Bromwich also explores continuities between material conditions brought about by historical criminal laws affecting adolescent sex workers and these current "protective" regimes. She concludes by suggesting law reform that would be consistent with what Sara Ruddick calls "maternal thinking," namely the repeal of "protective" confinement laws in Canadian provincial and territorial jurisdictions where they are currently in force.

Anonymous, "Acceptance, Love, Peace," SWANS Story Box Project

This artwork is part of a community project created in partnership with Sex Workers Advisory Network Sudbury and Myths and Mirrors Community Arts. Committed to building safer and more inclusive communities for sex worker peers, women with lived experience in sex work and their allies worked together and individually to artistically express aspects of themselves through "story boxes." The outside of the boxes represent the artists' public selves while the interior spaces represent their private worlds. This piece has been contributed to this anthology anonymously (but with the permission of the artist). The poetic aspect of the project was inspired by Ella George Lyon's poem "Where I am from."

Elizabeth Cunningham, "Excerpts from The Maeve Chronicles*"*

The Maeve Chronicles are a series of award-winning novels featuring a feisty Celtic Magdalen who is no one's disciple. In this fictional treatment she is also a non-repenting whore and mother. When author Elizabeth Cunningham toured with her novels, an audience inevitably asked, "Why did you make have to make her a whore?" Although no scriptural evidence proves Mary Magdalen to be a prostitute, sixth-century Pope Gregory gave official sanction to the legend, conflating her with the unidentified penitent who washes Jesus' feet with her tears. As Cunningham reminds us, any woman can be branded a whore if she steps out of line. The excerpts are taken from novels *The Passage of Mary Magdalen* and *Bright Dark Madonna.*

Shiloh Sophia, "Love Called My Name" (painting and poem)

Through ritual and intentional creativity, Shiloh Sophia encourages women to connect with the archetypal feminine and guides them through powerful and healing painting and writing programs such as the Mystery of Mary Magdalene, a class in which women can explore the identity of Mary Magdalene and what she means to them. The early church brands her as a whore, yet The Magdalene Movement embraces her as the wife of Christ, a mother, and even a potential sacred sex priestess. Painting the Magdalene helps women connect with the essence and love of the divine feminine within and with their own unique identities.

PJ Starr, Juliana Piccillo, Mama B and Gary Bullock on behalf of the Red Umbrella Babies Collective, "Red Umbrella Babies: By Sex Worker Parents and Their Children"

The chapter by the Red Umbrella Collective explores what a group of writers have learned in the process of constructing representations of themselves as sex workers and mothers. Asserting that the act of speaking up for sex workers and their families is its own rebellion against the silence, the collective shares experiences of its members as they take steps to develop their own work to represent themselves. *The Red Umbrella Babies* is a forthcoming anthology of writings, poetry, and artwork created by sex worker parents and the children raised by them. The anthology is edited by sex worker parents who are also writers, photographers, filmmakers, and artists.

Rebecca Bromwich, "All at Once"

"All at Once" is a painting done in acrylic on canvas that seeks to depict symbols associated with motherhood (the pram) and sex work (the red umbrella and boots) with the embodied subject of a woman linked to all of the symbolic objects, all of the social identities. The painting is an attempt to bring together many aspects of women's lives and identities that are generally constructed as opposite to one another. In doing so, the artwork foregrounds the possibilities of understanding women's lives, in particular mothers' lives, in new and potentially more emancipatory ways.

Besi Brillian Muhonja, "For My Children"

Told within the dramatic medium, Dr. Brillian Besi Muhonja's narrative "For My Children" depicts an African woman who is forced into sex work and subsequently experiences the myriad failings of the US legal governance of foreign sex workers and victims of trafficking. Within the context of transnational sex and labour slavery, very little is reported on African women as a collective whole and even less as individuals. Dr. Muhonja's narrative highlights one mother's struggles with the complex experiences of separation and yearning for her original state of motherhood in her motherland, motherhood under slavery, the rejection of a forced, unwanted pregnancy, and the choices mothers make for their children.

Kristine Vandenberg, "Intersections of Violence, Space, Motherhood, and Culture in the Sexual Assault of Sex Workers"

Exploring the concept of brutality through intimacy and why sex is used as a weapon, this chapter takes a critical geographical approach to thinking through intersections of violence, space, identity, globalization, and culture as manifested in the sexual assault of sex workers. This violence, promoted by unstable identities in a globalized world, becomes a means to experience intimacy and to define the "other" and oneself. This chapter also looks at how sex workers who are mothers are characterized in media and legal frameworks and the ways in which they are understood as victims and also at how the marginalization of sex workers exemplifies and promotes violence on both individual and state levels.

Alicia Vera, "Eden Sleeps Next to Her Cell Phone"

During her studies at the Academy of Art University, photographer Alicia Vera became interested in women's issues and began to document the complex lives of sex workers. While working on a project about strippers in San Francisco, CA, she met Eden, a sex worker who chose to move past her negative experiences in the industry, including three arrests, so that she could continue escorting. Although Eden's mother disapproves of her choices, she supports her daughter. This photography project showcases one woman's struggle to find her identity.

Lilith Bridges, "'How Could I?' A Personal and Political Contemplation of Entering the Sex Trade"

Weaving personal narrative and socio-political theory, Lilith Bridges explores her own places of resistance and attraction to the sex trade. She examines notions of agency and constraints on choosing sex work in her Western culture. Bridges unpacks the stigma and subsequent risks associated with sex work and the challenging, often conflicting considerations and emotions that confront her as a woman, mother, wife, and community member thinking of selling sexual services. Looking to people with lived experiences in sex work for guidance, Bridges writes toward a deeper understanding of the complexities of the work; as an opportunity for personal healing and identity formation; and as an ally with a vision for a safe, inclusive, and respectful society for sex workers and their clients. This personal reflection is part of a longer piece published on her blog.

Valandra, "Protective and Proactive Mothering: Prostituted African American Mothers' Use of Intergenerational Family Networks"

This chapter provides a rare insight into how intergenerational extended family networks are a source of strength in African American families, challenging the scholastic focus on intergenerational dysfunction. The intersection of prostitution, poverty, and parenting within intergenerational family networks enhances and challenges mothering among prostituted African American mothers. Based on in-depth interviews with thirteen mothers exposed to prostitution and traumatic events, this chapter examines the parenting practices of mothers within the context of intergenerational family networks and touches on how values, beliefs, forgiveness, and spirituality can also play a role in mothers finding healing for themselves.

Jesse Maley, "Chained Heart"

As the adopted daughter of a preacher of a large evangelical church, Jesse Maley grew up very sheltered. She became intrigued by the sex work industry at fifteen years old when she read a *Cosmopolitan* magazine article about the life of an escort. Maley later became a prostitute and spent many years cycling in and out of the criminal justice system. Her life was in disarray when she chose to quit at all costs fourteen years later. To help other women escape the drama and stigmatization of sex work, in 2008 Maley created the organization Out of the Life offering a safe house, resources, support, as well as healing through a journaling and art program. This pencil drawing illustrates a woman named Asia who tried to escape her pimp by getting sent to jail for stealing. In jail, she attended an Out of the Life class, and she had planned to go to the organization's home. Tragically, shortly after her release, her body was discovered in a ditch. She had been brutally raped and tortured and her arms were cut off.

Aphrodite Phoenix, "Breaks"

Aphrodite Phoenix is a retired sex worker who is a mother, an author, and an ardent activist for sex worker's rights. Her penname is an homage to both the goddess of sexual love and the mythical bird that arose from ashes of chaos and destruction, flying to freedom. The archetypes symbolize her sensual, nurturing nature and tragic-turned-triumphant life experience. Published in a collection titled *AND THE POINT of All this Agony IS...?*, this short story is a fictionalized piece providing an intimate and detailed look into Phoenix's work, her set-up arrest, and the irony of legal governance "protecting" sex workers by detaining or incarcerating them.

Ariana Ochoa Camacho, "The Border Brothels and Sex Trafficking: Untangling Discourses from a Sex Work Frame"

Ariana Ochoa Camacho's chapter provides a critical discourse analysis of media coverage of "sex trafficking" along the U.S.-Mexican border. Ochoa Camacho argues that this analysis of news coverage of cross-border sex trade reveals a set of interlocking narratives that (re)draw and cement the gendered and racialized hierarchies of U.S. society while simultaneously obscuring the very social machinery that generates the border and the conditions of migration. In the dominant discursive frame found in media sites, woman, child, and innocence are conflated while western feminists embrace a traditional gendered role as mothers.

Oglivy and Mather, Buenos Aires, "Street Corner Moms"

Featured in an ad campaign created by the Association of Women Prostitutes of Argentina (AMMAR), this photograph by Los Vocalino and Patricio Gomez Lambí captures "Banksy-style" urban street art. The following translated text appeared with each ad: "86 percent of sex workers are mothers. We need a law to regulate our work." The ad intends to encourage regulation as well as respect for this profession. Spanning two sides of a building corner, the ad cleverly depicts a woman on one side and children on the perpendicular side. Only by viewing the artwork from the corner does the viewer realize that the prostitute is also a mother.

Anonymous, "Mama Tiger Rising"

This narrative offers a glimpse into the hopelessness experienced by one woman who enaged in survival sex work. The narrative tracks her emancipatory understanding of motherhood. The narrative opens with a threat mothers in sex work all too often experience from bureaucracy: separation from their children. The story flashes back to this woman's life as a sex worker and the pain she endures. Her frequent thoughts of death are personified as she suffers from years of abuse and rape. Once she discovers her pregnancy, she chooses sobriety, her suicidal tendencies dwindle, and she begins a new life, but due to a report received by social services, her ability to be a fit mother is scrutinized.

Satabdi Samtani and Elizabeth Trejos-Castillo, "Motherhood and Sex Work: A Negotiation of Identities"

This chapter looks critically at the discursive identities of sex worker, "good" mother, and "good" worker. The chapter explicates common themes in identity negotiation found in literature surrounding sex work and mothering. The authors then explore how mothering for sex workers runs contrary to the known societal narrative of the process of nurturing as a mother. The authors then conclude by advocating for construction of understandings of sex workers as "good" workers and for legalization of sex work in countries where sex work as a profession or prostitution in general is deemed illegal.

OUR INTENTIONS

This book seeks to excavate the space between the binary oppositions of sex work and motherhood, working from a notion that it is difficult and perhaps unhelpful to seek to draw hard lines between what Andrea O'Reilly has characterized as "outlaw motherhood" and sex work. This book hopes to raise political, policy, and philosophical questions in the minds of readers, not to answer them. We seek to incite readers to ponder what sorts of social activism and law reform work are called for in view of the ongoing realities of sex work, prostitution, and human trafficking, fraught as prostitution has often been with exploitation, abuse, illegality, and invisibilities, especially when the field is viewed through a theoretical lens shaped by a feminist orientation toward maternal thinking. Looking intersectionally at a variety of dimensions of social identity, such as race, ethnicity, and social class as well as gender, the contributions in this book invite readers to reflect on how women and mothers who work in the sex trade are understood in mainstream Canadian society and beyond. Readers are invited to consider what relationships contemporary debates about whether and how to legally regulate sex work in Canada and elsewhere have to the ways mothers are understood. Further, the chapters in this volume are intended to lead readers to question the implications of the way societies regulate and talk about sex work on the equality of women in general, and on mothers in particular.

We truly hope this book inspires conversations about, as well as new conversations between, women and mothers involved in sex work. Their lives, perspectives, material conditions, and voices have been neglected and ignored for far too long, and readers, policymakers, thinkers, theorists, and governments need to imagine them as subjects with agencies, not just objects of abjection or rescue, and to listen to their diverse needs, their desires, and their wants. This book has sought to open a space for new conversations about and involving mothers who are valuable, vulnerable, powerful, diverse, varied, volitional, agentic, and who are workers, specifically those involved in sex work.

[1]Academics working on this research include Frances Shaver, Kevin Walby, Rachel Phillips, and Bill McCarthy. Many of their findings have yet to be released but a description of projects being undertaken can be found the website *(Understanding) Sex Work* (University of Victoria).
[2]The full study is yet to be released. See the C-36 brief for details ("Bill C-36 and the Views").

WORKS CITED

Allen, G., S. Hawker, G. Crow. "Britain's Changing Families." *Handbook of Contemporary Families*. Eds. M. Coleman and L. H. Ganong. Thousand Oaks, CA: Sage, 2004. 302-316. Print.

Bassin, Donna, Margaret Honey and Meryle Mahrer Kaplan eds. *Representations of Motherhood*. Binghamton, New York: Vail-Ballou Press, 1988. Print.

Benoit, C. et al. "Gender, Violence and Health: Contexts of Vulnerabilities, Resiliencies and Care among People in the Sex Industry." *Proceedings: Building on the Evidence: An International Symposium on the Sex Industry in Canada*. Ottawa: Canadian Institute for Health Research, 2014. Web. 28 May 2015.

Bill C-36 2nd Session, 41st Parliament, *The Protection of Communities and Exploited Persons Act*.

"Bill C-36 and the Views of People Involved in the Sex Trade Industry." *Gender, Violence and Health: Contexts of Vulnerabilities, Resiliencies and Care among People in the Sex Industry*. CIHR. 20 June 2015. Pdf.

Brown, Brené. *The Gifts of Imperfection: Let Go of Who You Think You're Supposed to Be and Embrace Who You Are*. Center City, Minnesota: Hazelden, 2010. Print.

Bruckert, Chris and Stacey Hannem. "Rethinking the Prostitution

Debates: Transcending Structural Stigma in Systemic Responses to Sex Work." *Canadian Journal of Law and Society* 28.1 (2013): 43-63. Print.

Canada (Attorney General) v. Bedford. SCC 72. 2013. *Judgments of the Supreme Court of Canada*. 20 Dec 2013.

Crozier, Lorna and Patrick Lane, eds. *Addicted Canada*. Toronto: Greystone Books, 2001. Print.

Cunningham, Elizabeth. "Sacred Prostitution: The Whore and the Holy One." *Elizabeth Cunningham*. 2012. Web. 28 May 2015.

Cunningham, L. C. and C. Christensen. *Violence against Women in Vancouver's Street Level Sex Trade and the Police Response*. Vancouver: PACE Society, 2001. Print.

Ditmore, Melissa Hope. *Encyclopedia of Prostitution and Sex Work*. Westport, Connecticut: Greenwood Press, 2006. Print.

Dworkin, Andrea. *Pornography: Men Possessing Women*. New York: Putnam, 1981. Print.

Dworkin, Andrea. "Prostitution and Male Supremacy." *Life and Death*. New York: Free Press, 1997. 139-151. Print.

Ekberg, G. S. "Prostitution and Trafficking: the Legal Situation in Sweden." Paper presented at Journées de Formation sur la Mondialisation de la Prostitution et du Trafic Sexuel, Association Québécoise des Organismes de Coopération Internationale. 2001. Montréal, Québec, Canada. Print.

Gallagher, John. *Geisha: A Unique World of Tradition, Elegance, and Art*. London: PRC, 2003.

Garrison, Daniel H. *Sexual Culture in Ancient Greece*. Norman, Oklahoma: University of Oklahoma, 2000. Print.

Harding, M. Esther. *Woman's Mysteries: Ancient and Modern*. Boston: Shambhala Publications, 1990. Print.

Jeffreys, Sheila. *The Industrial Vagina: The Political Economy of the Sex Trade*. London: Routledge, 2009. Print.

Kaplan, Ellen. "Sex, Work and Motherhood: The Impossible Triangle." *The Journal of Sex Research* 27.3 (1990): 409-425. Print.

Kelm, M. *Colonizing Bodies: Aboriginal Health and Healing in British Columbia, 1900-1950*. Vancouver: University of British Columbia Press, 1998. Print.

Krusl, A., et al. "Criminalisation of Clients: Reproducing Vulnerabilities for Violence and Poor Health among Street-based

Sex Workers in Canada—A Qualitative Study." *British Medical Journal* June (2014): 1-9. Web. 28 May 2015.

Kuosmanen, Jari. "Attitudes and Perceptions about Legislation Prohibiting the Purchase of Sexual Services in Sweden." *European Journal of Social Work*. 14.2 (2011): 247-263. Web. 28 May 2015.

Kushner, Nina. *Erotic Exchanges: The World of Elite Prostitution in Eighteenth Century Paris*. New York: Cornell University Press, 2013. Print.

Lewinsky, Monica "The Price of Shame." *TED*. March 2015. Web 28 May 2015.

Lynne, J. A. M. "Street Prostitution as Sexual Exploitation in First Nations Women's Lives." Master of Social Work. University of British Columbia. 1998. Print.

MacKinnon, Catherine. *Feminism Unmodified*. Cambridge, MA: Harvard University Press, 1987. Print.

Morgan-Thomas, R. (The Global Network of Sex Work Projects). "Brief to the House of Commons Standing Committee on Justice and Human Rights on *Protection of Communities and Exploited Persons Act*—Bill C-36." *Parliament of Canada*. 5 Sept. 2014. Web. 28 May 2015.

New Zealand Prostitution Reform Act. *New Zealand Legislation*. 2003.

O'Reilly, Andrea. *The Twenty-First Century Motherhood Movement*. Bradford, Ontario: Demeter Press, 2011. Print.

Pearce, Diana. 1978. "The Feminization of Poverty: Women, Work, and Welfare." *Urban and Social Change Review* 11 (1978): 28–36. Print.

R v. Pickton. 2 SCR 198. Supreme Court of Canada. 2010. *Judgments of the Supreme Court of Canada*. 30 July 2010.

Raymond, Janice et al. "A Comparative Study of Women Trafficked in the Migration Process: Patterns, Profiles and Health Consequences of Sexual Exploitation in Five Countries (Indonesia, the Philippines, Thailand, Venezuela, and the United States)." *OAS.org*. Amherst, MA: Coalition against Trafficking in Women. 2002. Web. 28 May 2015.

Ruddick, Sara. *Maternal Thinking: Toward a Politics of Peace*. Boston: Beacon Press, 1995. Print.

Shaver, Fran. "Demystifying Sex Work." Paper Presented at When Sex Works: International Conference on Prostitution and Other Sex Work. September 27-29, 1996. UQAM, Montréal (QC). Web. 28 May 2015.

Shaver, Fran. "Prostitution: A Female Crime?" *In Conflict with the Law: Women and the Canadian Justice System*. Eds. Ellen Alderberg and Claudia Currie. Vancouver: Press Gang Publishers, 1993. n. pag. Print.

Sloss, Christine and Harper, Gary "When Street Sex Workers are Mothers" *33 Archives of Sexual Behavior* 4 (2004): 329–341. Print.

Soderlund, Gretchen "Running from the Rescuers: New U.S. Crusades Against Sex Trafficking and the Rhetoric of Abolition." *NWSA Journal* 17 (2005): 64-87. Print.

Starhawk. *Truth or Dare*. New York: Harper & Row Publishers, 1990. Print.

Tate, Claudia. "Maya Angelou." *Conversations with Maya Angelou*. Ed. Jeffrey M. Elliot. Jackson, Mississippi: University Press, 1989. 146-165. Print.

United Nations. *United Nations Protocol to Prevent, Suppress and Punish Trafficking in Persons*. 2000. Pdf.

University of Victoria. *(Understanding) Sex Work: A Health Research and Community Partnership*. 2012. Web. 28 May 2015.

Valenti, Jessica. *The Purity Myth: How America's Obsession with Virginity is Hurting Young Women*. Berkeley, California: Seal Press, 2010. Print.

Van der Meulan, Emily, et al. *Selling Sex: Experience, Advocacy and Research on Sex Work in Canada*. Vancouver: UBC Press, 2013. Print.

Webster, Bethany. "Why It's Crucial for Women to Heal the Mother Wound." *Womb of Light: The Power of the Awakened Feminine*. 2013. Web. 28 May 2015.

Weitzer, Ronald. "The Social Construction of Sex Trafficking: Ideology and Institution of a Moral Crusade." 35 *Politics and Society* 3 (2007): 447-475. Print.

West, C. M., L. M. Williams, and J. A. Siegel. "Adult Sexual Re-victimization among Black Women Sexually Abused in Childhood: A Prospective Examination of Serious Consequences of Abuse."

Child Maltreatment 5 (2000): 49-57. Print.

White, L. "Domestic Labor in a Colonial City: Prostitution in Nairobi, 1900-1952." *Patriarchy and Class: African Women in the Home and the Workforce*. Eds. S. B. Stichter and J. Parport. Boulder: Westview Press, 1988. 139-160. Print.

Williams, Cara. *Economic Wellbeing, Women in Canada: A Gender-based Statistical Report*. Statistics Canada, December 2010. Print.

The First Compassion

(The Sacred Prostitute on her "work")

COSI FABIAN

Sometimes, my body or mind being distracted,
A prayer is necessary –
So that Her grace may be felt
By me,
Through me.

Always
– each time –
I do then feel my vulva quicken,
Connecting supplicant to The Great Mother.
And She, touched by his
Youthful fervour,
Pours forth Her divine essence.

The men told us that the love
of their distant God was infinite
(As they tied us to the burning stakes).
But this is the First Compassion –
Constantly vivifying, never depleted.

So much Charity given –
And still they come,
And still they are fed.

MARIE HALD

Bonnie, A Life in Prostitution

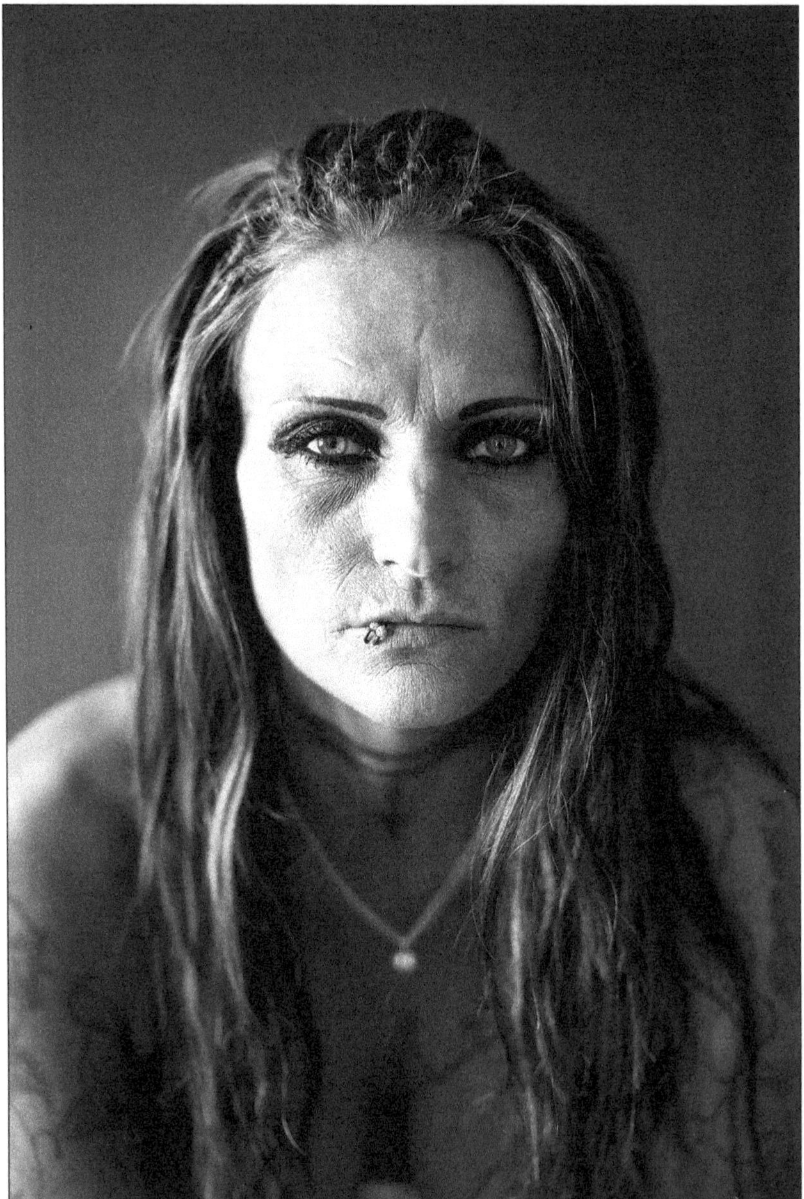

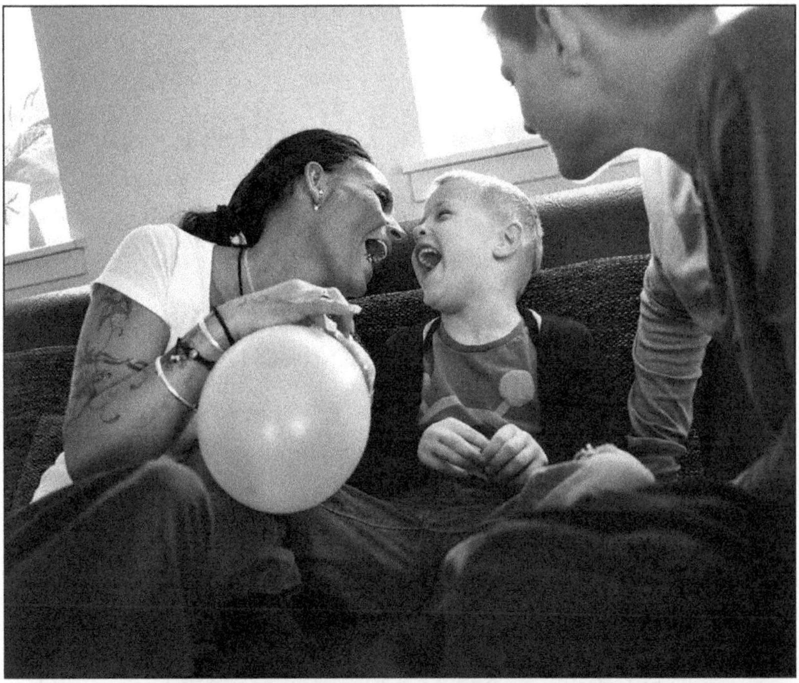

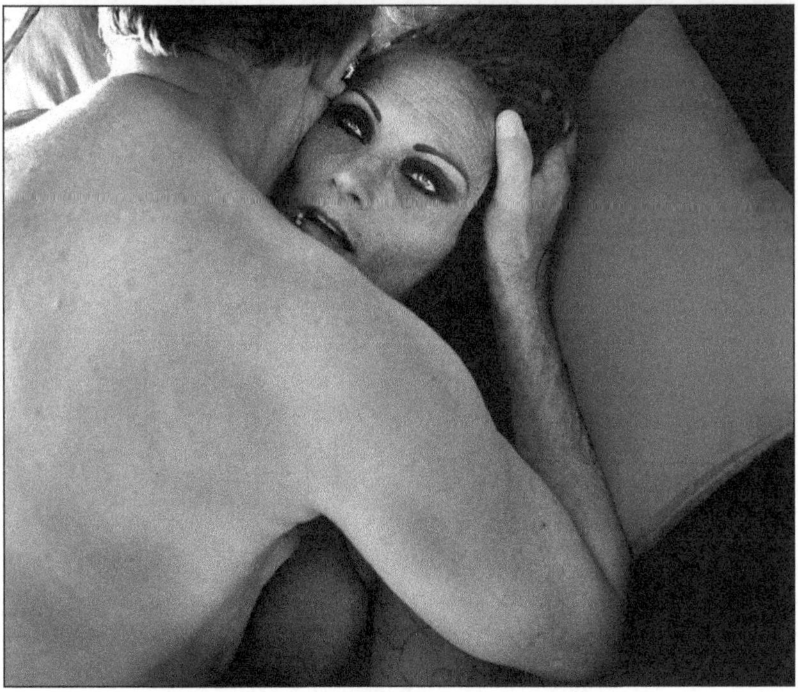

Photos: Marie Hald, 2014. Reprinted with kind permission.

The Spectrum of Motherhood

ALISON GRANGER-BROWN, GORDANA ELDJUPOVIC,
AMANDA STALLER, AND STEVEN MOORE

TRACY G. MCCLELLAND AND ROBERT NEWELL cite "Dalla [who] suggests that women involved in prostitution are seldom identified as parents" (436). We open our chapter with the story of a woman who is a mother. She was also an addict and for many years worked in increasing depths of the sex trade. Below, she tells her life story in all these roles to a friend from recovery. He held the pen and diligently recorded her narrative, scribing her uninhibited stream of memories. This story is our data, and as such, we allowed it to show us the way. This approach to data collection is valuable, not only in gathering complex and rich information, but also because it has the potential to heal. Indigenous research traditions, according to Four Arrows, Cajete and Lee, guide us to ensure that the "doing" of research must add value to those generous enough to give us a precious possession: their story. They continue, stating that similar to constructivism, Indigenous ontology believes there are multiple realities that are socially constructed; truth is not a fixed point, but constantly evolving, a point of balance, "perpetually created and perpetually new" (115). According to Smith, Indigenous research recognizes multiple ways to be either an insider or outsider researcher for which "the critical issue with insider research is the constant need for reflexivity" (137), as was the process for our storyteller.

This reflexivity is also a reminder of our social responsibility. We are all called into these relationships, as so much of anyone's identity is constructed by *us* and through interactions with *us*. We learn from our protagonist as she talks about being whomever anyone else wanted her to be; not just the johns, but we all play a role in constructing who she is and who she was. This is the struggle identified throughout: Who am I? Finally, she recognizes that she has been found. Actually, she was never lost, but her "self" was hidden by all the pressures of a difficult childhood and a judgemental society.

According to Oselin, "identities are fluid and can change depending on one's role and social positions, thus making identity transformations commonplace" (380). Oselin goes on to cite Stryker in explaining that identities are "parts of self, internalized positional designations and exist insofar as the person is a participant in structured role relationships" (382). Cooley's development of the concept the "looking-glass self," as described by Erickson et al., sheds further light on understanding the notion of identity(-ies) and role relationships. These authors suggest that "looking-glass self-concepts are the reflection of others' perceptions of us; in essence we are, or become, what we think others think we are" (780). Considering that "mothering in prostitution runs counter to the conventional view of mothering, it would not be surprising if it is commonly viewed as flawed" (Peled and Levin-Rotberg 44). We will add, following Cooley's notion of the looking glass, it is likely that it is also viewed as flawed by the "protagonist"—the mother. In other words, as Erikson et al. remind us, external perceptions translate into self-concepts that may aid in the understanding of "deviant" subgroups.

This chapter is about the evolution of identity, structured roles, and transformation: the reconciling of multiple events and the complexity of one's development from hurt through hope to healing.

There is no one story of prostitution and mothering according to McClelland and Newell, who conducted focus groups with twenty women who were mothers, substance abusers, and prostitutes. They pointed out that "although women in this study reported similar experiences, their personal experiences are unique to them and their children, and they do not represent a homogeneous group" (438). The present story is, therefore, a unique story that presents a temporal narrative rather than a snapshot view. This allows us to observe the fluidity of her identity: how her identify unfolds and changes throughout.

Independent of recording the storyteller's stream of memories, we reviewed studies on mothering and prostitution and identified main themes and factors highlighted by these studies. As expected, and as will be shown later in this chapter, all of these factors were present in her story. We used them as "anchors" to highlight experiences and aspects of her journey that research reports were not able to explain or capture. This paved the way to focus attention on the co-existence of opposing views, desires, and roles in the lived experience of prostitution, addiction, and mothering.

Our storyteller's journey will be presented in sections that reflect development and the stages of her life in prostitution, drug use, and mothering: her struggles and temptations. Each section of her narrative will end with comments by the co-authors of this chapter. Discussions highlight factors identified in the literature that our teller's story reveals. Following these discussions, we identify "missing" links, tracking what is not accounted for by these factors. These missing links are what makes the teller's story unique. Finally, we suggest that discerning what is not accounted for in the teller's story by existing research delineates areas of further research.

BEGINNINGS AND ENDINGS

I had a good view of the tree from the trailer window, and had stared at it many times this past year. I'm not entirely clear how I planned to use it; all I remember is being broken, sore, and exhausted. I didn't know how to live in my flesh: I was dying in order to live. It's difficult to explain when it all began, and how, and why. Maybe there is no one perfect explanation for any of life's choices and paths; all we can do is tell our story. Mine is one of rejection: first my biological father, but mainly my own of me.

I remember being sexually abused by the neighbor-boy, whose name I forget. At five, the offer of a fudgesicle was tempting enough for me to trust him. I didn't comprehend what was happening, but I made a promise to keep it a secret. Secrets became, from this time on, a way of life for me. My stepfather beat my mother regularly, and I saw it happen often. I couldn't tell anyone, for fear of getting in trouble, so I just kept it all inside, and vowed to take care of my little sister. We were afraid much of the time, as my mother drank a lot, and partied, and the beatings continued alongside all of this.

I was afraid most of the time. Nothing seemed permanent or "normal," and the secrets and lies I had to keep increased daily. I was the secret-keeper, persona unknown, and the responsibility weighed heavily on me. What I could not know then, was that this role was to become my norm, my default, throughout my life, helping me at times, to be sure, but mostly adding to my dis-ease with the world and the people I encountered.

In grade three, I began to have seizures; doctors prescribed medications, and I remember this was the first time I felt a positive attraction to the effects of drugs. I could, for a time anyway, escape myself and my reality. The fact that a pill could do this for me was fascinating. I remember feeling like my insides didn't match my outsides. I was one person at school and another at home, full of secrets and fears in both worlds. I didn't know who I was, or who I was supposed to be.

By seventeen, I had quit school, tried cocaine for the first time and loved it, and met a friend of a friend: much older than me; he had a car, and access to lots of cocaine. We partied, it seemed, almost all the time, and I quickly moved from doing straight cocaine to freebasing. Life's problems ceased to exist when I was high. To avoid the inevitable crash after using, I stayed high, which became a job in itself. I guess this is where sex work began, when I was working as a waitress in a smart restaurant in a ski resort. There were men, lots of them, always happy to give me money or drugs and to buy me anything. They were being nice to me so I would be "nice" to them. They were my "friends." They could easily have been my father, but when you get high you live in the moment, just this one moment.

DISCUSSION

There is a clear link between prostitution and substance abuse (Kennedy et al.; Kohm; McClelland and Newell; Sloss and Harper). Women employ one to manage the other. Women engage in the sex trade to obtain money for their drug use and/or they resort to drug use to make their way of earning money, sex as work, bearable. Regardless of how it starts, the outcome is the same—development of a strong link between two equally life-threatening, socially-unacceptable, and inherently-marginalizing lifestyles and ways of being:

> This vicious cycle of prostitution for drugs, under which more drugs are required to cope with the prostitution, and in turn more prostitution is required to afford drugs, drives the prostitute into deeper despair. Rather than affording women ultimate control over their bodies, prostitution quickly results in the ultimate loss of autonomy, power, and control over not only one's body, but over one's life. (Kohm 419)

The narrative presented in this chapter shows how the interdependence of prostitution and drug use evolved in the storyteller's life and how it was facilitated by vulnerability factors stemming from childhood. As Kohm points out, women enter prostitution "to attempt to overcome an upbringing of poverty and possibly abuse or lack of parental (particularly paternal) nurturing" (418). Rejection by her father was a significant factor for our storyteller, whose account highlights the lack of resources and sufficient stability for building a core identity, trust, and ability to recognize her own emotions, and observations: "I found independence through dependence on men."

Her way of making sense of an unstable, ever-changing environment was to develop a "matching," equally unstable, ever-changing identity of not knowing who she was. In Oselin's terms, as her story unfolds, we witness the fluidity of her identity depending on her role and social positions. Her "insides did not match her outsides." She became a "secret-keeper" and this in itself became a secret. Quick fixes and guaranteed drug highs became her "stability"—something she could always rely on.

ENTERING MOTHERHOOD

By the age of nineteen, I was pregnant and managed to stop doing cocaine throughout. However, the shame, guilt, and depression was overwhelming; everyone around me was happy, but I was not. I was not in love, just a place to live, all the while knowing I would start using again after giving birth: the cravings were just so strong. I would have to escape. We both kept trying; but our son went to his grandparents permanently as we were in and out of detox like a revolving door, chasing the rush to satisfy intense cravings. I was also getting into trouble with the law and just plain wearing out my body: doing anything for a fix and then treatment again.

I started prostituting myself during this time and each time I went out it got worse. I was young, with red hair and good looks, much-favoured by older men. The drug use had yet to take its toll, so I was able to command top prices, and even worked in an escort agency for a while, which was semi-safe: never a shortage of older men willing to pay for a young woman.

I carried a vagabond-bag with a toothbrush, condoms, and a change of clothes, bouncing around, never in one place for long—always on the move, running from I don't know what, but running nonetheless. Eventually, though, I met a guy at a treatment centre. He was again older than me, had money, and was funny. I came to realized that while men used me for sex, I used men for what they had to offer me. More money without a condom? Sure, why not? Some days I said no, but often yes ... more money equalled more dope.

It was during this time that I had my first bad date. He picked me up in a cab and took me to a park, where he began to beat and rape me. A dog scared him off. I don't know why I survived that night, but it didn't change my behaviour or routines. Immediately after the assault I went to a house—crack shack, really. All I wanted was to get high, and stay high, so I did. No point in going to the police; how much attention would they pay to a prostitute reporting a rape? That night a man overdosed in the shack and was found dead in the morning. None of this fazed me, but I remember thinking, "Shit just got real."

Sometime during this unsettled existence, I became pregnant again, only this time I used cocaine throughout, I couldn't stop. I hoped I would die soon; my mind was trapped in my growing body. No happiness this time, everyone wanted me to end it but I missed four appointments until it was too late. Perhaps deliberate? I don't know, but I gave birth to a baby girl; she was addicted to cocaine. Nothing happens in God's world by mistake and I called her Angel 'cos she was so beautiful and she kept me alive.

Two things are etched into my mind and heart from this time. The first is the tender, non-judgmental kindness of the doctor who delivered her; I hadn't felt the comfort and acceptance he offered me in a long time. There were no stern lectures and pitying looks: only quiet, calm dignity, given freely to one who didn't think she deserved it. The second thing occurred on the day I left the hospital. I was leaving, without her, and I visited the hospital chapel to ask for forgiveness for what I had done. How could I have brought her into this world addicted? I was so sorry I could not look after her. I must be a really bad person; nice people don't do that stuff.... I never really knew the difference between like and respect for myself.... I judged myself as bad rather than sick.

From the time I was young, I had witnessed men mistreating and dominating women. This doesn't mean I made a conscious choice to become a prostitute. I hooked and hustled because I needed the cocaine and later heroin with the cocaine. Even when working in so-called "safe" settings for prostitution, I was aware of the dangers. Men would not pay, or outright rob me, and sometimes they were violent. It didn't matter where I was: there were men willing to pay for sex.

I never sold myself cheap. I don't know how, but I never got to the point of hustling in the alleys for ten or twenty dollars. Later on, in what I refer to as my "disguise days," I turned also to theft and cons. I was tired and sore from the streets, and I needed drugs more often and in larger quantities in order to survive. I was in a living hell, full of remorse and desperately avoiding the thoughts of my children, and the life I led. I tried hard not to think about them and threw myself into being an actress, pretending.... Nobody knew I had kids: that's a matter of the heart. You don't sit in a crack shack and talk about matters of the heart. I made a trade-off: the living hell of prostitution and constantly being on the move was better in some strange but important way than the living hell of withdrawal and life without cocaine.

DISCUSSION

The segregation of thought and feelings about children is not uncommon among mothers who work in the sex trade. In a study by Sloss and Harper a "woman explained that while on the street, she 'locks out' her feelings and personal/family life, such that when she finishes working, she removes the 'blocks' and is the same non-working person" (335). This is well illustrated in our story. The storyteller states, "Nobody knew I had kids: that's a matter of the heart. You don't sit in a crack shack and talk about matters of the heart."

In order to protect her children, she gave them up. Once she gave up custody, safety no longer mattered. She needed and created a chaotic life to assist with forgetting. She "checked in and out from the heart." She was checking in and out of different parts of self and her roles as a way of self-preservation and as a result of realizing that she was not able to mother. As noted by McClelland and Newell, mothers often resorted to "negative coping strategies, such as increase in drug and alcohol consumption, with additional involvement in prostitution to fund them" (443), in order to deal with emotional difficulties associated with the despair of having to give up custody, or losing custody, of their children.

As with the memory of the kind doctor, McClelland and Newell's study showed supportive factors identified by twenty women who were mothers, substance abusers, and prostitutes: positive relationships, decent accommodation, and responsive services (such as drug clinics) with empathetic staff. Leaving the hospital without her child, via the chapel, reflects the shame, despair, and guilt associated with giving birth, becoming a mother and, yet, leaving the baby behind with a deliberate decision to do so, having assured herself that her child would stay within family. As is the case with the present storyteller, the literature documents the shame and guilt of both sex trade workers who tried to manage looking after their children while working the streets, as well as those who did not have custody of their children (Kohm; Sloss and Harper). "A feeling must be the truth, or so I thought. Negative emotions about myself reflect how things really are, it must be true. Now I know different: I had to learn to separate these from reality."

Of note is that the storyteller remembers her pregnancy in a similar way as she describes her vagabond bag. Did she have an alternative? Greater reflection on her pregnancy and what followed would cause unbearable pain. Instead of reflections and emotions, all her experiences and actions collided in her body: her pregnancy; earning money via selling her body; taking a risk to engage in unprotected sex for extra money; her body decaying; getting deeper into addiction. This was the core of who she was in that moment, and the secrets she kept—who she wanted to forget in order to preserve self. It is the fluidity of identity that kept her afloat.

THE PRICE

I met another guy at AA, and we got to know each other over a year or so. He was well employed, making him one of the most stable men I had met in a long time. We both used cocaine occasionally, even though we were in the program, but this time, his money supplied us well. There were warning signs: he bought and sold guns, and hoarded an arsenal in the house. He sold drugs, and later got into growing marijuana. Once again I was faced with the necessity of keeping secrets, and the fear of being discovered. I was with him for security, and here I was again, back into the vicious cycle of secrecy and fear. What he got from our relationship was often a mystery, but I was, I suppose, a trophy girlfriend, as well as a partner in his drug use. He bought me with a sports car, clothes, and vacations to tropical destinations. It seemed like a great life, but I always had an uneasy feeling, which makes my choice to marry him appear—even then—oddly masochistic: saying yes, without thinking, to the $6000 diamond ring.

I was in love with being in love, as I see it now, and even though I said yes, I didn't know what I was saying yes to. I got clean after having our first boy. I replaced my addiction to drugs and alcohol with other "isms": I used and abused over-the-counter drugs, such as Neo-Citron and Benadryl, to simulate a milder form of the oblivion I craved; I started to run, and became obsessed with losing weight; I shopped, using his money compulsively. I still attended AA, and became very involved in the local groups. Meanwhile, he continued to use, and even increased his drug use, eventually injecting heroin on a daily basis, sleeping most of the time he was not working, and suffering from serious mental health issues. I played the dutiful mother and wife for the sake of keeping up appearances. I worked at all the things typical housewives were supposed to do in the suburbs. I took the kids to soccer and play dates, kept the house clean, did the laundry, and cooked. I had a wonderful sense of connection with the two boys who were my third chance to be a mother. I loved snuggling with them, reading to them, playing with them, and taking them to parks and generally being the best mom I could be for my boys.

All was not well, however. I felt as if I had sold myself to this man in exchange for a "normal" life, which was a delusional sham. So desperate was I for calm, some shelter: I don't like thinking about it even now, years later. I felt so phony and shallow, and at the same time, accepting his gifts, and all the other luxurious and even mundane things he bought for me, and for the boys. I knew too much about his "operation" to be able to leave, or so I thought, as he did not trust me. I just kept looking the other way whenever possible and was constantly stressed and traumatized by all I had been through. I needed to stay strong for my children and to continue to keep up appearances. I looked better than I had in a long time, and I was healthy again, so how bad could it really be?

Things got worse and he became completely unavailable emotionally and had turned to degrading and sickening computer sex and pornography. (I shudder even now at the thought of these images and of his complete disregard for, or inability to, live a normal life.) I began to fantasize, and eventually to actually plan, a way out. I figured if I stayed around for a while longer, I could divorce him, and cash in on the settlement. I had no frame of reference to compare my life to, except for what I had already seen and lived.

Eventually, my decision was made for me; I caught him with a prostitute. Truth stared directly at me, and I reacted immediately, swearing to get even for this betrayal. What happened next—or what I did next—needs to be understood in the context of the immense pull of cocaine and dope. I was four years clean at this time, but the only reliable relief I knew was cocaine. It was as if six years of pain and suffering at the hands of this man had to be numbed. Couple this with a fierce desire to do to him what he had done to me, and six weeks later, I got loaded, and stayed loaded.

With both of us using again, I feared mostly for the boys. I needed to think of a way to keep them safe, so I started to talk of leaving. He threatened to kill me and the boys if I did leave, so I did the only thing I knew to do: I called Social Services. This was a huge risk, as I would certainly be questioned about our life. If I told even half of what I knew, I could ruin many people's lives. So, he held me as a virtual prisoner in my own home. Yet again, I was at the mercy of a man. We sold the house, and spent all the money on cocaine, dope, and alcohol. Our lives went to shit. I worked with Social Services to make sure my mom got the kids, and from then on, I was gone, in every sense: gone.

DISCUSSION

Some mechanisms of living a mainstream, middle-class lifestyle are not that different from what some sex trade workers do. As the storyteller said: "As I read this again, I realized that my thinking rested on the idea that if I couldn't be somebody within myself, I would have to marry somebody." This form of what could be considered prostitution may be more common than society recognizes. Mothers compromise themselves in order to provide for their children. One could argue that they "sell themselves" as "trophy wives" or "arm candy." The lifestyle they establish through these roles enables their children to have a nice house, extracurricular activities, and friends from "good homes." It enables children to have a life that is quite different from the lives of some children of prostitutes who live with their "working" mothers and who "have experienced varying degrees of neglect" (McClelland and Newell 441).

Keeping this in mind, we highlight the paradox that an aspect of the middle-class mother's life (for instance, continual investment in the "arm candy" image in order to preserve herself and her children's comfortable middle-class life) is not essentially different from findings that women continue or intensify their engagement in prostitution in order to provide for their children (Sloss and Harper).

For a number of years, the storyteller was able to manage checking in and checking out of her role. However, as the dysfunctional relationship with her husband intensified, her need for a "quick fix" also grew. She was no longer able to "keep the secret"; she resorted back to drugs. Her concern of losing custody due to being an unfit mother and an addict paradoxically led to staying clean and sober during her collaboration with Social Services. Although knowing that soon she would "check out" of the mother role, she did not give up on it until she ensured that her mother got custody of her children.

DYING INSIDE

I wanted to die. Instead, I said goodbye to Hello Kitty pajamas and found a pathway into my children's life.

I checked out completely, and proceeded straight downhill. I started to live out of a bag as I had ten years earlier, but this time I used wigs and clothing as disguises. Older now, not the young girl most men wanted, I decided to give men a fantasy, and for me, it was a chance to disappear. I didn't know who I was anymore. I cut off ties with my family, figuring that my children would be better off not knowing me: I stayed high 24/7. Everything had imploded—or exploded—and I was just debris from the wreckage. I knew nothing except the life of a junkie, and decided I was destined to live and to die eventually on the streets. Sex sells anywhere, so it didn't matter where I was. As long as I stayed high, I didn't have to think about my children, and what I had done to my life. Nothing mattered. I even brought cocaine into prison: a friend and I had a gig going, where I would pick up drops, and we would both get our fix inside. There were no serious attempts at detox or treatment for drug addiction in prison, so I just did my time, and walked out after my bit, and re-entered street life.

Once in a while, I would go to a drop-in centre for clothes, makeup, hot food, and a rest from the streets. My feet ached all the time, and I was developing sores on my body and face from picking at my skin when unable to get a fix. Disguises helped me attract "clients," and rob them if I could without too much trouble. It sounds strange, but I was happy, so long as I had money and cocaine. The oblivion I entered into with each hit on the pipe was more than a sensation: it was everything. It wasn't all bad on the streets either, while I encountered some violent men, I also met kind men, who would help me, and some became friends. I was back in the life, and this time, I was sure it would end with my death. I was a survivor—but this time, it was different. Gone was the youthful energy and "looks" that helped me survive my past on the street. I was so tired and had had enough overdoses to show me the true danger of my life, but I just wouldn't die.

Towards the end of this ten-year spree, I was completely beaten down, worn out, strung out, and needed the help of many more organizations than before. I was frequently using soup kitchens, outpatient programs, and programs for "at risk" women. Around this time, it was getting cold and I needed a place to stay, and money. A friend owed me, and said she was owed money by a man, who lived in a trailer not far from town. He said he would give us the money he owed, and even agreed to take me in temporarily, and take care of me while I looked for a place of my own. This led to a year that I cannot bear, even today, to think about. He didn't take care of me in any way, except to provide me with alcohol and drugs once in a while. For one year, he beat me constantly, and held me prisoner in his trailer. He was a blackout drinker, and I would often wake up with welts all over my body. He used a belt and his fists, even his teeth. He bit my toenail off at one point.

Caught once again in my addiction, I worked with him, stealing copper to sell to the scrap dealers, and even helping him and some of his friends to start a grow-op. Unlike my life with my ex-husband, there were no good times to balance the horror. He ripped out chunks of my hair, and bruised almost every part of my body, only to tell me afterwards that it was my fault, because I talked back to him. I did talk back to him; I am a strong woman who had survived street life for years. But for this year with him, I lived inside a paralyzing fear. Up in the bush, I was trapped, I knew no one, and to walk away seemed impossible. I did try once; he dragged me back to more beating. Looking at myself, "thoughts were bouncing off that mirror into my face." It became clear that the only way out would be suicide. The tree: glowing with life in the sunshine.

As I looked at the rope and the tree and realized the impossibility and futility, I felt a wave of despair, an overwhelming weakness overcame me. I just wanted out. It had been a grey and very dark winter, but as I stood there contemplating death, the clouds parted just enough to let a small bit of sunlight through. I dropped the rope and started walking to the light that shone through the haze and on towards the road to town.

I remembered one friend who might be able to help, so I began my change wearing only my baby girl Hello Kitty pajamas, a pair of boots, a coat, and—of course—several beers stashed in the pockets. I didn't know what I was doing; I just walked and kept on going. It took me all that day to hitchhike, with my only thought being, "Just make it to C, and she will know what to do." She did know, and got a friend to drive me to my sister's house. All I could think about or say—as I shook and shivered in the car—was, "Please, just get me to L's house, and she will take care of me." She did, and her first words were, "We're saying goodbye to Hello Kitty."

I detoxed with her, and have been sober ever since. She took me to AA, which I hated, but J told me to keep going, keep trying, and that she would never hurt me. That was when I started to believe for the first time that I never again had to feel the way I had for over twenty years. As I felt the warmth of J's hand in mine, and her words in my ear, I began to hope for the first time. J would not allow me to be a victim; she would not do things for me that she and I both knew I could do for myself.

The fight was on. Every brick they threw at me, I used to build a foundation for my recovery. Today, I am a recovered addict, who works with other addicts, including men, to help them the way others helped me. I recently graduated from college with a diploma in Addictions and Community Service Work. I have found a pathway into my children's lives that is perhaps not the "typical" mother role, but I let them decide how they needed to react to me, and so far it has been positive. I don't, and never did, expect to be able to simply walk back into their lives, announce my return, and think that all could be forgiven and forgotten. I now have grandchildren and attend family functions. Greeting my children with love, I then step back, allowing them to know me in their own time and in their terms.

My mother, after all these years, and with what she has done for my children, is one of the constants in my life, regardless of how far into my addiction I was to realize it at times. She bought me fitness clothes—not hooker clothes. I didn't know what to buy.... I am so grateful she took me to the hair salon: my hair was matted and chunks were missing.... I was so afraid of people judging me.... I even had to have a fake toe nail because he had bitten it off.

Since I have recovered, and now lead a life of service to other sufferers, I have rebuilt my trust in men through the other constant in my life. He was a friend of mine in high school who was always there for me, ready with a smile and a hug, supporting me and loving me through all my addictive behaviours and never using me. We are getting married, after a rough courtship, to say the least, and I have finally discovered who I am: I am....

DISCUSSION

Our storyteller's relationship with her mother requires closer examination. Lack of unwavering parental care, exposure to her mother's drinking and multiple partners have been, no doubt, contributing factors in the development of her path of "quick fixes" and keeping secrets. However, over time as her life evolved, her mother's behaviour became a protective factor and a major source of constancy. She referred to her mother as her "main support." It is precisely here, and through utilizing the temporal approach to the analysis of this issue, that the notion of hope is highlighted in this story. No matter how long the journey takes, there is always the possibility that with support, the mother may reunite with her children.

Kohm explains that "[a] potential loss of custody of a child is a major concern of a prostitute who wishes to remain a mother to her child" (425). By accepting to look after her grand-children, her mother eased her angst. In the long term, by doing this, she made the mother-child reunions possible. Therefore, our temporal approach to understanding the present story allows and encourages us to see the role of the mother (both the storyteller's and her mother's) as fluid and changing. A source of factors that at one point contributed to prostitution and addiction, at another time emerged and became a source of protective factors.

Her sister supported her to say goodbye to Hello Kitty pajamas and the identity they represented for her, while her mother took her to the hairdresser and for a pedicure to mask the injuries and damage from prolonged physical abuse. She bought her exercise clothes, which hookers usually do not wear. This is a seemingly simple intervention on the part of her mother, but in fact it assisted the storyteller in switching to a new identity and believing that she could be something else. To paraphrase Cooley, her mother's reactions were her "looking-glass"; the storyteller's self-concept became a reflection of her mother's perception of her, of her mother seeing her as someone who deserves to wear clothes that are not to advertise her body for sale. "There are many ways to heal from abuse, there is no right way, no tidy step by step, just getting down and dirty with yourself. I started to heal by washing floors ... literally."

CONCLUDING THOUGHTS

The present story highlights that one is a mother even when "checking in and out" of this role, and physiologically one will always be the mother. Future research could be well served by exploring the dominant social reaction to a mother seen to be ill or in trouble. It seems that society wants to respond. However, in contrast, as we separate the identity of mother out, leaving only prostitute, we abdicate responsibility and fall to blame, shame, and ostracization.

As Oselin, quoting Brown, points out, "Some individuals with 'deviant' identities were able to capitalize on them as they transitioned to a professional career" (383). This is true for those with addiction histories but does not appear to be the case for prostitutes, partly because the stigma attached to prostitution is extremely high and affects identities intricately connected to gender (e.g., sexually chaste, mothers). Oselin further shows that when one's role and identity are stigmatized, the individuals are assumed to be deficient, and this categorization allows for discriminatory practices enforced by the "normals" onto the stigmatized, "discredited" individuals.

The driving factor for our storyteller to leave her children was her addiction. Prostitution was "just" the means of getting drugs. At the beginning, she tells us that her story will be about how she rejected her own self and became whomever anyone wanted her to be. We highlight that she would not have been able to reject herself and become whomever anyone wanted her to be, had she not had assistance from the "normals," who willingly and knowingly engaged in buying a young woman's body for sex and asked her to be whomever they fantasized, because she needed money for the next "fix." For many years these transactions became her dominant "looking glass" due to her, understandably, having to temporarily forget that she was a mother to in fact preserve her mother-identity for the future.

WORKS CITED

Erickson, Patricia, Jennifer Butters, Patti McGillcuddy and Ase Hallgren. "Race and Prostitution: Gender, Myths and Experiences." *Journal of Drug Issues* 30.4 (2000): 767-788. Print.

Four Arrows, Gregory Cajete, and Jason Lee. *Critical Neurophilosophy and Indigenous Wisdom.* Rotterdam: Sense, 2010. Print.

Kennedy, Alexis M., Carlin Klein, Jessica T. K. Bristowe, Barry S. Cooper and John C. Yuille. "Routes of Recruitment: Pimps' Techniques and Other Circumstances That Lead to Street Prostitution." *Journal of Aggression, Maltreatment and Trauma* 15.2 (2007): 1-19. Print.

Kohm, Lynne M. "Women as Perpetrators: Does Motherhood Have a Reformative Effect on Prostitution?" *Fordham Urban Law Journal* 33.2 (2006): 407-429. Print.

McClelland, Tracy G. and Robert Newell. "A Qualitative Study of the Experiences of Mothers Involved in Street-based Prostitution and Problematic Substance Use." *Journal of Research in Nursing* 13.5 (2008): 437-447. Print.

Oselin, Sharon S. "Leaving the Streets: Transformation of Prostitute Identity within the Prostitution Rehabilitation Program." *Deviant Behavior* 30.4 (2009): 379-406. Print.

Peled, Einat and Tal Levin-Rotberg. "The Perceptions of Child

Protection Officers toward Mothering in Prostitution." *Social Service Review* 87.1 (2013): 40-69. Print.

Sloss, Christine M. and Gary W. Harper. "When Street Sex Workers Are Mothers." *Archives of Sexual Behavior* 33.4 (2004): 329-341. Print.

Smith, Linda. *Decolonizing Methodologies: Research and Indigenous Peoples*. Dunedin: University of Otago, 1999. Print.

Portrait of Maya Angelou as a Dancer

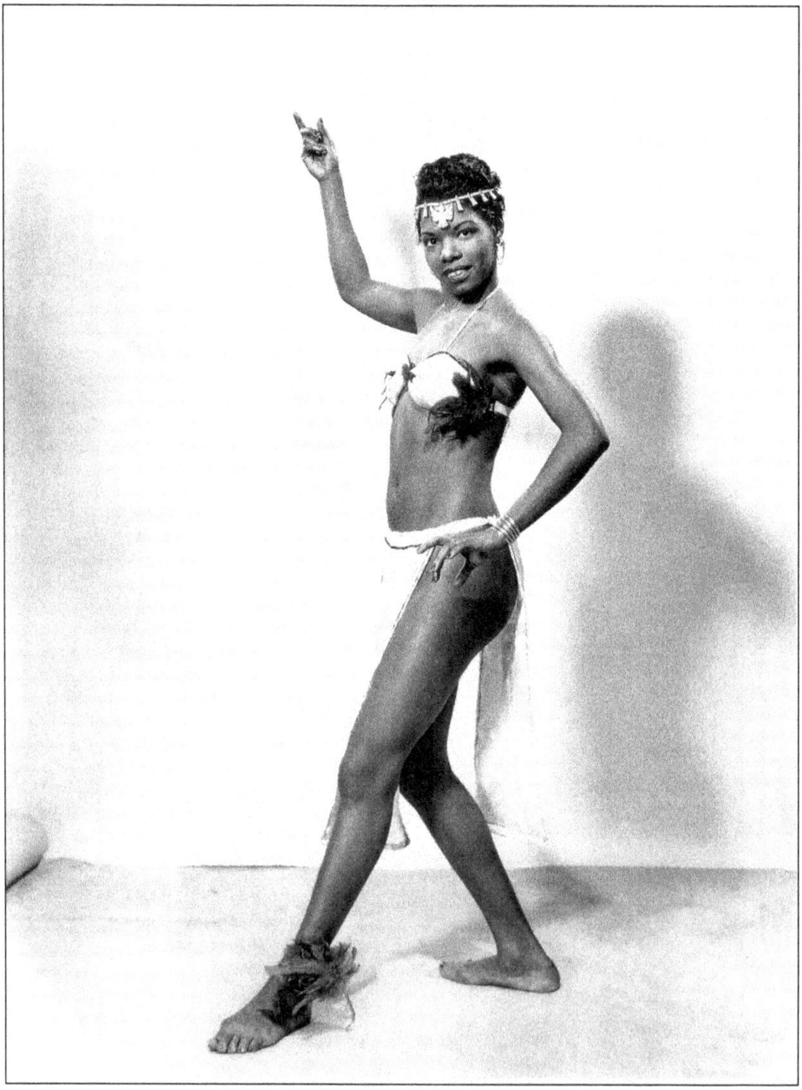

Photo: Michael Ochs Archives/Getty Images, circa 1950

Excerpt from *Gather Together in My Name*

MAYA ANGELOU

DURING THIS TIME WHEN MY life hinged melodramatically on intrigue and deceit, I discovered the Russian writers. One title caught my eye. Not because I felt guilty raking in money from the doings of prostitutes but because of the title's perfect balance. Life, as far as I had deduced it, was a series of opposites: black/white, up/down, life/death, rich/poor, love/hate, happy/sad and no mitigating areas in between. It followed *Crime & Punishment.*

The heavy opulence of Dostoevsky's world was where I had lived forever. The gloomy, lightless interiors, the complex ratiocinations of the characters and their burdensome humors, were as familiar to me as loneliness.

I walked the sunny California streets shrouded in Russian mists. I fell in love with the Karamazov brothers and longed to drink from a samovar with the lecherous old father. Then Gorki became my favorite. He was the blackest, most dear, most despairing. The books couldn't last long enough for me. I wished the writers all alive, turning out manuscripts for my addiction. I took to the Chekov plays and Turgenev, but always returned to the late nights, after I had collected my boodle, to the Maxim Gorki and his murky, unjust world.

My dance teacher, who took no personal interest, wore the most outlandish clothes. Her long dark skirt, gathered, fell to just above her ankles. The blouses were of Mexican persuasion and were worn off her thin shoulders. Ropes of colorful beads and thong sandals completed her costume. She looked odd enough for admiration.

I copied her clothes, and when not dressed in the white-blouse, black-skirt waitress uniform, I could be seen haunting the libraries, a tall thin black girl in too-long skirts and senorita blouses, which might have been sexy had I had the figure and/or attitude to complement them. Alas, I didn't.

Upon reflection, I marvel that no one saw through me enough to bundle me off to the nearest mental institution. The fact that it didn't happen depended less on my being a good actress than the fact that I was surrounded, as I had been all my life, by strangers. The world of waitress, dreamer, madam and mother might have continued indefinitely, except for another of life's unexpected surprises.

I didn't insist on any rules in my little whorehouse by the side of the road except one: no all-night dates, no matter what the temptation. I wanted the money without name, the ease without strain. I never wanted any tricks to be in the house when I arrived, hence the signal with Hank.

One evening I sat in a taxi on the darkened street (I never took my automobile to the whorehouse) and waited for the light to go off on the porch. The driver, who also bought trade, and I walked into the house.

I stood in the center of the tiny living room, which smelled of Lysol and smoke and incense, hemmed in by the driver, the women and Hank, and by the furniture, which threatened to oust us all at any moment. Beatrice and Johnnie Mae erased any budding aspirations I had for owning things. Now that they had money, their acquisitive natures came into their own. The total filling up of the living room was so gradual that it was as if the existing furniture gave birth nightly to smaller and even larger images of itself.

Hank passed me the cigar box of money.

"Damn, turn the damned radio off till we get business settled. You can't hear a shitting thing." I had taken to cursing to round out my image. The two women no longer took any interest in me, except possibly to hate my arrogance and envy my authority. I couldn't care less.

I had not finished recovering their chits and was about to turn to the cabdriver when a drunk, half-dressed white sailor stumbled through the bedroom door. He had nothing on below the blue middy. There was a moment's hush when the women and Hank looked at me. I was hypnotized at the man's nudity and couldn't take my eyes off his white, soft, dangling penis.

Beatrice ran to him. "Honey, I told you to stay—"

"What's going on? Who are these folks?" His accent was lower Mississippi, and he looked as naked and white and ugly and drunk and nasty as anything I could think of.

Beatrice herded him back into the room.

In those seconds, I became a child again. Unreasoning rage consumed me. The low-down sneaking bitches—I had told them to have the place cleared before I got there. They had probably had tricks there every night and I hadn't even questioned them. I could have gone to jail or worse. After all I'd done for them, their whorish hearts were so ungrateful that I had been subjugated to looking at the sickening aspect of a white man's penis.

I turned to Hank, and lumbering toward me, he said, "Rita, swear to God, I thought they was all gone."

Johnnie Mae allowed a little of her jealousy to show. "I don't see nothing wrong myself. You come over here every night collecting money, acting like you somebody's pimp. But you too good to turn a trick. And you keep this big rough sonofabitch watching us all the time. Well, you can kiss my black ass."

Her rudeness didn't surprise me. I would not have moved an eyebrow at anything anymore. The driver stood mesmerized by the event.

I gave the cigar box to Hank. "Hank. Do you want a whorehouse, complete with whores? You've just been given one." I turned to the women, gathering all my injured dignity. "And, ladies, you decided in the beginning that you were going to screw me one way or the other. Look at us now. Who did the screwing?"

Beatrice's voice keened, sharpened and moved through the room like a swinging razor. "If it hadn't been for you, we'd be living like we always did."

"Yes, in the street or back in some white woman's kitchen."

Johnnie Mae swelled up as if she had taken in more air than it was possible to release. "Be goddamn careful how you talk to her, you big-nose bitch."

It was time to go. These lying heathens were not above attacking me. And after all I'd done for them.

"Hank, if you want this place, it's all yours." And one parting shot to the traitors: "At least I'm leaving you better off than I found you. You've got enough secondhand furniture to start your own Goodwill store." And to the cab driver: "Will you please take me home."

I stood straighter, separating myself from the stench of my present environment, and started out. Johnnie Mae's rage propelled her after me. I reached the door just as she stretched her hand for me. I put on a little speed, not wanting to appear to be running, and escaped down the steps as she and the cabdriver collided in the doorway. He extricated himself in a hurry, more than a little terrified of getting caught between two restless tribes. Johnnie Mae, thwarted, for I had gained the sidewalk, screamed out into the quiet darkness: "You bitch! You think the police don't want to know how you bought that car. You better not drive it again. I'll have the vice squad on your ass."

I don't know how I continued walking to the cab. Her threat and the sound of her screech had stabbed me to the quick as surely as it had pierced the night. The wretch would put the cops on my trail and I'd lose my car, go to jail and be put out of Mother Cleo's. I was sitting in the back of the taxi when a numbing thought sidled across my brain like a poisonous snake, I might be declared an unfit mother and my son would be made a ward of the court. There were cases like that. The tiny glands on my armpits opened and closed to the pricking of a thousand straight pins.

"Please take me home, and I'm sorry for that terrible outburst." Fear still rode the front seat with the driver and he lost no time in depositing me at my destination. I paid him, tipped him grandly and inundated him with praise for his reliability and courtesy and lack of familiarity. I don't think he heard a word, and before I reached the front door, his tail lights had turned winking around the corner.

During the exotic buying sprees, I hadn't though to get luggage to hold my new acquisitions. I heaped piles of my clothes and my son's into the suitcases Bailey had given me in San Francisco. I had made up my mind that come daybreak, my son and I were going to make a run for it. If the police caught me, they'd catch me at the railway station or on the train, not a sitting duck waiting passively to be arrested. When I had finished cramming as many things as possible into the bags, I sat down to ready until daybreak.

Since childhood I had often read until the gray light entered my room, but on that tense night it seemed like sleep had allied itself with my enemies, and along with them was determined to overpower me, do me down. I tried sitting in a chair and sitting cross-legged on the bed. A knock awoke me. It was Mother Cleo.

"Rita, you left your light on again. You going to start helping me with the electricity. You don't know how much it cost..." She was moving away from the door, and her words reached down the hall.

I came to full attention and checked my luggage, my money and my story again.

"Mother Cleo, my mother is sick in San Francisco. She telephoned me at the club last night, so I have to go home." I had followed her into the kitchen. She put down her cup and looked at me with such sympathy. I almost wished I wasn't lying.

"Oh, you poor thing. She ain't bad off, is she?"

"Oh, nothing serious." I wanted to calm her fears.

"Well the, you won't be long. You'll leave the baby?"

"Oh no. She wants to see him. And I'll tell you the truth"—as if I could—"I'm not coming back soon."

"Aw, don't tell me that. I've come to look on you as family."

"Mother Cleo, I appreciate everything you've done for us. And I want you to have this." I laid fifty dollars on the table. "My boyfriend sent it to you as a present."

She beamed and I saw the tears start to form.

"Now, don't cry. We'll come back sometime. I wish you'd bathe the baby while I'm taking a bath, and then we'll hit the highway."

Her last words to me as she and Mr. Henry helped me to the car were attributes to my acting and successful deceit.

"You're just what I wanted for a daughter. You smart and mannerable and truthful. That's what I like most. You living a Christian life. Keep up the good work. God bless you and the child. And your mother."

I tore down the morning streets as if the hounds of hell were coming to collect my soul. The baby responded to the two-wheel curve-taking by giving out air-splitting screams. My "Hush, baby" and "it's all right, baby" could have been unheard whispers. He felt my panic and seemed to want the world to know that he was just as a afraid as his mother.

At the train station, I wiped the steering wheel and unstrapped the baby. I left the car parked in a No Parking zone, and as far as I know, it is there to this day.

I was racing away with my son on my hip and sheer fright in my heart. My general destination was Arkansas where I had grown up. But the particular goal of the journey was the protective embrace of Mrs. Annie Henderson, the grandmother who had raised me. Momma, as we called her, was a deliberately slow-speaking, right-thinking woman. And above all, she had what I lacked most at the moment. Courage.

* * *

"You sure are starting at a good time. The radio said rain today."

I sat in an uncomfortable chair and watched the two women.

Clara looked up at me and explained. "Tricks walk in the rain." She laughed. "I'm sure I don't know why. If I was them, I'd rather stay in my own bed." She laughed again. "By myself." Chuckle.

Bea's voice interrupted Clara's amusement. "Goddam. Don't say nothing like that, you'll put the bad mouth on the day. I want to be in bed with ten tricks by noon. It's already nine o'clock and I haven't even broke luck yet."

Carefully applied make-up did not disguise the woman's hard features. When I met her the night before, I had decided she wasn't nearly as nice as Clara, and although I would work with her, we'd never become friends.

"New girl gets to break luck." Clara laid on a little authority. "You know how it goes."

The language was new but its meaning was clear, and I wanted above all things not to appear stupid and not to display my immobilizing nervousness. I tried to concentrate on what the women were doing. Their fingers darted making knots in strings of heavy white twine.

Bea looked up at me, disdain a mist across her face. "You a cherry, ain't you?"

"Yes." Lying would get me nothing.

"Well, that's a thirty-second business. Once you turn the first trick, you'll be a 'ho. A stone 'ho. I mean, for life." She grinned sourer than a rotten lemon, but her make-up and jewelry and air of abandoned sex gave her a hint of glamour.

Clara wedged in a peacemaker's tone. "Well, that won't be so bad, will it? I mean, you're a whore."

"Hell yes. I'm a damn good one. I'm a mud kicker. In the streets I make more money by accident than most bitches make on purpose." She rolled her head and twisted her body. "And it's more action, too. I mean the lights and tricking all night until the sun comes up."

I wondered why she left the streets.

"I just got too hot. I was getting busted two, three times a week. So my daddy brought me down to the crib. Let the heat get off. Then I'll be back switching and bitching and getting merry like Christmas."

They both stood up and shook out strings in their hands. Clara walked to the living-room door and attached two strings to tacks over the lintel. She took matches form her robe pocket and lighted the ends that swung lazily near the floor.

"You burn string in the morning for luck, Rita. When it reaches the first knot the tricks begin to walk."

Bea had left the room to place string over the other doors.

Clara went back to her uneasy chair.

"Now, Rita, let's have a little talk. You were so tired when L.D. brought you in here last night, I thought I'd wait till morning to tell you how I run this place." I pulled my attention from the little red mouths that were nibbling up the string.

"L.D. said your work name was Sugar. I think that goes with you. You so young and quiet. Now, here's how it goes. In your room you have a tablet, and when you take a trick he pays me; and after, I sign your book. If you didn't have a man of your own, I'd give you your money at the end of the day and you could leave. But what'll happen is, at the end of the week Lou will come and I'll give it to him. He'll straighten out your bills, room rent, board and liquor." She caught herself. "Course, you don't drink and soft drinks are free. Then you get your day off and get to stay all night with your man.

"All my tricks are Mexican. They're fast but not too clean. Each girl has her own trick pan and towels. You wash them first and after. Then you take fresh water and wash yourself good. Since you're a cherry, I have to tell you that Mexicans aren't built very large, but don't open your legs wide. They are tricks, not your old man, so don't try making love to them. That's why they call them tricks."

Clara's superstition about burning string had already disenchanted me, and her conversation on deception of customers erased any respect I had for her. The only way I could be in the business was to give due service for the money paid. I decided privately that I would make each trick (each man) happy and forget the unbearable loneliness that sent him out in the rain searching for love.

"They walk in here," she continued, " and take their choice of you or Bea. L.D. said you shouldn't use make-up and ought to keep on those junie flip clothes. That's all right with me. When you get regulars, Bea is not allowed to pull them, unless you're busy and they can't wait. That's the same with her steadies. Anything you want to know, ask me."

The doorbell rang.

"See Rita! Look at that string." The red dot had reached a knot on one of the strings. "Trick time."

Bea came running into the room, and the sound of her footsteps was a little more audible than my heartbeat. The moment of truth had gotten stuck in my throat and saliva refused to go around it.

Clara went to open the door.

"Hello, Papa, come in. I've got something special for you today." She stage-whispered, "A school girl."

My God, she was lying. I was already going to be a whore. Take this man's hard-earned money, go to bed with him without love. Why add lying to it?

They came in view. Clara had her arm around the shoulders of a short little fat man who wore matching gray khaki pants and shirt. He looked Indian.

"Sugar, come over and say hello to Papa Pedro."

I walked over as if I were being introduced in my mother's living room.

"*Buenos dias, Señor Pedro.*"

His eyes left my flat chest and narrow hips. "*Oh. Hablas español?*"

My mind flinched at his use of the familiar. It should only be used between family members, close friends and lovers, according to my high school teacher.

"*Sí. Yo lo puedo hablar.*"

"Okay Sugar. Take him in the back and show him a good time."

Bea's voice hacked through from the corner. "Yea Pedro. If she don't give you enough, you can see me after. Remember last time?"

His glance didn't stay two seconds in her direction.

Clara took us both by the hand. "Come on, you two. You're wasting time." And drew us to my bedroom door. "Get in there and have fun."

I found my voice. "*Viene con migo, señor.*"

He stood in the middle of the floor, looking like a bemused Akim Tamiroff. I had to say something but didn't know how to say "take your clothes off" in Spanish, so I asked him how he was. He said well. I pulled off all my clothes during the long pause and he opened his pants. Dignity rode his face bareback.

I washed him and all I remember of my first great slide into the slimy world of mortal sin is the scratching of the man's zipper on my upper thighs.

* * *

At sundown Bea washed her face and spent a few minutes in Clara's bedroom. She came out clicking her purse shut.

"I'm nearly shame to show this little money to my daddy. I've spoiled that man." She looked at me, and without the cosmetic she was ten years younger. "How you feel?"

I didn't know how I felt. I said, "All right, thank you."

"Clara, you ought to get the news over to the camp. Tell them that you got a cherry. Maybe that'll stir up some tricks." She walked to the door, shaking her hips from side to side. "You won't be a cherry long, better git it while the gittin's good. See you all in the morning." She slammed the door behind her.

Clara followed and snapped a double lock, then drew a chain across the door.

"Sugar, you better take a long bath. Put some Epsom salts in to take out the soreness."

I said nothing because I thought nothing.

"Don't worry, you didn't do so good today, but then, you're just starting. Give you a few tips. Don't take off all your clothes. It takes too long. And remember, the men come here to trick, not to get married. Talk to them dirty but soft. And play with them."

She hmphed to herself.

"You got it easy. I was turned out with white men. They want to talk all the time. They tell you how beautiful you are and how much they love you. And wonder what you're doing being a whore all the time they're jugging in you and paying for it. Then when they get finished they got the nerve to ask you how you liked it. And talk about your freaks! White men can really think of some nasty things to do."

She started to her room and turned. "One thing I can say about my daddy"—her lips prissed and she lifted her nose and wiggled it—"he doesn't want me to do anything freakish. No matter how much money is involved. I like that." She rubbed her hands down her sides complimenting herself. "Better get your bath. Dinner'll be ready soon."

I sat thinking about the spent day. The faces, bodies and smells of the tricks made an unending paisley pattern in my mind. Except for the Tamiroffish first customer, the others had no individual characteristics. The strong Lysol washing water stung my eyes and a film of the vapor coated my adenoids.

I had expected the loud screams of total orgasmic release and felt totally inadequate when the men had finished with grunts and yanked up their pants without thanks. I decided that, being black, I had a different rhythm from the Latinos and I all had to do was let myself learn their tempos.

Clara gave me salts and bath oil and I continued examining the day in fingernailfuls. I was intelligent and I was young. I could teach myself the craft and make loads of money. L.D. might be able to settle his debts before the month was up.

The woman who came in daily at five o'clock to cook reminded me of my grandmother and I had to avert my eyes when she placed dinner on the table.

I reassured myself. I was helping my man. After all, there was nothing wrong with sex. I had no need for shame. Society dictated that sex was only licensed by marriage documents. Well, I didn't agree with that. Society is just a conglomerate of human beings, and that's just what I was. A human being.

For the next week, I vied with Bea for the attentions of Pedros, Josés, Pablos, and Ramóns. I brushed up on my Spanish and tried with little success to include *tú* in my enticing come-ons. The women's conversations interested me more than the tricks' visits. Men came to Clara's house singly, and rather than having an air of celebration, they all seemed to be ashamed of their own presence and at the same time resigned to be there. I never found one man who considered how I might or might not enjoy those three-minute sojourns in the cell-like room. And for my part, I accepted Clara's signature on my tablet as a symbol of being paid in full.

Bea made an attempt at friendliness one morning. She came into the house early and settled on a stiff chair opposite me.

"Sugar, how do you like it?"

Her voice was kinder than usual, which surprised me, and as I had no ready answer, I muttered, "Well, it's ... a new—"

"New? Screwing ain't new, is it?" She slipped back into sarcasm easily.

"No. That's not what I meant."

"Well, don't worry about it. You'll break in."

"I won't be doing this long." I had to separate myself from the insinuation.

"Like hell. Wait till you make a nice piece of money. Then your daddy will give you a little white girl."

"A what? What would I do with a little white girl?"

She laughed a tight little laugh. "Not 'a' white girl. You don't know what 'white girl' is?"

"I don't know what you mean." I was trying to withdraw.

"They call cocaine 'white girl'. Some people call horse 'white girl' too. I don't mess with heroin, though. It makes me sick. But wait till your daddy gives you some coke. Kiss the baby!" Hugging herself, she coasted away for a second on her thought.

I wouldn't tell her that L.D. didn't even want me to smoke pot, but she seemed to pick the thought out of her mind.

"They won't let you smoke hemp, though. They say it makes a

'ho too frisky. 'Hos get their heads bad and forget about tending to business."

Clara came in bringing coffee, and Bea plunged into conversation with her.

"You know what we did last night? Daddy took me down to a gambling game in Firebaugh ... You know who I saw? ... Haven't seen that bitch in a month of Sundays ..."

I didn't know the people she was talking about and couldn't have cared less what she did the night before, but she had given me something to think about. Since she spoke from experience, she was probably right. But she was talking about pimps and I knew L.D. wasn't a pimp. He was a gambler. I couldn't allow myself to entertain corrosive thoughts. All I had to do was my best to help him and keep my thoughts clear and unpolluted. I decided I wouldn't even mention the conversation to L.D.

In the long waits between customers, Bea and Clara talked about money, their old men, other whorehouses and their old men and travel to nearby towns and their old men. They both called their men "Daddy," their voices tightened into lurid imitations of baby talk. Their faces softened and their lips pouted (Clara could wrinkle her nose and wiggle it like a bunny).

I wondered if prostitutes, as one, suffered from an Electra complex and were motivated by a need to have a daddy, please a daddy and finally make love to a daddy.

"My daddy says he's going to take me to Hot Springs for the season." Bea sat in her chair by the door and shook her delight.

"Daddy and I went to the Kentucky Derby last year. We had a ball." Clara began to shake her nose. "Everybody was there. I met sports from New York City and Detroit and Chicago."

"My daddy says those eastern pimps are colder than a whore's heart in Nome. I believe him too. Look at their faces. They chilly. If they don't kill their whores, they make them wish they were dead."

"Well, my daddy didn't never hit me except when I needed it. Oh, he whip my ass then. Better believe it. But no scars. He ain't never left a scar on me."

Bea grinned as if she had outwitted the men. "They ain't crazy. They wouldn't hurt their little money-makers."

Their conversations were tightly choreographed measures and

since I didn't know the steps, I sat on the sidelines and watched. They would hardly be interested in my dance career, or my son, or the books I'd read. And I flatly, on principle, refused to call L.D. "Daddy." I mean, I protested to myself, my father Bailey Johnson Sr. was in San Diego, posturing and er'ring his pretentious butt off. Daddy Clidell was my one-time stepfather but he and Mother had signed divorce papers. Mother's men, whom I had called Daddy Jack, Uncle Bob or Hanover Daddy, came and went with such regularity that whatever name I tacked on after the paternal title escaped me after a few months. I decided I wouldn't discuss L.D. at all. They were too cynical to understand that we were in love and that after I had helped him out of trouble, after he had a divorce, we were going to be married and live in a dream house with my son and lots of flowers. I would not share my plan with hard-hearted whores.

Despite my youth and high school clothes and stilted Spanish, I wasn't popular at Clara's. The men preferred Bea. She had a swing in her hips and a knowing smile that I couldn't imitate. Then, Mexican farm workers obviously had no erotic fantasies starring teenage black girls; the came to a whorehouse for a whore, and Bea answered their needs.

***

"Have a good time, you all." Clara waved to L.D. and me from the steps. He didn't acknowledge her but I turned and waved.

In the car, he wore the same sour face he'd had when he returned from talking with Clara in the bedroom. Fear that he didn't love me anymore iced my bare arms. When I first moved to Clara's, he had assured me. "Don't worry about going to bed with other men. It'll just make me love you more. You're doing it to help Daddy." He hugged me too. Now I remembered and supposed he had thought so at the time. But when face to face with the reality, he found me disgusting. For the first time since I went to Clara's, I began to feel unclean. I was Lady Macbeth. All the waters in the world wouldn't wash away the fingerprints of the men who had mauled me. I had been stupid to let him talk me into doing something that would turn him from me. He needed love. He needed a good woman to love him, especially now while he was in trouble with the big boys. But instead of using the brain I was inordinately proud of, I had let him down. His life was so unstable (the big diamond ring and expensive car were symbols of insecurity), and when I had a chance to introduce some order into his world I had fluffed it. It was clear I'd never see him again, since waves of hate radiated from him as rhythmically as the heat trembled up from the highway. We rode in silence until we reached Stockton.

"Where do you want to go?" His question popped like a whip.

"To pick up the baby."

The steering wheel almost came off in his hand.

When he parked the car, he made no move toward getting out, so I opened my door and had to ask, "Will you take us for a ride?"

"Close the door, Rita. I better talk to you."

Now it would come. The bad words, the insults, and all rightly placed. I closed the door.

"I talked to Clara. And there wasn't hardly any money at all. I don't think you tried."

"L.D., I did. I tried with all my heart." Relief flooded my brain. If that was all he was worried about.

"Clara says you sit around like a judge, never saying anything to them. And that you talk to the tricks in Spanish like a goddam schoolteacher."

"L.D., I'm sorry. I just don't know what to do. But I promise I'll try harder. Don't be angry, Lou."

"Another thing, you haven't called me Daddy. All the—I'm supposed to be your daddy." He was fierce suddenly. "Remember that."

I said, "Yes, Daddy," and hated it. Later on I'd be able to tell him the Electra story and explain why I hated my own father and expand my theory about prostitutes and their men. I knew he wouldn't appreciate being thought a pimp and we'd be able to lose "Daddy" from our vocabulary, unless he allowed my son the right to so address him.

"I can't take you all out today, but here, pay the woman, and here's ten dollars. You go to a picture show, but don't keep him all night. Take him back to her and I'll come over to your place this evening."

"Yes, Lou." He wasn't angry any longer.

"Daddy?" he prompted.

"Daddy." I smiled and bided my time.

Excerpted from Angelou, Maya. Gather Together In My Name *(New York: Random House, 1974: Chapter 27). Reprinted with permission from Random House.*

Continuing the Policy Debate

Canadian Prostitution Legislation and the Implications for Sex Workers

S. VERLYN BATEMAN

SOCIETY IS FASCINATED BY and highly obsessive about the topic of prostitution, which has been seen as a social ill in the form of public nuisance, vice, and corrupted evil throughout modern Western history (Jeffrey; Oosenbrug). At this public site multiple perspectives, ideologies, and moral positions collide. The issue of prostitution has not been settled morally or legally, although Canada has attempted many incremental approaches during various political party conventions and also within municipal to federal levels. The very prominence and attention the topic receives indicates how serious this issue is to Canada (Backhouse).

Social policies, with the goal of reducing or eliminating prostitution, have not been successful to date (Kuo), as prostitution is a policy-resistant industry (Wagennar and Altink). The current thought on crime approach impacts the players involved in prostitution: sex workers have faced the consequences of legislation criminalizing prostitution, yet sex work persists. Stigma and demeaning stereotypes are propagated, such as linking prostitution with drugs and criminal gangs. With divergent and contentious views, punitive legislation, and the lack of harm-reduction interventions, many of the dangers of prostitution are, this chapter suggests, related to enacted policies based on prevailing attitudes. The dynamic between prostitution and morality has been made, but this has not been well connected with a dominant ideology. To do so would provide further clarity and understanding in debating the complex issue of prostitution policy.

This chapter argues that the study of prostitution and prostitution legislation is deeply intertwined with two dominant political ideologies, neoliberalism and neoconservatism; thus this area is a legitimate site of inquiry to explore the efficacy of these moral positions encoded in social legislation. This chapter attends to these moral assumptions and their implications on prostitution as found in contemporary Canadian policy. Reflecting a gendered phenomenon, this paper focuses on female sex workers, the statistical majority represented in the sex work industry. This is not to ignore other genders; rather, the diversity of types of prostitution increases the difficulty in studying this phenomenon. As all sex workers do not engage in prostitution for the same reason, the uniqueness of each story cannot be encapsulated by one narrative, further muddying motivational understandings of prostitution and the difficulty in creating one policy for all.

Studying prostitution and working with sex workers[1] have been very difficult for researchers and social service providers, given the dynamic and hidden nature of sex work particularly after increasing criminalization (Benoit et al.). The dynamics of who has power in society, who benefits and alternatively who loses, are in part controlled by legislation. Thus, social policies have a direct impact on the life circumstances of both individuals and groups (Gil, *Confronting Injustice*). Social policies are inherently created with dominant political ideologies at the heart of the approach, where the divisions within society's values, morals, and views on tradition become evident. Examining prostitution legislation is one way of understanding and describing the relationship between richly embedded ideology and the ramifications of this for sex workers and other stakeholders.

This chapter argues that Canadian prostitution law contains significant neoconservative, morality-influenced legislation rather than evidence-influenced legislation. To accomplish this, *The Protection of Communities and Exploited Persons Act* (2014) is analyzed. The Act is shown to embody social legislation representation of moral neoconservatism. Rather than offer a solution to the posited social problem, as social policy should do, the Act serves to further marginalize those involved in prostitution and will not be effective in eliminating prostitution. The Act negates the social-structural roots of patriarchy, classism, and racism and positions the players in prostitution as abusive sexual deviants exploiting passive female victims directly and the moral good of society more generally. This chapter argues that this, in sum, will further place sex workers in danger of societal stigma, psychological internalized stigma, and continued violence.

The chapter will unfold in the following way: First, Canadian political ideology will be explored to understand and describe what impact belief structures have on contemporary prostitution policy, including the implications and limits of the moral basis of ideology. Cultural conceptualizations of sex workers are next discussed in conjunction with divisive feminist positions on prostitution. Looking outside Canada, other legislation models are investigated to have a larger understanding of international concerns and values. Two different models are discussed in depth to determine whether either one may be the most comprehensive in dealing this social issue for Canada. Finally, *The Protection of Communities and Exploited Persons Act* is deconstructed and analyzed to understand how and why it was created. This chapter is a contribution to the academic and policy dialogue on this social issue, as only limited attention has been paid to the relation between prostitution, social policy, and the moral dimension of political ideology (Wagennar and Altlink).

IDEOLOGICALLY INFUSED GENDER AND SEXUALITY POLITICS

Ideology is understood as a largely unconscious (Lakoff) system of socially shared beliefs, attitudes, and knowledge positions on social needs (Thorisdottir, Jost and Kay). The need to study political ideology in conjunction with prostitution policy is integral to understanding the dimensions of power, as the prevailing ideological rationalities determine how knowledge is processed and controlled (Lemke). This determines who benefits and what world views are valued, both of which shape the broader context of the society through social policy formation. This has a cascading top-down effect from the elites and media to the population, justifying the current social and economic order (Thorisdottir, Jost and Kay). At present, neoliberalism and neoconservatism hold a coalition with varying interests, both collaborating and opposing each other at different sites.

Each ideological position has a way of framing, explaining, and solving social policy problems. These in turn, can be understood as attempts to control the production of knowledge and ideas in and about the social world, which has an effect of dynamically forging and imposing social identities for groups (Mullaly). Focusing on political ideology in the discussion of prostitution legislation in Canada requires an unpacking of the underlying values, beliefs, and attitudes inherent in prostitution legislation discourse. Neoliberalism and neoconservatism will be explored as these frameworks dominate the formation of ideas on social and economic issues.

Neoliberalism can be viewed as a rationality or political ideology of contemporary capitalism, where competition is the universal rule of government and free markets regulate the economy and all of social life (Dardot and Laval). This is a major shift away from the Keynesian welfare state beliefs, shifting the roles and responsibilities of government and citizens (Brodie). As a result, individual responsibilization and reduced social spending are now taken for granted as the way to move forward. Neoliberalism is also an international hegemonic force, engaging in depoliticalization of social and political issues, viewing responsibilities and failures as due to the individual (Brown). As such, there is a notable absence of shared social care and a social safety net.

Neoliberalism holds no moral or ethical concerns. Under this regime, each citizen is expected to be an entrepreneur or small business owner by marketing themselves, upgrading skills, and selling goods or services for their market value. The onus of deciding to engage in selling sexual services as a commodity is one's own personal choice, with the consequences falling on the individual (Scoular and O'Neill). The sex industry can be described as "the child of neoliberal capitalism" (Phipps 77) that contributes, rather than hinders, the economy. From this perspective, individuals are required to take control of their own health and well-being as social programs and services are minimal. Less social spending, such as child care benefits and maternity leave, has particularly negative impacts on women's lives, as they are the ones who perform the bulk of unpaid work (Braedley and Luxton). According to neoliberal theory, the artificial assistance of the welfare state is not needed as all citizens are inherently equal players in charge of their own economic growth. The resulting inequalities are due to citizens not selling their services or the low worth of these services on the market. As such, prostitution is accepted and sex workers sell sexual services as a commodity on a contractual basis, aiming to maximize their profits in competition with others.

Neoliberalism does not hold enough support from political constituencies to keep power without partnerships with other ideologies, as it is politically and economically unstable (Peck). Neoconservatism, which favours tradition, authority, and national customs, is added to the dominant political pool. In addition, moral absolutism—accepting positions of good or evil on issues; rarely embracing grey areas—is apparent (Uhlmann, Poehlman and Bargh). Social justice concerns such as violence against women can be a concern for this ideology (depending on the political objectives current at the time), which further amplifies the complexities of ideology (Feldman and Johnston). Jost and colleagues argue that neoconservatism's main focus is fear and terror management, meeting the need for structure, simplicity, order, and certainty. Under neoconservative ideology, sexuality must be controlled by morality via traditional norms such as heterosexual marriage and enforced through laws (Gotell). Citizen's private lives are under the lens of the state, with significant costs to not adhering to moral expectations. The more ground neoconservatism gains in the minds of people, the greater losses will be seen in terms of bodily sexual autonomy (Acar and Altunok). When confronted with concerns of social change, neoconservatism responds with punishment, religiosity, and strict morality (Jost et al.). Getting tough on crime is seen as the answer; deeper investigation or the implementation of social programs or economic safety nets are not.

Without state control, sexuality is seen to cause moral decay and a decline specifically in the hetero-normative family and more generally in social order. This perspective stems from patriarchal morals, for which prostitution is understood as fundamentally sinful (Kuo). Illustrating a neoconservative lack of belief in structural root causes, Acar and Altunok draw attention to the fact that violence against women is rarely connected to gender inequality but rather with an emphasis on laws and punishment as the corrective means. Women need to be protected by men from men that harm them; this will ultimately protect the family system. In this instance sex workers are conceptualized as passive victims in need of saving and clients as criminal offenders. Can gender equality, as a social value, be accomplished by increasing Criminal Code offenses? Neoconservatism answers that it can.

The combined forces of neoliberalism and neoconservatism help to determine the dynamic, rather than static, reproduction of gender inequality and control over women's bodies and their sexuality. There is an ebb and flow that exists between neoliberalism and neoconservatism. At various times and with various issues, one may reign supreme, or new meanings may be created. A product of this ideological junction is that social concerns such as gender equality are transformed into individual problems that then have market solutions (Brown). The root causes of social problems and crime are not a major component in this worldview. Instead of the existence of social problems exacerbated by underlying, poverty, inequality, or class, neoconservatism offers this answer: This individual infringed on communal standards of traditional morality. Moral purity and justice work hand in hand with neoconservative ideology, as "people are apt to embrace ideological opinions that are in line with their ideas about what is fair and moral and, once adopted, ideological opinions are likely to influence beliefs about what is just and appropriate" (Thorisdottir, Jost and Kay 16). Omitting the root causes of crime, or any social problem, the post-welfare solution involves higher levels of policing and other forms of social control (Peck). Both kinds of interventions are quite evident in the case of prostitution policy, as this chapter will demonstrate.

The symbolic and working relationship between neoconservatism and neoliberalism functions to meet the goals of maintaining the political and legal power of the .01% and, at the same time, to keep public morality in check and women controlled (Kuo). Both sides agree on amassing wealth while avoiding an examination or rectification of social inequalities. Neoconservatives desire to keep the focus of this accumulation of wealth centred on the mythical benefits of hard work and superior intelligence (Kolozi). As such,

Christian family tradition and work ethics coexist, somewhat uncomfortably, with a free-market, entrepreneurial approach (Brown).

Neoconservatives have religious limits as to what can be sold. For example, neoconservatives cannot support obscenity, such as pornography and prostitution, while neoliberals have no issues making a profit from socially disrupting materials and services, provided the profit is accomplished in the context of the rule of the market. Phipps sums up the divergent views of prostitution among neoconservatives and neoliberals as a "tension between 'sex-as-recreation' and 'sex-as-romance'" (80). Canadian social policy is shaping contemporary morality and women's roles: Women are morally permitted to engage in sex only in marriage and for the purpose of procreation. Under neoconservative thought, sex work and motherhood cannot coexist and are diametrically opposed. This is particularly resonant in terms of the community-focused aspects of neoconservative ideology. Should a sex worker raise children, this would expose them to poor social values. Social exclusion, barriers to health support, and internalized stigma and shame (Sloss and Harper) have been found to be dominant themes for mothers working in prostitution.

Since the 1980s neoliberalism and neoconservatism have been in a somewhat tense political coalition, one that blends social regulation with free-market goals (Steger and Roy). Both positions have strong views on realms where prostitution is situated: role of women in society, crime, morality, punishment, finances, and labour. Neoconservatism attributes crime to individual faults where neoliberalism views crime as a rational choice decision based on an economic cost-benefit payoff (Lemke). Morality comes into play only as the actor weighs which action to take based on the expected risk outcome. As self-responsible players, there are no structural factors such as poverty, gender, or racial discrimination that play a role in decision-making (Lemke).

Neoconservatism also ignores such interactions and factors in choices made, confidently summing up these players as largely immoral. Wendy Brown speaks to the pull toward neoconservatism's strong belief in the role of morality as an adjunct to neoliberal ideology. In terms of punishment, neoconservatives desire long incarceration sentences and the rehabilitated reform of sex workers into morally appropriate women. Retribution via incarceration is an important point in this discussion. Emotion-based and immediate responses to crime, such as calling for longer minimum sentences, are quite compelling to the fearful public yet are not supported as effective in reducing recidivism or acting as a strong initial crime deterrent. A North American meta-analysis comprised of over 330,000 offenders found that prison sentences are not crime deterrents; imprisonment functions as a costly form of retribution (Gendreau, Goggin and Cullen). This payback has the potential to provide closure for victims as "justice has been served," yet these punishments largely function to appease social needs inherent in conservative values. After a sex worker has been incarcerated for any number of prostitution-related charges, she faces a permanent scarlet letter for her perceived poor morality. At this point, many fields of employment are closed off to her as are many social relations, particularly due to the stigma of a criminal record. Minimum-wage jobs may be open to her. For homeless women without an address, maintaining employment is often incredibly difficult. A single mother providing for dependents would need to balance child care and employment, often leaving little money remaining.

THE CANADIAN APPROACH TO PROSTITUTION

Prostitution was framed as a public nuisance of vagrancy at first; colonial Canada inherited British laws that focused on street-level prostitution (Gotell). Between 1839 and 1972, under the Vagrancy Act women had to account for their presence on the streets (Jeffrey); simply being a sex worker in public was punishable (Backhouse). The very presence of prostitution puts society in the morally uncomfortable position of dealing with women and sexuality. From the 1860s to the 1900s women engaging in prostitution received negative public attention. This debate was framed as the sexual exploitation of young women who must have been coerced into prostitution, and outcries for the social purity of sexual morality were made (Backhouse). Even 150 years ago, the same issues were raised as now with remarkably similar interventions, which will be shown herein to be derivatives of conservative ideology. Fears surrounding prostitution were first related to moral purity, but later this shifted to a fear of disease contagion during the World Wars (Hayes-Smith and Shekarkhar). At this time there was a great concern of female sex workers spreading sexually transmitted infections to men, implicating women as the vessels of disease.

One hundred years later, political debates about sex work and prostitution rage on. The Fraser Special Committee on Pornography and Prostitution was established in 1983 to gather more information on obscenity issues from various stakeholders. The Committee noted a lack of public agreement on what should be done about prostitution and suggested regulatory changes to continue to criminalize public nuisance prostitution while decriminalizing prostitution conducted in private (Oosenbrug). Placing this into political context, the Committee was mandated under a Liberal government. In 1985, a Conservative government was elected. Less than two weeks after the Fraser report was released, the Conservative[2] government announced Bill C-49, which included criminalizing communication for the purposes of prostitution in addition to other criminalized acts, all of which were quite different from the spirit of the Fraser Report (Jeffrey). The result of the work of the committee, two years of research and information gathering, produced little or no response in terms of influencing government legislation (Oosenbrug). This is possible because findings from committees and commissions are not legally binding; there is no obligation to implement.

As will be discussed later, this incongruence was duplicated in the 2013 Bedford Supreme Court case. This was also under the power of the Conservative government, and demonstrate a pattern of behaviour when ideology confronts evidence. This repetition of Canadian Conservative governments in disregarding evidence and permitting neoconservative morality to be the basis of policies is disconcerting, particularly as prostitution is not the only social policy target. Canada is an example of "debates about prostitution ... policy that [have] all the characteristics of a 'dialogue of the deaf': the angry reiteration of original positions, the unwillingness to listen to the opponent's point of view, the demonization of those who think differently" (Wagennar and Altink 284).

Moving away from domestic debates, Canada has international obligations after ratifying various agreements in relation to prostitution. Canada did not sign on to the 1949 *United Naitons Convention for the Suppression of the Traffic in Persons and of the Exploitation of the Prostitution of Others*. Notably, Article 6 of the *Convention* prohibits regulation of prostitution while Article 16 moves toward the prevention of prostitution. As Canada did not hold an abolitionist approach to prostitution in 1949, the *Convention* was not ratified by Canada (Barnett and Nicol). Globally, the issue of human trafficking is seen as a fairly unified issue in the broader concern to eradicate human rights abuses. Canada has signed onto UN conventions against forced prostitution and human trafficking of women and children, such as the 1979 UN *Convention on the Elimination of All Forms of Discrimination against Women* and the 1995 *Beijing Declaration and Platform for Action*. At the international level, the debate surrounding prostitution is joined with other issues such as human trafficking, violence against women, and child prostitution. A protectionist stance by way of stopping or incarcerating criminals with tough sentences is proposed, which is in line with neoconservative ideology.

Systematic oppression, as a consequence of such ideology, is a pertinent concept in the analysis of prostitution policy. Sex workers frequently experience socially and legally sanctioned subordination, which includes law enforcement, related policy, and current social norms. Policies are a strong force affecting daily lives and social realities of groups in society (Gil, *Unravelling*). Social policy is not created in a vacuum: who determines what constitutes a social problem also holds power in society. In the case of prostitution law, the government's ruling political party and courts often dominate this discussion, with lesser players on the margins of the debate. In the past several years the old issue of prostitution has been revamped to include exploitation with a focus on children and women. This updating of the issue has created an easier case to sell to the public and thus gain more ground for support (Weitzer).

CONCEPTIONS OF IDENTITY

The elites (small groups who control disproportionate shares of social power) construct discourses of the lives of "othered" groups to further their goals and socio-economic positions. These social identities are fashioned by the ruling groups, creating the excluded "other" (Dominelli), and can be encoded in formal legislation or, more informally, in policy. These constructions must therefore be sold to the public, and any group that fosters different ideas must be discredited. Established beliefs may be contradicted, which can result in binary positions. For example, sex workers are seen as: victims versus free agents; coerced versus free actors; and oppressed versus empowered (Carpenter; Phipps). Further, construction of sex workers as victims can also be used to dehumanize sex workers: only seeing them for their method of economic survival. Sex workers are not commonly conceptualized as people, family members, or mothers.

All-or-nothing positions transform a complex issue into a simple one, which is easier to package and sell. Most often, prostitution is located somewhere in between these polarized notions. The media and government now portray sex workers with one prevailing voice: that of the lost, victimized, and trafficked woman. Due to stigma, prostitution is often kept private and anonymous, so there is no dominant narrative stemming from sex workers themselves (Wagenaar and Altink). Given the hidden nature of prostitution, there is still little information about sex worker conditions (Gall) and even less about sex purchasers (Harrington). The complexity and diversity of prostitution should not be ignored in the formation of prostitution legislation. This creates a difficulty: how can polarized positions be accounted for in one policy that will speak to the lives of all sex workers?

Positioning all sex workers as victims is ideologically powerful as it aligns radical feminists and some liberal concerns about patriarchy and female oppression with a conservative moral obligation to protect women. A. Jordan argues that feminists are using patriarchal oppressive social norms aimed at controlling women. Other writers provide support for a conservative and feminist partnership to take on the sex industry together, irrespective of their positions on other social issues (Gotell; Weitzer). No matter the linkage, neoconservative and radical feminists have joined together to tackle obscenity and the sex industry. A splitting of feminist beliefs is witnessed. Now broad and decentralized, there is no single view of the origin or effects of prostitution (Oosenbrug). The polarized conceptions of prostitution and sex workers will be next explored via international comparisons.

INTERNATIONAL APPROACHES

Globally, there is a great divide in positions about the formation of prostitution legislation, from abolition, asymmetrical criminalization (client is criminalized, sex worker is not), regulation (such as business licenses), decriminalization, and legalization. Two fairly opposing positions, as they manifest in Sweden and New Zealand, are reviewed in this paper. These nations have some commonalities as developed countries with a similar population. Both are parliamentary constitutional monarchies with elected prime ministers and were early players in the women's suffrage movement. The prostitution legislation changes in question were made between 1999 and 2003 in these countries and both approaches claim to hold feminist support (Harrington). In terms of gender equality over recent years, Sweden rates among the highest in the world, with New Zealand closely following (World Economic Forum, 2006; 2014). In sum, there are sufficient similarities between these two countries to compare approaches to prostitution legislation without great hindrances.

Sweden implemented the *Sex Purchase Act* in 1999, which is now known internationally as the "Nordic Model" of asymmetrical criminalization: only the purchaser of sexual services is criminalized. This policy implementation addresses the Swedish government's social and moral positioning of sex work as unacceptable. Prostitution is always considered exploitive, being harmful to women, children, and society. The goals of the reform law were aimed at creating a deterrent to clients thereby decreasing the number of sex workers in order to promote gender equality (Chu and Glass). This functions as a legally mandated cultural norm of what is deemed acceptable sexual behaviour. Sex worker voices were not included in the policy debate (Harrington), which speaks to the paternal and moral positioning of the elite. Further, Sweden lumps prostitution and human trafficking together, as prostitution can never be voluntary in the government's opinion, or if it is voluntary, that is irrelevant (Waltman).

Research on Sweden's asymmetrical criminalization model has yielded curious and contentious results. In 2010, it was estimated that there were a total of six hundred sex workers in Sweden including men and trans* persons (Kelly, Coy and Davenport). The low number of street-level sex workers recorded was highly praised by the Swedish government, declaring that criminalization was a success, with numbers halved. The reduction in numbers of visible sex workers is attributed to the criminalization law (Waltman). It is important to note some years were not studied therefore this data represents an incomplete picture.

In addition to visible street-level prostitution, the Government of Sweden stated that indoor prostitution amounts to approximately 66 percent of sex work. Addressing the assertion that prostitution has migrated to other countries or turned indoors or to more hidden locations, "no information, empirical evidence, or other research suggests that this has actually occurred" (Waltman 147). However, a 2010 Swedish government document pointed to the dramatic increase in sex worker numbers in neighbouring countries. A study on violence against sex workers was conducted among the sex workers still working in prostitution. The police led an investigation into the rate of violence sex workers experience; the results showed no increase but made the casual connection between the existence of prostitution and violence (Waltman). As police are one of the most common perpetrators of violence to sex workers (Deering et al.), one could question their objectivity in conducting such a study. Further, law enforcement services specialize in law enforcement, not in understanding the sexual or physical assault experiences of marginalized groups.

The majority of research done on the Nordic Model is in Swedish, with little translated into English (Dodillet and Ostergren). There is questionable evidence as to the Swedish government's assertions that asymmetrical criminalization has decreased street-based sex work as much as stated. Government reports present no conclusive evidence to back these claims (A. Jordan). Independent and international research has determined that there is no accurate data to indicate that prostitution is decreasing, yet an increase in danger for sex workers was found (Chu and Glass; CPHA; Levy and Jakobsson; UNAIDS; UNDP). Dodillet and Ostergren also speak to the discrepancy between the stated success of the policy and actual data: these researchers believe that the Sex Purchase Act of 1999 has not decreased prostitution or acted to deter clients but rather increased rates of stigma. Research has found that more street sex workers have moved into illegal brothels or are displaced in other nearby countries, which decreases the visibility of prostitution in Sweden (Chu and Glass).

Beyond physical and psychological dangers, such criminalization can be understood as reproducing race, class, and gender discrimination (Kuo), as often the targets are poor women of colour. These women do not conform to neoconservative morals and are subjected to socially constructed discrimination. This marginalization of identities and sexual behaviours serves to negatively impact many aspects of sex workers lives. The implementation of criminalized sex purchasing involves the increased use of courts, policing efforts, and community resources. In 2008 a total of seventy-six people pled guilty to or were sentenced for attempting to purchase sex in Sweden, and all received fines (Dodillet and Ostergren). The effects on sex workers are more perverse. As prostitution is increasingly criminalized, sex workers have little protection from discrimination and assault, and poor access to legal protection (UNDP). This legislation reform is used as a method of placing Sweden on a high moral ground to serve as an international example of striving for gender equality while stigmatizing those involved in prostitution (A. Jordan). The marketing and selling of the Nordic Model has been positively received internationally with many countries, such as the UK and Canada, adopting very similar laws thereafter.

New Zealand is another model to consider, as this country decriminalized prostitution in 2003. New Zealand is a socially liberal and progressive country that has been a forerunner for social equality and in reducing legal barriers: women were given the vote in 1893, homosexual sex was decriminalized in 1986, and in 1987 a needle exchange system was created (Barnett et al.). New Zealand views sex work as work, assuming a public health, harm reduction, and human rights perspective (Farvid and Glass; Fitzgerald and Abel). This model uses the neoliberal values of self-responsibility and decision-making freedom without a moral filter on earnings. Sex workers weigh the risks and benefits individually, as rational actors in a free market. The prostitution legislation reform does not address structural oppression or gender inequality (Harrington).

This is a notable shift from moralistic-based legislation. Early in its history, New Zealand adopted British obscenity and contagious diseases laws. The women's rights movement, gay movement, and HIV/AIDS of the 1970s and 1980s led to greater support for public health initiatives, including a campaign that garnered support for sex workers' rights (J. Jordan). In 1996, three sex workers were murdered and three sexually assaulted, which resulted in cries for decriminalization to increase the safety of sex work. This reflects a human rights perspective and a questioning of the moralistic basis underlying female agency and freedoms (J. Jordan). These political changes were not done without an external push. The New Zealand Prostitutes' Collective (NZPC) was formative in connecting with politicians and spearheading the movement (Barnett et al.), illustrating the neoliberal value of self-governance. The NZPC partnered with legal, academic, and public health stakeholders to jointly draft the prostitution reform bill, with campaigning done over many years. The drafting of the bill started in 1994, and after several revisions, it came into effect in 2003.

The media holds a dominant position of proliferating conservative discourses on prostitution rather than informed knowledge from experts in the field, including sex workers themselves (Fitzgerald and Abel). After New Zealand decriminalized prostitution, research was conducted on media reporting, which found that crime and drugs were frequently reported as integral components in prostitution, as well as a highly exaggerated numbers of sex workers (Fitzharris and Taylor). Further media studies were done, resulting in the same negative construction of street-level prostitution as before the legislation reform, particularly in reference to breeching social codes of expected femininity (Favrid and Glass). Newspaper and TV representations of sex workers and the topic of prostitution have great power to sway the public and policy dialogue. Sex worker data and stereotypes are often intentionally misrepresented to gain emotional support for morally based positions on the issue (Weitzer). Along with the media, historical, religious, and other traditional beliefs have impacted the conception of a sex worker's identity, providing a neoconservative cultural knowledge, which has influenced policy and legislation.

According to reliable estimates, the country has approximately 2,332 women involved in the sex industry (Kelly, Coy and Davenport). Research between 2003 and 2006 noted the media presented neutral comments, yet articles from politicians expressed mostly conservative moral views (Fitzgerald and Abel). Results of decriminalizing prostitution indicate very positive results, including lower stigma and violence as well as better access to medical resources (CPHA). All of these are linked with an increased quality of life. New Zealand federal reports have not indicated an increase in the number of sex workers since implementation of the legislation, and also noted that the Prostitution Reform Act continues to have a positive impact on the health and safety of sex workers (Fitzharris and Taylor; Ministry of Justice, "Report"). The Prostitution Law Review Committee completed a final report five years after the legislation reform came into effect and found no specific link between crime and prostitution, no increase in under-age sex workers, and no increase in human trafficking, and it suggested that if street-based prostitution were criminalized, it would go underground and result in increased risks (Fitzharris and Taylor).

New Zealand academics and public health professionals believe that other countries do not recognize this model or the past decade of positive results. The New Zealand experience was listed in documents taken into consideration in the drafting of the Canadian Protection of Communities and Exploited Persons Act (Department of Justice, "Annex"). Yet there is no mention or discussion of this in Canadian publications related to the Act. The Nordic Model, on the other hand, was highly praised and made considerable mention of (Department of Justice "Backgrounder") although the reliability of data on the Nordic Model is highly suspect, as previously indicated. At this site, there is a large discrepancy between international prostitution legislation, research, and value-based frameworks.

Canada has intentionally chosen to ignore health and safety research evidence in favour of implementing a blanketed morally conservative approach. This raises questions into whether Canada has the physical and mental well-being of female sex workers in mind. This powerful stance sends a message of expendability when sex workers violate in-group norms of womanhood. If citizens do not commit to personally adopting conservative moralistic virtues, the indirect outcomes are likely violence, incarceration, stigma, and poor health. Fundamentally, regardless of moral positioning, how dedicated is Canada to the health and safety of all our citizens? Are Canadians subject to the neoliberal, self-responsibilization scheme, the neoconservative moral values acting as barriers to equitable health outcomes, or another framework? In the following sections, this will be examined.

COURT RULING

There have been several court challenges over the years by sex workers and sex worker groups who spoke out against Canada's alleged unconstitutional and harmful prostitution laws. These court cases pertain to achieving increased legal protection and improving health outcomes by removing harmful laws (Barnett and Nicol). One case was recently successful at the Supreme Court of Canada (SSC) level. *Bedford v. Canada* brought forward constitutional challenges insisting that present laws interfered with Charter rights as enacted legislation created an almost impossibility for sex workers to legally and safely engage in prostitution.

Specifically, the sections rendered invalid by the SCC in the Criminal Code were: keeping a common bawdy-house (s. 197, 210); living off the avails of prostitution (s. 212); and communicating in public for the purpose of prostitution (s.213). The bawdy-house law prohibited sex workers from working together indoors to enhance safety. In making sex workers unable to hire bodyguards, s.212 was deemed too broad, as not all who profit from prostitution are pimps (Department of Justice "Backgrounder"). This forces sex workers to comply with laws that place them in dangerous situations and renders them unable to discuss use of safer sex practices such as condoms (CPHA). In 2013, the SCC gave the government one year to correct this situation and institute new legislation that does not breech basic Charter rights. After significant research, the Court made suggestions for the government to consider in creating a Bill. The end result was The Protection of Communities and Exploited Persons Act, which contradicted the spirit of the SCC decision and many of these recommendations. The Bill became legislation in 2014 under a Conservative government.

ACT CREATION, CHANGES, AND CONCERNS

Canada has accepted recommendations from the Council of Europe that advocated for asymmetrical criminalization of the purchase of sex as the best way to prevent and combat human trafficking (Department of Justice "Backgrounder"). During the second reading of Bill C-36, The Minister of Justice Peter MacKay said that the criminal punishments for the purchase of sex and advertising sex (now both illegal activities) are in line with the punishments for human trafficking (Parliament of Canada). The very name of the Act addresses society as a predominant concern first and then sex workers after. Some sex workers are exploited, but how can an act regarding exploited persons represent all sex workers, including those who are not exploited. The Act excludes the neoliberal foundations of human agency and freedom of choice as possibilities for engaging in prostitution. The assumption that all sex workers must be exploited persons is reminiscent of Sweden's model, which places select social values in high regard and ignore research evidence.

The very title of the Act is indicative of a distinct trend in neoconservative thought. The term "prostitution" is given to the public packaged as human trafficking, which is highly problematic and evident of convoluted definitions. Prostitution is the action of selling sexual acts for money or goods. This is an informal contractual arrangement between two or more consenting adults where the seller and buyer hold agency and decision-making capabilities. Sex trafficking involves coercion and the use of power in recruiting, transporting, and/or harbouring people for sexual exploitation (UNDP). Prostitution is not a cause of human trafficking (UNAIDS; Weitzer) and cannot be dealt with as a human rights abuse (UN Women).

In recent years the terms "human trafficking" and "prostitution" have become increasingly synonymous (Abel; Gall; Weitzer). This is due in part to moral and paternal understandings of women's bodies as targets of social control (Phipps). The state is deemed better able to determine women's best interests, the protection of women, and rules surrounding bodily autonomy than the individual female (Kuo). This belief contradicts the neoliberal view in which there are no ethical or moral limitations on women selling sexual services as a commodity. She has proprietary rights to do with her body as she chooses. Here, instead, the protective, traditionalist stance of neoconservative ideology is obvious. The elite law makers, largely Caucasian men, have complete power to decide what actions are prohibited and how to make sure these actions are refrained from.

The process of linking prostitution and sex trafficking is a powerful one with global ramifications. The United States has strings attached to international financial support provided to other nations, particularly developing nations. For HIV/AIDS funding, countries must not support legalized prostitution in order to receive funding (Hayes-Smith and Shekarkhar). In the case of human sex trafficking, international NGOs must be against the legalization and regulation of prostitution (Weitzer). This belief is reflected in U.S. domestic research. A 2014 U.S. Department of Justice document on the urban commercial sex industry includes both sex trafficking and adult prostitution together in one definition (Dank et al.). The top ten findings of the study confusingly refer to both terms as inherently the same and make links to crime, gangs, and weapons. Research such as this is unreliable as multiple prostitution terms are conflated (A. Jordan). Sweden and Canada, as well, are guilty of convoluting the definitions of human trafficking for sexual purposes and prostitution. Such research, international definitions, and agreements have an impact on the creation of domestic prostitution policy and legislation.

The process of Bill C-36 receiving royal assent indicated that at all readings only the Conservative members voted in favour. The Liberals, NDP, and Bloc voted against it. As the Conservatives held the majority of seats, even with all other political parties dissenting at each reading every time, the Bill was passed (Open Parliament). Conservative politics and neoconservative ideology have aligned, acting not in accordance with research and evidence on the subject but with patriarchal positioning of women in society. The most recent changes to prostitution legislation have created tougher laws that contravene the Supreme Court of Canada's recommendations and quite likely the Charter. At present the client purchasing sex is criminalized (also known as asymmetrical criminalization), and sex advertising and communication for the purpose of purchasing sex work are illegal.

These changes would presumably be legally justified under current Canadian law; however, this may not be the case. The Canadian Bar Association (CBA) is concerned that, as selling sex is technically legal, the government may be increasing the danger of an already risky (but legal) activity and violating s.7 of the Charter by preventing sex workers from protecting themselves through working with others and hiring bodyguards (National Criminal Justice). Further, the updated communicating and advertising laws are at odds with s.2(b) of the Charter. Here, neoconservative morality politics take tremendous steps forward, perhaps pushing legal limits. Less than two months before Bill C-36 was enacted, the CBA warned that sections of Bill C-36 could very well be successfully challenged under the Charter, rendering them invalid. The Canadian government response in this new legislation was to purposefully ignore the SCC decision and CBA recommendations to implement likely illegal legislation. This is explained as a goal of the moral crusade against prostitution—eliminating any form of support at all costs.

GOALS OF THE ACT

The objectives of the Act are to reduce the demand for prostitution, taking an abolitionist stance based on beliefs that all sex work is sexually exploitive (Department of Justice, "Bill C-36"). A radical feminist position is partnered with neoconservatism in viewing prostitution as a manifestation of violence against women. This view is elaborated through a neoliberal take on one's free will and weighs the costs and benefits of obtaining sexual services, which is the main tenant behind deterrence measures (Hayes-Smith and Shekarkhar). Further, the deterrence model posits that if punished once, the offender will desist from doing such activity. By enacting a hard stance to cut off demand, all such problems are believed to end. Objectives are to protect sex workers from exploitation as well as the community from possible harms; to achieve this, the Government of Canada formulated new criminal charges (Department of Justice, "Background"). The Act proposes to protect people by fining or incarcerating clients purchasing sex and sex workers who will naturally commit an illegal act. If guilty of purchasing sexual services, one would be fined five hundred dollars plus a possible jail sentence of up to five years. If this offense was conducted near a daycare for instance, the fine is doubled (Department of Justice, "Backgrounder").

A latent goal of the Act is to strengthen Canada's family values moral crusade, criminalizing those who do not conform to this social norm "under the auspices of protecting the vulnerable from exploitation" (Brock and Teixeira 308). The negative impact of these social values and codified laws on the lives of sex workers must be carefully considered. Moving away from an overt concern with a public nuisance and toward stopping exploitation signals a change to social goals enshrined in the law. Harsher criminal sanctions now imposed are infused with neoconservative ideology. Feminist arguments deployed to support the legislation that say it is about protecting women are smoke screen for a moral agenda (Caroline). This paternalistic construction of women is forcibly re-implemented to revalue women in traditional roles as chaste and virtuous, dependent on and protected by chivalrous men (Cikara et al.). Any other positioning presents a challenge to the prevailing neoconservative ideological beliefs of women's position in society. Women engaging in sex work through a non-conformist expression of sexuality and taking explicit control over their own bodies contradicts neoconservative positioning. Thus, these women must either be passive victims or criminals (Caroline). Correspondingly, "good" women are praised, receiving incentives to follow social order, while "bad" women are labelled criminals and face stigmatization (Cikara et al.). Neoconservative ideology grasps to maintain legal and social control over women, partnering when needed with feminists but always following traditional moral codes of conservative family values to regulate gender roles and expectations.

As the purchase of sex is now an offense and communication laws are tighter, there is reason to believe that sex workers will not be able to screen their clients as well, potentially placing them in physical danger (Hayes-Smith and Shekarkhar). The Act does not embody an understanding or concern for underlying social and economic conditions involved in prostitution, or the inherently complex nature of prostitution. The very name of the Act is suggestive of such: the protection of communities, as in protecting societal norms first and foremost. The Act is concerned with solicitation and communication, particularly in areas where a child under the age of eighteen could reasonably be present. Therefore, as a child could reasonably be in most outdoor spaces, there are great concerns that sex workers will not have the appropriate time to screen clients and negotiate safer sex practices. This places sex workers at an increased risk of violence and contracting sexually transmitted infections (CPHA).

A LIKELY SOLUTION?

Sex work and prostitution are socially divisive topics, the regulation of which involve multiple levels of jurisdiction, hundreds of players, and a wide range of interests. At the federal level, the Act has been created and implemented as Canada's latest response to issues involving prostitution by framing this as exploitation and linking prostitution with human trafficking. In the recent past, Canada has attempted to use lower jurisdictions to control the sex industry. Barnett and Nicol offer that implementation on the local level can address area-specific issues, which cannot be done on an overarching, one-fits-all approach. The use of provincial and municipal power is a dynamic and flexible method to consider; yet this undermines the social values inherent in the federal law. Some cities in Canada have attempted to create regulated business licensing of prostitution, although the end result was failure (Lewis and Maticka-Tyndale). The licenses applied for were used for businesses such as massage parlors and escort agencies, as there is no legal license for prostitution in Canada. This was made possible as general business licenses are under municipal jurisdiction. Zoning by-laws have also been used in various cities to limit the location of the local adult sex industry (Barnett and Nicol). This again falls under municipal jurisdiction. One problem with this approach is the inequality it could create for sex workers in different regions of the country. In more conservative areas, there would likely be higher control, while in more liberal cities, there may be local incentives to focus on public health and harm reduction. Again, morality is at play against best evidence.

Within the context of the new laws, will all law enforcement—from city police services to the Royal Canadian Mounted Police—consistently use the same approaches? What resources and efforts will be used to enforce giving out fines to the purchasers of sexual services? Further increasing criminalization legally supports police intervention in the form of prostitution raids. Zatz raises concerns over selective enforcement of legislation, as this could be used to harass and control women of colour, resulting in further worsening of racist and classist issues. Looking at the impact this legislation has had to date, four months after the new legislation, there are news reports indicating police forces are using discretion and generally not implementing the new law (Eschner). Other players are concerned about the safety of Canada's sex workers. Ontario's premier Kathleen Wynne has voiced serious concerns about the legislation, although she offered provincial compliance, leaving law to the courts (Leslie). It is interesting and ironic that Wynne is leaving law to the courts, as the Supreme Court of Canada had no say in creating this Bill. The Government of Canada has provided twenty million dollars of funding for programs aimed at those interested in exiting sex work (Department of Justice, "Backgrounder"). What will the content of these programs be, what agency will design them, and when will they come into effect? What about the sex workers that decide to remain in prostitution? More questions are raised than answers address.

Recent research on the impact of criminalization on Canadian sex workers provides a grim outlook on the future under the new Act. An 18-month British Columbia study on street-based sex workers using substances reported strong evidence that criminalization policies negatively impacts sex workers' lives, in particular, rates of violence against women increase (Shannon et al.). Support for structural interventions to combat gender-based violence was suggested, such as affordable housing and increased availability of drug treatment programs. These solutions quickly hit a roadblock: the Ontario Ministry of Municipal Affairs and Housing predicts a harrowing future for social housing, stating that "in 10 years, federal spending for social housing in Ontario will be $267 million less than it is today, declining to zero by 2033." The lack of emphasis placed on social housing and other social concerns is reflective of neoliberal ideology, which posits little social spending as an ideal state of affairs. By 2033, that is exactly what we will have for Ontario's social housing. The likelihood of increasing long-term structural interventions is low.

The role of policing in prostitution is important to note here. Rather than benign or helpful, many studies have reported coercion, physical assault, and sexual assault from police officers, which were found to have the strongest correlation with violence against female sex workers (Shannon et al.). These data are supported by a 2014 multi-city study on over two hundred sex workers, noting that only fourteen percent of sex workers felt that police treat sex workers fairly (Benoit et al.). Those responsible for enforcing the law can be a threat to female sex workers' health outcomes, leading to serious unintended consequences. Client criminalization can be viewed as invalidating sex workers' control over their bodies and, just as important, their human agency. This serves to further stigmatize, as sex workers are viewed as helpless victims (UNAIDS). UN Women feel strongly that criminalization of the sex worker or the purchaser violates rights to health and self-determination.

The Canadian Public Health Association (CPHA) takes the perspective that harm reduction, addressing the social determinants of health and structural violence may be the best policy solutions. Recognizing that policies have dramatic impact on the socio-economic lives of sex workers, "poverty, homelessness, and trauma that result from inequitable policy, social and economic forces contribute to involvement in the sex trade" (CPHA 4). The CPHA gives support to the idea that regulating prostitution as a business is the best approach in addition to: 1) exploring the link between engaging in prostitution and the structural determinants of health, and 2) incorporating harm reduction methods. These suggestions involve funding social programs for economic stability.

Unfortunately, these suggestions are in conflict with the neoliberal limited social spending budget and the neoconservative moralistic outcry against prostitution. Rather than assuming a moral position, Jordan advocates for evidence-based potential solutions, created with input from all stakeholders. This input would need to hold weight, unlike the the report of the Fraser Committee, which was disregarded and used rather as a symbolic measure taken to appease interests groups desiring to have their voices heard.

CONCLUSION

This chapter has covered the multiple and conflicted ideologies present in Canadian prostitution policy to explore political goals, moral values, and positions. Addressing the social issue of prostitution by implementing legal controls and moral approbation is unlikely to eliminate or greatly reduce prostitution. It is highly unethical for governments to increase harms to sex workers when research has overwhelmingly shown a positive relationship between increased criminalization and increased violence (Caroline). Marginalized women who work in prostitution are being used as a political tool to strengthen the neoconservative moral agenda on traditional gender roles and gender positioning in society. This conceptualization attempts to silence alternative positions, with prostitution as only one site of neoconservative ideology. For example, American alcohol prohibition, rich with conservative values, uses a similar attempt to suppress the public's natural immorality. This resulted in the increase of illegal international trade of unregulated alcohol and drugs, putting millions of dollars into criminal organizations and increasing corruption and incarceration rates (Chambliss). This illustrates the breadth and history of conservative moral control. Continuing down this avenue is highly problematic, as moral regulation cannot ever function as equitable social justice.

Western culture purports a "tough on crime" approach to prostitution, which is rooted in neoconservative ideology and the moral disgust with non-traditional sexual arrangements outside of a heterosexual marriage. This has constructed discourses framing prostitution as a social evil that must be severely punished, and this action will cause this behaviour to be expunged from society. This belief structure joins emotional reactions to social problems, ignoring the consequences if both are not acknowledged separately. Rather than using evidence-informed data, the powerful voices of the elite are able to strategically override the dialogue with morally rich emotional appeals. Conversely, it is much harder for academics and sex worker union groups to obtain the same media coverage to disseminate other ideas to weaken the legitimacy of the neoconservative argument. This is further complicated because there is little accurate data on the nature of prostitution and sex workers. Finally, to add to this argument, there are already existing crimes such as sexual and physical assault, harassment, forcible confinement, attempted murder, etc. How will adding another criminal offense protect women in prostitution? All of these components combine to form the dialogue of the deaf.

Rather than offering a novel solution, as the Nordic Model has been stated to be, the Protection of Communities and Exploited Persons Act functions as another conservative penal moral order. Whether there has been some positive effect from Sweden's reformed prostitution policy is unknown as the data are highly confounded and English reports are few. The New Zealand model places sex workers as independent, rational players, employing more neoliberal principles. Either way, a critical perspective is missing—one that unpacks the social structures and economic power dynamics that reproduce the conditions necessary for prostitution (Farvid and Glass). New Zealand's position to decriminalize prostitution has effectively been ignored by Canada, as neoconservatism cannot imagine loosening the tight hold over control of women's sexuality. Such legislation works to further entrench not only these beliefs but also the use of fines and incarceration, which have been shown to weaken crime deterrence. In the end, because of emotion-based beliefs in the sacredness of traditional family values, especially including constructs of the "good" mother, women are further placed in harm's way. For Canadians, this takes the form of more missing and murdered Aboriginal women and sexually assaulted women who are blamed for what they were wearing at the time of their attack. Is this the socially just and progressive Canada we want for our future?

[1]A note on language: Wagennar and Altink suggest that it is impossible to write about prostitution policy without having a personal moral involvement in this issue. They differentiate between the terms sex work(er), prostitution, and prostitute. This paper will speak of the act of prostitution, defined as selling a sexual service, and of the sex worker, as the person engaging in the act. The term sex worker is used as a broad category and also to indicate and provide solidarity, as the term was originally coined to do, yet is rarely used by sex workers themselves (Quan). The term "prostitute" will not be included, except for when making reference to specific historical elements in original terminology.
[2]Conservative governments and conservative ideology are not synonymous, although both often reflect traditional, moralistic qualities.

WORKS CITED

Acar, F. and G. Altunok. "The 'Politics of Intimate' at the Intersection of Neo-Liberalism and Neo-Conservatism in Contemporary Turkey." *Women's Studies International Forum*. 41 (2013): 14-23. Print.

Backhouse, C. B. "Nineteenth-Century Canadian Prostitution Law. Reflection of a Discriminatory Society." *Social History* XVIII.36 (1985): 387-423. Print.

Barnett, T., C. Healy, A. Reed, C. Bennachie. "Lobbying for Decriminalization." *Taking the Crime Out of Sex Work*. Eds. G. Abel, L. Fitzgerald, C. Healy and A. Taylor. Bristol: The Policy Press, 2010. 57-74. Print.

Barnett, L. and J. Nicol. "Prostitution in Canada: International Obligations, Federal Law, and Provincial and Municipal Jurisdiction." Library of Parliament Background Paper. 2012. Pdf.

Benoit, C., C. Atchison, L. Casey, M. Jansson, B. McCarthy, R. Phillips, B. Reimer, D. Reist, F. M. Shaver. "Gender, Violence and Health. Contexts of Vulnerability, Resiliencies and Care among People in the Sex Industry." *(Understanding) Sex Work*. November 18, 2014. Pdf.

Braedley, S. and M. Luxton, ed. "Competing Philosophies: Neoliberalism and the Challenges of Everday Life." *Neoliberalism and Everyday Life*. Montreal: McGill-Queen's University Press, 2010. 3-22. Print.

Brodie, J. "Canadian Women, Changing State Forms, and Public Policy." *Women and Canadian Public Policy*. Toronto: Harcourt Brace & Company, 1996. 1-30. Print.

Brown, W. "American Nightmare: Neoliberalism, Neoconservatism, and De-Democratization." *Political Theory* 34 (2006): 690-714. Print.

Canadian Public Health Association (CPHA). "Sex work in Canada." 2014. Web. 28 May 2015.

Caroline, A. "Criminal Justice, Extreme Pornography and Prostitution: Protecting Women or Promoting Morality? *Sexualities* 14. 3 (2011): 312-333. Print.

Carpenter, B. *Re-Thinking Prostitution*. New York: Peter Lang Publishing, Inc., 2000. Print.

Chambliss, W. J. "Another Lost War: The Costs and Consequences of Drug Prohibition." *Social Justice* 22.2 (1995): 101-124. Print.

Chu, S. K. H., and R. Glass. "Sex Work Law Reform in Canada: Considering Problems with the Nordic Model." *Alberta Law Review* 51 (2013): 101–124. Print.

Cikara, M., T. L. Lee, S. T. Fiske, P. Glick. "Ambivalent Sexism at Home and at Work: How Attitudes toward Women in Relationships Foster Exclusion in the Public Sphere." *Social and Psychological Bases of Ideology and System Justification*. Eds. T. Jost, A. C. Kay, H. Thorisdottir. New York: Oxford University Press, 2009. 444-462. Print.

Council of Europe. "Prostitution, Trafficking and Modern Slavery in Europe." *Parliamentary Assembly*. 2014. Web. 28 May 2015.

Dank, M., B. Khan, P. M. Downey, C. Kotonias, D. Mayer, C. Ownes, L. Pacifici, and L. Yu. "Estimating the Size and Structure of the Underground Commercial Sex Economy in Eight Major U.S. Cities." The Urban Institute. 2014. Pdf.

Dardot, P. and Laval, C. *The New Way of the World: On Neoliberal Society*. London: Verson, 2014. Print.

Deering, K. N., A. Amin, J. Shoveller, A. Nesbitt, C. Garcia-Moreno. "A Systematic Review of the Correlates of Violence against Sex Workers." *American Journal of Public Health* 104.5 (2014): E42-E54. Print.

Department of Justice. "Backgrounder. Protection of Communities and Exploited Persons Act." Government of Canada. 2014. Web. 28 May 2015.

Department of Justice. "Bill C-36, Protection of Communities and Exploited Persons Act: Technical Paper." Government of Canada. 2015. Web. 28 May 2015.

Department of Justice. "Annex A—Bibliography." Government of Canada. 2015. Web. 28 May 2015.

Dodillet, S., and P. Ostergren. "The Swedish Sex Purchase Act: Claimed Success and Documented Effects." Paper presented at the International Workshop: Decriminalizing Prostitution and Beyond: Practical Experiences and Challenges. The Hague. 2011. Pdf.

Dominelli, L. *Anti-Oppressive Social Work Theory and Practice.* New York: Palgrave MacMillan, 2002. Print.

Eschner, K. "Are Cops Turning Their Backs on Feds' New Hooker Law?" *Now Toronto*. 2015. Web. 28 May 2015.

Farvid, P., and L. Glass. "'It Isn't Prostitution as You Normally Think of It. It's Survival Sex': Media Representations of Adult and Child Prostitution in New Zealand." *Women's Studies Journal* 28.1 (2014): 47-64. Print.

Feldman, S., and C. Johnston. "Understanding the Determinants of Political Ideology: Implications of Structural Complexity." *Political Psychology* 35.3 (2013): 337-358. Print.

Fitzgerald, L. and G. Abel. "The Media and the Prostitution Reform Act." *Taking the Crime Out of Sex Work*. Eds. G. Abel, L. Fitzgerald, C. Healy, A. Taylor. Bristol: The Policy Press, 2010. 197-216. Print.

Fitzharris, P. and A. Taylor. "Review of the Prostitution Reform Act." *Taking the Crime Out of Sex Work*. Eds. G. Abel, L. Fitzgerald, C. Healy, A. Taylor. Bristol: The Policy Press, 2010. 105-118. Print.

Gall, G. *Sex Worker Union Organizing: An International Study*. Hampshire: Palgrave MacMillan, 2006. Print.

Gendreau, P., C. Goggin, and F. T. Cullen. *The Effects of Prison Sentences on Recidivism*. Ottawa: Solicitor General Canada, 1999. Print.

Gil, D. G. *Unravelling Social Policy: Theory, Analysis, and Political*

Action towards Social Equality. Vermont: Schenkman Books Inc., 1992. Print.

Gil, D. G. *Confronting Injustice and Oppression. Concepts and Strategies for Social workers*. New York: Columbia University Press, 1998. Print.

Gotell, L. "Policing Desire: Obscenity Law, Pornography Politics, and Feminism in Canada." *Women and Canadian Public Policy*. Ed. J. Brodie. Toronto: Harcourt Brace & Company, 1996. 279-318. Print.

Government of Sweden. "Selected Extracts of the Swedish Government Report SOU 2010:49: The Ban against the Purchase of Sexual Services. An Evaluation 1999-2008." 2010. Pdf.

Harrington, C. "Prostitution Policy Models and Feminist Knowledge Politics in New Zealand and Sweden." *Sex Res Social Policy* 9 (2012): 337-349.

Hayes-Smith, R., and Z. Shekarkhar. "Why is Prostitution Criminalized? An Alternative Viewpoint on the Construction of Sex Work." *Contemporary Justice Review* 13.1 (2010): 43-55. Print.

Jeffrey, L. A. "Prostitution as Public Nuisance: Prostitution Policy in Canada." *The Politics of Prostitution* . Ed. J. Outshoorn. Cambridge: Cambridge University Press, 2004. 83-102. Print.

Jordan, A. "The Swedish Law to Criminalize Clients: A Failed Experiment in Social Engineering." American University Washington College of Law. Issue Paper 4, April 2012. Web. 28 May 2015.

Jordan, J. "Of Whalers, Diggers and 'Soiled Doves': A History of the Sex Industry in New Zealand." *Taking the Crime Out of Sex Work*. Eds. G. Abel, L. Fitzgerald, C. Healy. A. Taylor. Bristol: The Policy Press, 2010. 25-44. Print.

Jost, J. T., J. Glaser, A. W. Kruglanski, F. J. Sulloway. "Political Conservativism as Motivated Social Cognition." *Psychological Bulletin* 129.3 (2003): 339-375. Print.

Kelly, L., M. Coy, R. Davenport. "Shifting Sands: A Comparison of Prostitution Regimes across Nine Countries." 2010. Pdf.

Kuo, L. *Prostitution Policy: Revolutionizing Practice through a Gendered Perspective*. New York: New York University Press, 2005. Print.

Kolozi, P. "The Neoconservative Critiques of and Reconciliation with Capitalism." *New Political Science* 35.1 (2013): 44-64. Print.

Lakoff, G."Why Political Psychology is Important." *Social and Psychological Bases of Ideology and System Justification*. Eds. T. Jost, A. C. Kay, H. Thorisdottir. New York: Oxford University Press, 2009. xiii-xv Print.

Lemke, Thomas. "'The Birth of Biopolitics': Michel Foucault's Lecture at the College de France on Neoliberal Governmentality. *Economy and Society* 30.2 (2001): 190-207. Print.

Leslie, K. "Ontario Will Follow Prostitution Law despite Concerns, says Kathleen Wynne." *The Star*. 19 Dec 2014. Web. 28 May 2015.

Lewis, J., and E. Matika-Tyndale. "Licensing Sex wWork: Public Policy and Women's Lives." *Canadian Public Policy* 26.4 (2000): 437-449. Print.

Levy, J., and P. Jakobsson. "Sweden's Abolitionist Discourse and Law: Effects on the Dynamics of Swedish Sex Work and on the Lives of Sweden's Sex Workers." *Criminology and Criminal Justice* 14.5 (2014): 593-607. Print.

Ministry of Justice. "Report of the Prostitution Law Review Committee on the Operation of the Prostitution Reform Act 2003." 2008. Web. 28 May 2015.

Mullaly, B. *Challenging Oppression. A Critical Social Work Approach*. Oxford University Press: Ontario, 2003. Print.

National Criminal Justice Section and Municipal Law Section of the Canadian Bar Association. "Bill C-36, Protection of Communities and Exploited Persons Act." Canadian Bar Association. 2014. Pdf.

Ontario Ministry of Municipal Affairs and Housing. "Long-Term Funding for Affordable Housing. Federal Housing and Homelessness Funding to Ontario is Declining." 2014. Web. 28 May 2015.

Open Parliament. "Bill C-36. Protection of Communities and Exploited Persons Act." *Open Parliament*. 2014. Web. 28 May 2015.

Oosenbrug, L. D. "Prostitution, Patriarchy and the 'Whore' Stigma. Examining Prostitution Theory and Policy in the Netherlands, Sweden and Canada." Masters thesis. University of Alberta, 2007. Print.

Parliament of Canada. 41st Parliament, 2nd session. *House of Commons Debates*. 2014.Web. 28 May 2015.

Peck, J. *Constructions of Neoliberal Reason*. New York: Oxford University Press Inc., 2010. Print.

Phipps, A. *The Politics of the Body. Gender in a Neoliberal and Neoconservative Age*. Cambridge, UK: Polity Press, 2014. Print.

Quan, T. "The Name of the Pose: A Sex Worker by Any Other Name?" *Prostitution and Pornography. Philosophical Debate about the Sex Industry*. Ed. J. Spector. Stanford University Press: California, 2006. 341-348. Print.

Scoular, J., and M. O'Neill, M. "Regulating Prostitution." *British Journal of Criminology*, 47.5 (2007): 764-778. Print.

Shannon, K., T. Kerr, S.A. Strathdee, J. Shoveller, J. S. Montaner, M.W. Tyndall, M. W. "Prevalence and Structural Correlates of Gender Based Violence among a Prospective Cohort of Female Sex Workers." *British Medical Journal* 339 (2009): b2939. Print.

Sloss, C. M., and G. W. Harper. "When Street Sex Workers are Mothers." *Archives of Sexual Behaviour* 33.4 (2004): 329-341. Print.

Steger, M. B., and R. K. Roy. *Neoliberalism: A Very Short Introduction*. New York: Oxford Press Inc., 2010. Print.

Thorisdottir, H., J. T. Jost, A.C. Kay. "On the Social and Psychological Bases of Ideology and System Justification." *Social and Psychological Bases of Ideology and System Justification*. Eds. T. Jost, A. C. Kay, H. Thorisdottir. New York: Oxford University Press, 2009. 3-26. Print.

Uhlmann, E. L., A. T. Poehlman, J. A Bargh. "American Moral Exceptionalism." *Social and Psychological Bases of Ideology and System Justification*. Eds. T. Jost, A. C. Kay, H. Thorisdottir. New York: Oxford University Press, 2009. 27-52. Print.

UNAIDS. "The Legal Status of Sex Work. Key Human Rights and Public Health Considerations." Briefing note. Feb 2014. Pdf.

UNDP. "Global Commission on HIV and the Law. Risks, Rights and Health." 2012. Pdf.

UN Women. "Note on Sex Work, Sexual Exploitation and Trafficking." 2013. Pdf.

Waltman, M. "Prohibiting Sex Purchasing and Ending Trafficking: The Swedish Prostitution Law." *Michigan Journal of International Law* 33 (2011): 133-157. Print.

Wagenaar, H. and S. Altink. "Prostitution as Morality Politics or

Why It Is Exceedingly Difficult to Design and Sustain Effective Prostitution Policy." *Sex Research Social Policy* 9 (2012): 279-292. Print.

Weitzer, R. "The Social Construction of Sex Trafficking: Ideology and Institutionalization of a Moral Crusade." *Politics and Society* 35.3 (2007): 447-475. Print.

World Economic Forum. "The Global Gender Gap Report 2006." 2006. Pdf.

World Economic Forum. "The Global Gender Gap Report 2014." 2014. Pdf.

"Voices" from *Dear Life*

ALICE MUNRO

WHEN MY MOTHER WAS GROWING UP, she and her whole family would go to dances. These would be held in the schoolhouse, or sometimes in a farmhouse with a big enough front room. Young and old would be in attendance. Someone would play the piano—the household piano or the one in the school—and someone would have brought a violin. The square dancing had complicated patterns or steps, which a person known for a special facility would call out at the top of his voice (it was always a man) and in a strange desperate sort of haste which was of no use at all unless you knew the dance already. As everybody did, having learned them all by the time they were ten or twelve years old.

We were dressed up. At the country dances my mother remembered, there was never any appearance in those sassy square dance outfits you would see later on television. Everybody wore their best, and not to do so—to appear in anything like those frills and neckerchieves that were the supposed attire of country folk—would have been an insult to the hosts and everybody else. I wore a dress my mother had made for me, of soft winter wool. The skirt was pink and the top yellow, with a heart of the pink wool sewn where my left breast would be one day. My hair was combed and moistened and shaped into those long fat sausage-like ringlets that I got rid of every day on the way to school. I had complained about wearing them to the dance on the grounds that nobody else wore them. My mother's retort was that nobody else was so lucky. I dropped the complaint because I wanted to go so much, or perhaps because I thought that nobody from school would be at the dance so it didn't matter. It was the ridicule of my school fellows that I feared always.

My mother's dress was not homemade. It was her best, too elegant for church and too festive for a funeral, and so hardly ever worn. It was made of black velvet, with sleeves to the elbows, and a high neckline. The wonderful thing about it was a proliferation of tiny beads, gold and silver and various colours, sewn all over the bodice and catching the light, changing whenever she moved or only breathed. She had braided her hair, which was still mostly black, then pinned it in a tight coronet on top of her head. If she had been anybody else but my mother I would have thought her thrillingly handsome. I think I did find her so, but as soon as we got into the strange house I had to notice that her best dress was nothing like any other woman's dress, though they must have put on their best too.

The other women I'm speaking of were in the kitchen. That was where we stopped and looked at things set out on a big table. All sorts of tarts and cookies and pies and cakes. And my mother too set down some fancy thing she had made and started to fuss around to make it look better. She commented on how mouthwatering everything looked.

Am I sure she said that—mouthwatering? Whatever she said, it did not sound quite right. I wished then for my father to be there, always sounding perfectly right for the occasion, even when he spoke grammatically. He would do that in our house but not so readily outside of it. He slipped into whatever exchange was going on—he understood that the thing to do was never to say anything special. My mother was just the opposite. With her everything was clear and ringing and served to call attention.

Now that was happening and I heard her laugh, delightedly, as if to make up for nobody's talking to her. She was inquiring where we might put our coats.

It turned out that we could put them anywhere, but if we wanted, somebody said, we could lay them down on the bed upstairs. You got upstairs by a staircase shut in by walls, and there was no light, except at the top. My mother told me to go ahead, she would be up in a minute, and so I did.

A question here might be whether there could really have been a payment for attending that dance. My mother could have stayed behind to arrange it. On the other hand, would people have been asked to pay and still have brought all those refreshments? And were the refreshments really as lavish as I remember? With everybody so poor? But maybe they were already feeling not so poor, with the war jobs and money that soldiers sent home. If I was really ten, and I think I was, then those changes would have been going on for two years.

The staircase came up from the kitchen and also from the front room, joining together into one set of steps that led up to the bedrooms. After I had got rid of my coat and boots in the tidied-up front bedroom, I could still hear my mother's voice ringing out in the kitchen. But I could also hear music coming from the front room, so I went down that way.

The room had been cleared of all furniture except the piano. Dark green cloth blinds, of the kind I thought particularly dreary, were pulled down over the windows. But there was no dreary sort of atmosphere in the room. Many people were dancing, decorously holding on to each other, shuffling or swaying in tight circles. A couple of girls still in school were dancing in a way that was just becoming popular, moving opposite each other and sometimes holding hands, sometimes not. They actually smiled a greeting when they saw me, and I melted with pleasure, as I was apt to do when any confident older girl paid any attention to me.

There was a woman in that room you couldn't help noticing, one whose dress would certainly put my mother's in the shade. She must have been quite a bit older than my mother—her hair was white, and worn in a smooth sophisticated arrangement of what were called marcelled waves, close to her scalp. She was a large person with noble shoulders and broad hips, and she was wearing a dress of golden-orange taffeta, cut with a rather low square neck and a skirt that just covered her knees. Her short sleeves held her arms tightly and the flesh on them was heavy and smooth and white, like lard.

This was a startling sight. I would not have thought it possible that somebody could look both old and polished, both heavy and graceful, bold as brass and yet mightily dignified. You could have called her brazen, and perhaps my mother later did—that was her sort of word. Someone better disposed might have said, stately. She didn't really show off, except in the whole style and colour of the dress. She and the man with her danced together in a respectful, rather absentminded style, like spouses.

I didn't know her name. I had never seen her before. I didn't know that she was notorious in our town, and maybe farther afield, for all I knew.

I think that if I was writing fiction instead of remembering something that happened, I would never have given her that dress. A kind of advertisement she didn't need.

Of course, if I had lived in the town, instead of just going in and out every day for school, I might have known that she was a notable prostitute. I would surely have seen her sometime, though not in that orange dress. And I would not have used the word prostitute. Bad woman, more likely. I would have known that there was something disgusting and dangerous and exciting and bold about her, without knowing exactly what it was. If somebody had tried to tell me, I don't think I would have believed them.

There were several people in town who looked unusual and maybe she would have seemed to me just another. There was the hunchbacked man who polished the doors of the town hall every day and as far as I know did nothing else. And the quite proper- looking woman who never stopped talking in a loud voice to herself, scolding people who were nowhere in sight.

I would have learned in time what her name was and eventually found out that she really did the things I could not believe she did. And that the man I saw dancing with her and whose name perhaps I never knew was the owner of the poolroom. One day when I was in high school a couple of girls dared me to go into the poolroom when we were walking past, and I did, and there he was, the same man. Though he was balder and heavier now, and wearing shabbier clothes. I don't recall that he said anything to me, but he did not have to. I bolted back to my friends, who were not quite friends after all, and told them nothing.

When I saw the owner of the poolroom, the whole scene of the dance came back to me, the thumping piano and the fiddle music and the orange dress, which I would by then have called ridiculous, and my mother's sudden appearance with her coat on that she had probably never taken off.

There she was, calling my name through the music in the tone I particularly disliked, the tone that seemed to specially remind me that it was thanks to her I was on this earth at all.

She said, "Where is your coat?" As if I had mislaid it somewhere.

"Upstairs."

"Well go and get it."

She would have seen it there if she herself had been upstairs at all. She must never have got past the kitchen, she must have been fussing around the food with her own coat unbuttoned but not removed, until she looked into the room where the dancing was taking place and knew who that orange dancer was.

"Don't delay," she said.

I didn't intend to. I opened the door to the stairway and ran up the first steps and found that where the stairs took their turn some people were sitting, blocking my way. They didn't see me coming—they were taken up, it seemed, with something serious. Not an argument, exactly, but an urgent sort of communication.

Two of these people were men. Young men in Air Force uniforms. One sitting on a step, one leaning forward on a lower step with a hand on his knee. There was a girl sitting on the step above them, and the man nearest to her was patting her leg in a comforting way. I thought she must have fallen on these narrow stairs and hurt herself, for she was crying.

Peggy. Her name was Peggy. "Peggy, Peggy," the young men were saying, in their urgent and even tender voices.

She said something I couldn't make out. She spoke in a childish voice. She was complaining, the way you complain about something that isn't fair. You say over and over that something isn't fair, but in a hopeless voice, as if you don't expect the thing that isn't fair to be righted. Mean is another word to be made use of in these circumstances. It's so mean. Somebody has been so mean.

By listening to my mother's talk to my father when we got home I found out something of what had happened, but I was not able to get it straight. Mrs. Hutchison had shown up at the dance, driven by the poolroom man, who was not known to me then as the poolroom man. I don't know what name my mother called him by, but she was sadly dismayed by his behaviour. News had got out about the dance and some boys from Port Albert—that is, from the Air Force base—had decided to put in an appearance as well. Of course that would have been all right. The Air Force boys were all right. It was Mrs. Hutchison who was the disgrace. And the girl.

She had brought one of her girls with her. "Maybe just felt like an outing," my father said. "Maybe just likes to dance."

My mother seemed not even to have heard this. She said that it was a shame. You expected to have a nice time, a nice decent dance within a neighbourhood, and then it was all ruined.

I was in the habit of assessing the looks of older girls. I had not thought Peggy was particularly pretty. Maybe her makeup had rubbed off with her crying. Her rolled-up mousey-coloured hair had got loose from some of its bobby pins. Her fingernails were polished but they still looked as if she chewed them. She didn't seem much more grown up than one of those whiny, sneaky, perpetually complaining older girls I knew. Nevertheless the young men treated her as if she was someone who deserved never to have encountered one rough moment, someone who rightfully should be petted and pleasured and have heads bowed before her.

One of them offered her a ready-made cigarette. This in itself I saw as a treat, since my father rolled his own and so did every other man I knew. But Peggy shook her head and complained in that hurt voice that she did not smoke. Then the other man offered a stick of gum, and she accepted it.

What was going on? I had no way of knowing. The boy who had offered the gum noticed me, while rummaging in his pocket, and he said, "Peggy? Peggy, here's a little girl I think wants to go upstairs."

When I came downstairs with my coat on they were still there, but this time they had been expecting me, so they all kept quiet while I passed. Except that Peggy gave one loud sniffle, and the young man nearest to her kept stroking her upper leg. Her skirt was pulled up and I saw the fastener holding her stocking.

For a long time I remembered the voices. I pondered over the voices. Not Peggy's. The men's. I know now that some of the Air Force men stationed at Port Albert early in the war had come out from England, and were training there to fight the Germans. So I wonder if it was the accent of some part of Britain that I was finding so mild and entrancing. It was certainly true that I had never in my life heard a man speak in that way, treating a woman as if she was so fine and valued a creature that whatever it was, whatever unkindness had come near her, was somehow a breach of a law, a sin.

What did I think had happened to make Peggy cry? The question did not much interest me at the time. I was not a brave person myself. I cried when chased and beaten with shingles on the way home from my first school. I cried when the teacher in the town school singled me out, in front of the class, to expose the shocking untidiness of my desk. And when she phoned my mother about the same problem and my mother hanging up the phone herself wept, enduring misery because I was not a credit to her. It seemed as though some people were naturally brave and others weren't. Somebody must have said something to Peggy, and there she was snuffling, because like me she was not thick-skinned. It must have been that orange-dressed woman who had been mean, I thought, for no particular reason. It had to have been a woman. Because if it had been a man, one of her Air Force comforters would have punished him. Told him to watch his mouth, maybe dragged him outside and beaten him up.

So it wasn't Peggy I was interested in, not her tears, her crumpled looks. She reminded me too much of myself. It was her comforters I marvelled at. How they seemed to bow down and declare themselves in front of her.

What had they been saying? Nothing in particular. All right, they said. It's all right, Peggy, they said. Now, Peggy. All right. All right. Such kindness. That anybody could be so kind.

It is true that these young men, brought to our country to train for bombing missions on which so many of them would be killed, might have been speaking in the normal accents of Cornwall or Kent or Hull or Scotland. But to me they seemed to be unable to open their mouths without uttering some kind of blessing, a blessing on the moment. It didn't occur to me that their futures were all bound up with disaster, or that their ordinary lives had flown out the window and been smashed on the ground. I just thought of the blessing, how wonderful to get on the receiving end of it, how strangely lucky and undeserving was that Peggy.

And, for I don't know how long, I thought of them. In the cold dark of my bedroom they rocked me to sleep. I could turn them on, summon up their faces and their voices—but oh, far more, their voices were now directed to myself and not to any unnecessary third party. Their hands blessed my own skinny thighs and their voices assured me that I, too, was worthy of love.

And while they still inhabited my not yet quite erotic fantasies they were gone. Some, many, gone for good.

Excerpted from: Alice Munro. Dear Life *(Toronto: McClelland & Stewart, 2012). Reprinted with permission.*

Cosmic Creatix

MONIQUE MARIE DEJONG

She weaves her hips,
syncretic serpentine undulations of infinity.

Hidden and unraveled for lifetimes,
Her ever-expansive womb grid surges,
reawakening worlds of women
to their true Templedoms.

Like a river once meandering, She cannot be contorted
into linear paths – Her venomous wildness and
fearful asymmetry gathers and swells,
retracing Her original, curvaceously carved fullness,
ravaging towns in Her wake.

If you banish Her darkness, She still lingers,
seeping into any crevice. Her smallest movements
make ships' timbers tremble, solar systems collapse.

Cavernous symbols decoded,
revealing new mysteries
of embodied presence.
If you follow the Darkness,
it leads to Light.

Remember the calling of the Snake Priestess
the Weaver of the sacral-heart tapestry,
    the Mother of whores, lovers, and virgins,
    the Keeper of innocence and sacred sensuality,
    the Creatrix of the cosmos,
    the Legendary Self,
for forgetting has been the greatest poison,
yet the greatest gift.

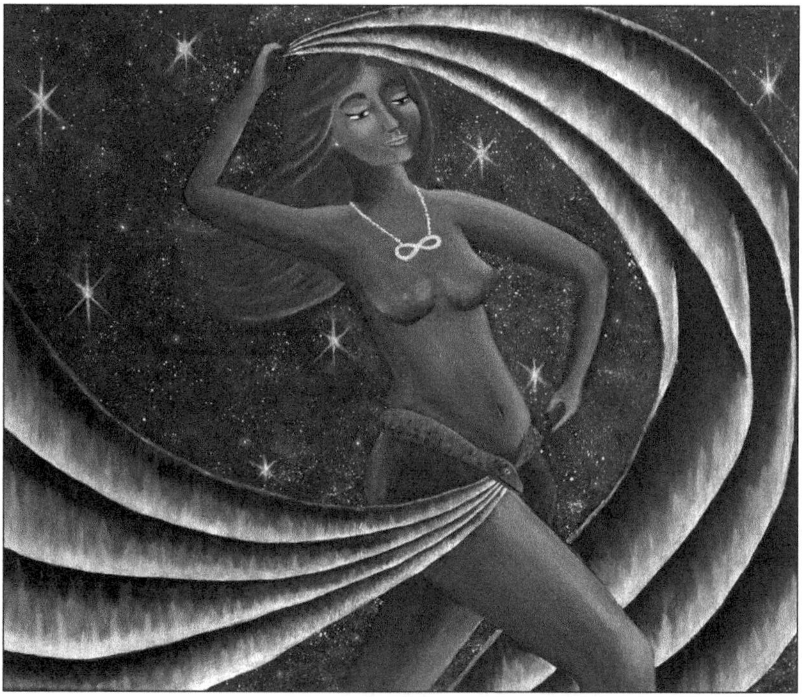

Sacred belly dancer creating the cosmos.
Monique Marie DeJong, "Cosmic Creatrix," 2015, acrylic on canvas, 60cm x 50cm.

Maternal Thinking About Adolescent Mothers Engaged in Sex Work

Moving Toward Alternatives to "Secure Care"

REBECCA BROMWICH

> *I can't go home, but it would be fruitless to stay here, waiting to be picked up by the police. I can't even run away from here because there's nowhere to go without getting caught.*
> —Evelyn Lau, age 14, *Diary of a Runaway Street Kid*

IN THE ABOVE EXCERPT FROM HER MEMOIR detailing her two years living on the street and working intermittently as a prostitute at the age of fourteen, Evelyn Lau highlights the lack of favourable options with which she was faced. Similarly, in a novel that blurs fictionalized narrative with autobiography called *Lullabies for Little Criminals*, Heather O'Neill's protagonist, a teenage girl growing up in contemporary Montreal, is incarcerated in a juvenile detention centre for a month for, as she puts it, "dating a pimp." This intervention is understood by the adolescent narrator as one in a series of confinements and abuses, and neither helps her leave prostitution, nor escape her "pimp" boyfriend Alphonse. It also does not provide her security or support in her difficult relationship with her heroin-addicted father. It becomes apparent that forced confinement of this adolescent involved in sex work does not help her.

While O'Neill's narrative is fictionalized, and Lau's memoir dates from a generation ago, the eventuality that adolescents involved in sex work are often forcibly detained, purportedly for their protection, is contemporary fact. As discussed in the introduction of this book, while a good deal of public debate and significant efforts toward law reform are currently being expended to modify the legal regime concerning adults who engage in sex work in Canada, the state of the formal law concerning criminalization of adolescent sex workers and the "protective" detention of adolescent sex workers is not in flux. The purpose of this chapter is to problematize existing "secure care" regimes governing adolescent girls involved in sex work in an effort to complicate understandings of sex work and motherhood for which the subjects concerned are adolescent girls in Canada. Despite the prevalence of grand narratives of liberal progress (especially the widely accepted assumption that a "rights revolution" in Canada since the 1960s has proven emancipatory for formerly disenfranchised marginal groups [Clement]), it is the argument of this chapter that government of adolescent girls' agencies, and the perpetuation of systems of knowledge and power that make their sexual agencies unthinkable, has not progressed to a more emancipatory formulation over the past few decades. Rather, in formal legal regimes and discourses of protection, the sexual agencies of adolescent girls, in particular adolescent girls who are engaged in some form of sex work, as well as adolescent girls who are mothers and especially adolescent mothers who are engaged in sex work, may even be rendered invisible more profoundly now than in the past.

When sexuality is considered, an adolescent girl is a problematic subject, and an adolescent mother is a particularly difficult subject in late modern Canada. Protective regimes in domestic and international child protection law tend to provide a binary set of social categories of "child" and "adult," notwithstanding the existence in criminal legal regimes of an intermediary category of adolescence as in the *Youth Criminal Justice Act* (YCJA) in Canada. Adolescent girls, particularly those who are mothers, whether or not they engage in the sex trade, are troublesome for this system of social categorization in that they often "look like" adults and, by definition, engage in many behaviours, including parenting and sexual acts associated with adulthood. They may engage in sex work as survival behaviour, especially if they are "thrown away" or have run away from dysfunctional homes (Greene, Ennett, and Ringwalt). The agencies, desires, and capacities of adolescent girls are not well conceptualized or made easily visible in late modern discourses of the child and the girl (Karaian).

In the protective discursive and legal frameworks of child sexual abuse and child protection laws, there is a binary jump from child to adult at age eighteen. However, adolescents clearly experience a gradual transition from dependency to autonomy in their capacities and agencies, including their sexual expression, agency, and capacity to consent. The United Nations Convention on the Rights of the Child (UNCRC) both reflects the consensus of a large number of countries on child protection issues and has an influential role in shaping their social policy agendas. Notably, the UNCRC defines "child" as any person under the age of eighteen. In consequence, adolescent girls are "children" and adolescent mothers are children having children in this framework. Even so, the right to sexual expression is included in the UNCRC. Similarly, Canada's Criminal Code was amended in 2008 by means of the Tackling Violent Crime Act to increase the age of sexual consent in Canada from fourteen to sixteen. However, according to Statistics Canada survey data, as of 2003, at least twenty-eight percent of Canadians aged fifteen-seventeen are sexually active, many of those with more than one partner (Statistics Canada). Further, people who are older than the age of eighteen occupy different and unequal social positions from one another and can be vulnerable to exploitation in much the same manner as sixteen and seventeen year olds. The material conditions experienced by subjects embodied as adolescent girls are much more complicated than formal legal discourses of child protection contemplate.

THE "SECURE CARE" LAWS

The preponderant understanding of sex work by adolescents in Canada is through the lens of the discourse of child sexual abuse (Brock). This dominant understanding is not the only analysis of sex work by adolescents available. Significantly, in a 2013 Canadian compilation, Emily Van der Meulan and her co-authors (in their chapter "We Speak for Ourselves: Anti-colonial and Self-determined Responses to Young People Involved in the Sex Trade") provide arguments and narrative about adolescents involved in sex work that are not subsumed within the discourse of child sexual abuse, but rather pay more attention to the agencies of these young people, and take seriously their existence as knowledge producers, not just objects. Nonetheless, recent understandings of prostitution-related policy strategy by governments across Canada locate youth prostitution in child sexual abuse discourse. Without dismissing the significance of sexual abuse and exploitation of young adolescent women and girls, it is important to acknowledge that discourses of the child victim are being used as technologies to enable neoliberal governments and their officials to take Draconian measures in the fields of criminal law, privacy law, and child protection, in all instances resulting in serious constraints on subjects' agencies not in the guise of punisher but "protector." Adolescent sex workers, the majority of them girls, are neither seen as punishable criminals nor as entrepreneurial workers but rather as victims of sexual abuse in need of protection: protective regimes in provincial and territorial jurisdictions are deployed as governmental technologies against adolescent girls suspected of involvement in sex work, as a means to seek to eradicate sex work involving those not yet adults.

While it is not officially understood as imprisonment, under the guise of protection or "secure care," what is effectively tantamount to incarceration of adolescents for involvement in sex work—or even suspected and unproven involvement—or socially frowned upon expressions of sexual agency remains legal. Alberta was the first Canadian jurisdiction to pass a "secure care" law (the Alberta government introduced the *Protection of Children Involved in Prostitution Act* [PCHIP Act]). As amended, this law allows for the forced detention of young adolescent women for an initial period of five days up to two consecutive, twenty-one-day periods of detention. Numerous other provinces followed suit and have enacted or proposed similar laws. These protective custody regimes do indirectly and covertly what *Juvenile Delinquents Act* (JDA) of 1908 did directly and overtly: they perpetuate the same sort of incarceration of adolescent girls for expressions of sexual agency—and for maternal thinking and mother work—that the now-much-maligned statutes of the twentieth-century before the *Young Offenders Act* (YOA) did.

However, whether young adolescent women continue to be incarcerated for sexual impropriety under current child protection regimes is questionable. Where female adolescents are concerned, values that inform interpretation of what is the "best" in the "best interests of the child" standard has historically been fraught with patriarchal assumptions and problematic racial and class biases in the context of child welfare law. Just as administration of the JDA and related statutes were problematic in that they treated young adolescent women differently depending upon their class, race, and particularly aboriginal heritage, there is scholarship and statistical evidence supporting the contention that contemporary child welfare legislation continues to disproportionately affect the lives of racialized and economically marginalized young women generally, especially aboriginal young women (Busby et al.; Monture).

Within the child welfare systems of Canada's provinces and territories, there remain problematic contexts in which young adolescent women continue to be effectively incarcerated as a result of allegations about their sexual behaviour. Detention under the auspices of child protection legislation is a prevalent but controversial method of regulating child prostitution and of controlling illicit drug use by teens. Child protection laws are used to coercively detain—effectively to incarcerate—adolescents for protective reasons related to sexual behaviour in several provinces. A number of tactics have been used to facilitate this. Some jurisdictions simply include prostitution among the criteria for classifying a child as in need of protection. Others have enacted "secure care" legislation that authorizes involuntary detention of minors engaged in prostitution or who are suspected of involvement in drug use (Busby et al.).

Protection legislation in many provinces provides social services authorities with the power to remove the child at risk of prostitution and to place him or her into the child welfare system. British Columbia, Alberta, Saskatchewan, and Prince Edward Island explicitly refer to prostitution in their child welfare legislation. These provincial laws allow a child to be found in need of protection and to be involuntarily detained if he, or, more commonly, she, has been or is likely to be sexually abused or exploited. In addition to the basic provisions noted above, courts in British Columbia and Alberta can issue a restraining order if reasonable grounds exist to believe that a person has encouraged or coerced, or is likely to encourage or coerce, a youth involved in the child welfare system to engage in prostitution.

Alberta has enacted the *Protection of Children Abusing Drugs Act* (PChAD), Saskatchewan's parallel law is called the *Youth Drug Detoxification and Stabilization Act*, and Manitoba has passed the *Youth Drug Stabilization (Support for Parents) Act*. All of this legislation provides for involuntary detention of youth who are involved in substance abuse. British Columbia's legislature has assented to legislation that deals with both drug abuse and prostitution but has indicated it will not be proclaimed in force. Similar laws exist respecting child prostitution. Alberta passed the *Protection of Sexually Exploited Children Act*. This law provides for involuntary detention of youth who are involved in prostitution. Saskatchewan, Ontario, and British Columbia have introduced or effected similar legislation.

Critics of these laws often focus on the efficacy of the legislation. They contend that forcibly confining an adolescent woman who is suspected to be involved in prostitution has little proven positive effect and in fact may be counter-productive from the perspective of ending her involvement with the sex trade in the long run. The argument often is that offering help when young adolescent women want or need it, such as assistance with unplanned pregnancies and access to social assistance, will be more assistive to them than creating a climate of fear of incarceration by the state. Provision of appropriately designed voluntary community and social services are arguably far more effective in providing a woman a path out of prostitution in the long term. Addressing her poverty and victimization by various kinds of abuse could be much more effective than forcibly confining her (Busby et al.). As David Barrett has contended with reference to strategies to "rescue" child prostitutes in the United Kingdom, providing assistance to adolescent sex workers when they seek it, and advising them of its availability, is likely to have more efficacy than forcible attempts to confine and control them. Strategies that confirm their agency and empower them to change their lives would be more useful than control mechanisms that confirm their passivity.

In addition to being ineffective measures to protect adolescents, child protection regimes that forcibly detain young adolescent women are also problematic in terms of making them invisible, constraining and punishing young subjects' sexual agencies or, in legal language, impinging on a young woman's rights to liberty and autonomy. A determination may be made under child protection statutes that results in a long period of what is tantamount to incarceration without the procedural safeguards or presumption of innocence that would be afforded her in a criminal court. While a child protection order is levied in language that sounds benevolent, it can result in the same sort of forced confinement a woman would face in jail, which is tantamount to incarceration.

CONTEXTUALIZING "SECURE CARE" IN CANADA'S COLONIAL HISTORY

In Canada, protection of women (especially mothers) in general, and young adolescent women in particular, has a problematic history, especially where sexuality is concerned (O'Reilly). This is a history characterized by a troubling relationship between regulation of morality, sexual behaviour, criminalization of sex work, "protection" of adolescent girls, and adolescent maternity. Young adolescent Canadian women's sexual agencies have been alternately punished and rendered invisible based on a colonial settler geography that limits girls' agencies on matrixes of race and class has been written in to both laws about sex work and child protective regimes that penalize adolescents for engaging in sex work under the guise of protection.

Controlling young adolescent women's sexual agency and containing their sexual and reproductive potential agencies have been integral elements to regimes under which adolescent girls are both penalized and protected. Young adolescent women were historically incarcerated for sexual "impropriety." Evidence of such impropriety could include becoming pregnant with illegitimate children by men deemed socially inappropriate fathers. Incarceration of adolescent girls was used to deal with conduct that would not be considered criminal were it undertaken by a male under the JDA and related quasi-criminal/regulatory and protective statutes in effect across Canada. Until the *Young Offenders Act* came into effect in 1984, the most common offence for which young adolescent women were locked up was the status offence (meaning an identity, not a particular impugned act) of "incorrigibility," and more specifically the behaviour that most often founded an allegation of incorrigibility was sexual impropriety. And, things being as they are, especially before contraception became legal, the best evidence of such impropriety was pregnancy.

From 1908 onward, the *Juvenile Delinquents Act,* with its regime of status offences, criminalized teen motherhood in certain circumstances for young adolescent women up to sixteen or eighteen years of age depending upon the jurisdiction. From 1897 to 1958, in Ontario, the *Female Refuges Act* provided at Section 17 for young women up to age twenty-one to be incarcerated for incorrigibility. The *Indian Act* provided for charges for young adolescent women in provisions that prohibited things such as the consumption of alcohol and a general offence of "profligacy." Delinquent status as a result of these general status offences could be evidenced by pregnancy.

Incarceration of young adolescent women for sexual impropriety and for motherhood of "illegitimate" children took place in the context of white European imperialism and settler colonialism (McLaren). Performance of femininity was enforced by the criminal law as it related to young adolescent women. As Joan Sangster has pointed out, incarceration of young adolescent women in Canada was undertaken in ways that were similar to practices across North America whereby young adolescent women's sexual conduct was a central concern of the courts. Allegations of sexual promiscuity were a major reason that judges resorted to closed custody sentences. Allegations of sexual misconduct would often become the central issue, no matter what the original charge or concern of the charging authorities was, whether those authorities gained jurisdiction under the Indian Act, provincial legislation, police powers, or the allegations were raised by someone from the young adolescent woman's family. This focus on young women's sexual behaviour was related to broader social contexts of eugenics and white supremacy.

Passed in 1908, revised in 1929, and remaining in force until 1982, the JDA (discussed above) was very euphemistic in its tone. It applied generally to both males and females but young adolescent women were arrested and incarcerated under its auspices for very different reasons than were young adolescent males. Acting in the "best interests" of an adolescent was the highest priority under the legislation. The JDA saw the state as a sympathetic, patriarchal guardian whose actions were intended to treat the juvenile as a misguided child in need of care and supervision. The JDA contained a definition of delinquency that went beyond codified adult crimes specified in the *Criminal Code* to include "sexual immorality or any similar form of vice." Jurisdiction of the Juvenile Court under the JDA extended as well to cases that concerned neglected, abused or otherwise "incorrigible" or uncontrollable children. After a finding of delinquency, an open-ended jurisdiction of the state over these children lasted until their twenty-first birthday.

Young adolescent women across Canada did not receive equal treatment under these historical laws. The operation of the JDA was by no means uniform across jurisdictions and time. Provincial legislation was even more obviously divergent across Canada. The vague offence of "incorrigibility" was enforced selectively. Race and social class, and especially aboriginal heritage, were other complicating factors leading to differential treatment of young adolescent women across Canada. For instance, anti-Chinese racism was a particularly virulent motivating force behind construction of some young adolescent women's relationships as criminal in Canada. As Joan Sangster has noted, aboriginal young women were stereotyped as wild and out of control before any conduct on their part specifically evidenced "incorrigibility," a systemic bias that contributed to high levels of incarceration of aboriginal young women under the JDA.

In general, too often under the JDA, moral regulation and sexual control as well as performance of proscribed gender roles were rigidly enforced against Canadian young adolescent women. The JDA "dealt with" adolescents labelled as delinquents expressly in the "best interests of the child." Forcible confinement, which was actually incarceration, was euphemistically termed "training." Other times, "incorrigibility" meant running away from a battering father, stepfather, or male relative, or sexual and physical abuse in their homes.

Perhaps the most famous case of an adolescent Caucasian Canadian woman criminalized for a sexual liaison and resultant motherhood is that of Velma Demerson who was arrested at her father's request for being "incorrigible" under the Female Refuges Act (Demerson). The first person recounting of her story by "delinquent" Velma Demerson and chronicling of it by Professor Constance Backhouse in her book *Carnal Crimes* brought to public prominence problems related to incarcerating young women for "incorrigibility" in relation to sexual activity and pregnancy, as well as abuse of young adolescent women within carceral institutions (Backhouse).

Demerson's incorrigibility was founded on her romantic relationship with and pregnancy by Harry Yip, a Chinese man. Demerson offered to marry the father of her child at her trial. This suggestion was rejected by the Court. Harry Yip was never charged with anything. Demerson was incarcerated for this incorrigibility, during which time she gave birth at the Mercer Reformatory. Before giving birth, Demerson was experimented on in sadistic ways by a physician at the reformatory. Experiments on her genitals and abdomen while she was pregnant involved the injection of chemicals that likely compromised her son's health. Her son, Harry Junior, was taken from her once he was three months old. Demerson eventually regained custody of her son after her release. In this case, at a time when white children born out of wedlock in Canada were often quietly adopted, or their young parents were swiftly married before the birth, it is evident that racism too played a considerable role in the determination of which teen pregnancies and sexual behaviours by girls might give rise to a finding of delinquency and which might instead be corrigible by a swift marriage or a discreet absence and adoption.

The JDA and provincial legislation like the Female Refuges Act created a highly discretionary youth justice system that left police, judges, and probation officers to do whatever they deemed to be in a young woman's "best interests." The fact is that under these historical laws, girls were locked up and sometimes even medically tortured and sexually assaulted ostensibly for "their own good." The JDA lacked legislative guidelines governing jurisdiction and sentencing. Statutory language and court practices not only failed to afford but also actively discouraged representation of young accuseds by counsel. These problems in turn led to disparities and injustices across Canada regarding who was under juvenile court authority and in what ways they were treated. What was understood to be "good" for young adolescent women was defined in the interests of what were perceived to be greater goods than their individual autonomy or liberty. Additionally, these laws afforded system actors a wide discretion to project their own fears or cruel whims onto girls subjected to the system. What was considered most important was the moral development of Canada's children in general and the creation of a morally pure nation, contemplated as a white one.

Young adolescent women were rigidly regulated by juvenile justice law as it existed in Canada historically. Young adolescent women were forced into socially desired activities and socially sanctioned relationships and were required to comply with subordinate gender roles by threat of criminal sanction. The labour of young adolescent women was channelled by the JDA, Female Refuges Act, and related statutes into working-class, paid employment and to the bearing of and caring for socially sanctioned white children. Inter-racial unions, like Demerson's, were seen as undesirable. Further, aboriginal women's mother work was consistently derogated and discouraged in a society that simply did not value aboriginal children being born and certainly actively prevented cultural transmission by aboriginal mothers to their children by apprehending children at young ages and sending them to residential schools.

State actors crafting and administering the JDA, as expressly stated under the legislation, believed they were acting in the best interests of the young adolescent women concerned. Problematically, under this regime protection of the young adolescent women's moral virtue and socialization into appropriate (and subordinate) gender roles were understood to be things like "light, soap and water" (Valverde) that were integral the building both of Canada as a nation and the moral development of teenage girls. What was considered to be best for young adolescent women was referential to distorted, masculinist, colonial understandings of the good. In the "rights revolution" that characterized Canadian politics in the mid-twentieth century (Clement) critics ultimately attacked the JDA for paternalism, informality of processes, and failure to protect the basic legal rights of adolescents.

In response to these and other criticisms, the *Young Offenders Act* eliminated all status offences (such as truancy, incorrigibility, and sexual immorality). Delinquency is no longer a legal status in Canada. Culpability for the purposes of the criminal law is confined to only criminal offences. The YOA also provided young offenders with the right to legal representation and established strict rules of evidence and proof throughout court proceedings. The YOA reframed the criminal law with respect to youth to form a youth justice system that stresses the accountability of the offender and the protection of society while still recognizing special needs of youths. Reflecting this, its dispositions ranged from reprimands, fines, probation, and community service to secure custody to a maximum carceral term of ten years. The contemporary *Youth Criminal Justice Act* (YCJA), which came into force in 2003, continues the rights-based regime of the YOA.

CONCLUSION: ALTERNATIVE LEGAL APPROACHES

I have argued that, where adolescent sex workers and adolescent mothers are concerned, the widely celebrated narrative of the ascendancy of the "rights revolution" in Canadian law is seriously undermined by the problematic continuity between "secure care" laws and historical criminal laws that all lock up girls "for their own good." By another name, I have argued that the "secure care" statutes effectively either preserve or reinstate the status offences of promiscuity and incorrigibility. Consequently, they deploy discourses of child sexual abuse to reinscribe patriarchal views of what constitute the "best interests" of young adolescent women or children and continue to make unthinkable and invisible the agencies, including sexual agencies, of adolescent girls.

Factors, contexts, and issues relating to the involvement of adolescents, particularly young women in sex work, are complex. Their agencies are certainly constrained by their developmental capacities, and they are vulnerable in ways adults are not. I have not disputed that sexual exploitation of young adolescent women and girls is a serious social problem in Canada as it is elsewhere. However, measures taken to alleviate the social problem of sexual exploitation and abuse of young adolescent women and girls both can be and need to be sufficiently nuanced to appreciate that state action which coercively confines these young Canadians in a manner that is tantamount to incarceration is counterproductive and oppressive.

In *Canada (Attorney General) v. Bedford*, the Supreme Court of Canada in December 2013 struck down existing laws that prohibited activities that would help ensure the safety of sex workers: prohibitions on the existence of brothels (or safe spaces for sex work to take place) and on "living off the avails" of prostitution as well as on solicitation for prostitution were struck down by the Court. While not directly binding as precedent on the protective confinement laws, this decision affords reasoning that is consistent with, and even cries out for, an amendment or repeal of the "secure care" laws.

Maternal thinking involves contemplating solutions to social problems that focus on "protection, nurturance and training ... care and respect" (Ruddick; O'Reilly). Ruddick identifies the "maternal standpoint" as a way of looking at all children and other people as human. Caring for and respecting the embodied agencies of adolescent girls involved in sex work would be manifested by approaches used in social services apparatuses and laws that support those agencies and afford them opportunities to live lives free from abuse and exploitation without oppressing or effectively incarcerating them as agents. It would not, I would argue, be consistent with the current "secure care" laws.

Not every Canadian jurisdiction has passed "secure care" laws. A notable exception is Saskatchewan. The Saskatchewan government rejected efforts by advocates to enact secure care laws in 1999. Other jurisdictions could follow suit and either refuse to enact "secure care" laws or repeal the ones currently in force. Comparative analysis of Saskatchewan's approach makes clear that reform to the child protection regimes that effectively incarcerate adolescent girls involved in sex work is imaginable and could be done quite easily if the political will existed to make it so.

WORKS CITED

Barrett, David. *Child Prostitution in Britain: Dilemmas and Practical Responses.* London: The Children's Society, 1997. Print.

Backhouse, Constance *Carnal Crimes: Sexual Assault Law in Canada*, 1900-1975. Toronto: Irwin Law, 2010. Print.

Brock, D. *Making Work, Making Trouble: Prostitution as a Social Problem.* Toronto: University of Toronto Press, 1998. Print.

Busby, Karen, et al. *In the Best Interests of the Girl Child: Phase II Report.* Canada: Alliance of Five Research Centres on Violence. January 2002. Print.

Clement, Dominique. "Canada's Rights Revolution: Social Movements and Social Change, 1937-1982." *History of Rights.* Vancouver: University of British Columbia Press, 2008. Print.

Demerson, Velma. *Incorrigible.* Toronto: Laurier Press, 2004. Print.

Greene, J., S. Ennett, and C. Ringwalt. "Prevalence and Correlates of Survival Sex among Runaway and Homeless Youth." *American Journal of Public Health* 89.9 (1999): 1406-1409. Print.

Karaian, Lara. "Consensual Sexting and Child Pornography: Legal and Cultural Controversies." *Gender, Sex, and Politics: In the Streets and Between the Sheets in the 21*st Century. Ed. Shira Tarrant. New York: Routledge, forthcoming 2015.

Lau, Evelyn. *Diary of a Runaway Street Kid.* Toronto: Harper Collins, 1995. Print.

McLaren, Angus. *Our Own Master Race: Eugenics in Canada, 1884–1945.* Toronto: McClelland and Stewart, 1990. Print.

Monture, Patricia "A Vicious Circle: Child Welfare and the First Nations." *Canadian Journal of Women and the Law* 3.1 (1989): 1–17. Print.

O'Neill, Heather. *Lullabies for Little Criminals.* Toronto: Harper, 2006. Print.

O'Reilly, Andrea. *The Twenty-First Century Motherhood Movement.* Bradford Ontario: Demeter Press, 2011. Print.

Ruddick, Sara. *Maternal Thinking: Toward a Politics of Peace.* Boston: Beacon Press, 1995. Print.

Sangster, Joan. "'She Is Hostile to Our Ways': First Nations Girls Sentenced to the Ontario Training School for Girls, 1933–1960." *Law and History Review* 20 (2002):1 Print.

Valverde, Mariana. *The Age of Light, Soap, and Water: Moral Reform in English Canada, 1885-1925*. Toronto: McClelland & Stewart Inc., 1991. Print.

Van der Meulan, Emily et al. *Selling Sex: Experience, Advocacy and Research on Sex Work in Canada* Vancouver: University of British Columbia Press, Press, 2013. Print.

LEGISLATION AND CASE LAW

Canada (Attorney General) v. Bedford. SCC 72. 2013. *Judgments of the Supreme Court of Canada*. 20 Dec 2013.

Emergency Protection for Victims of Child Sexual Abuse and Exploitation Act, S.S. 2002.

Juvenile Delinquents Act R.S.C. 1908.

Protection of Sexually Exploited Children Act R.S.A. 2005.

Rescuing Children from Sexual Exploitation Act S.O. 2002 (not yet in force).

Tackling Violent Crime Act SC 2008 c.6.

United Nations Convention on the Rights of the Child

Young Offenders Act R.S.C. 1985, c. Y-1.

Youth Criminal Justice Act R.S.C. 2002, C-1.

ANONYMOUS

"Acceptance, Love, Peace"

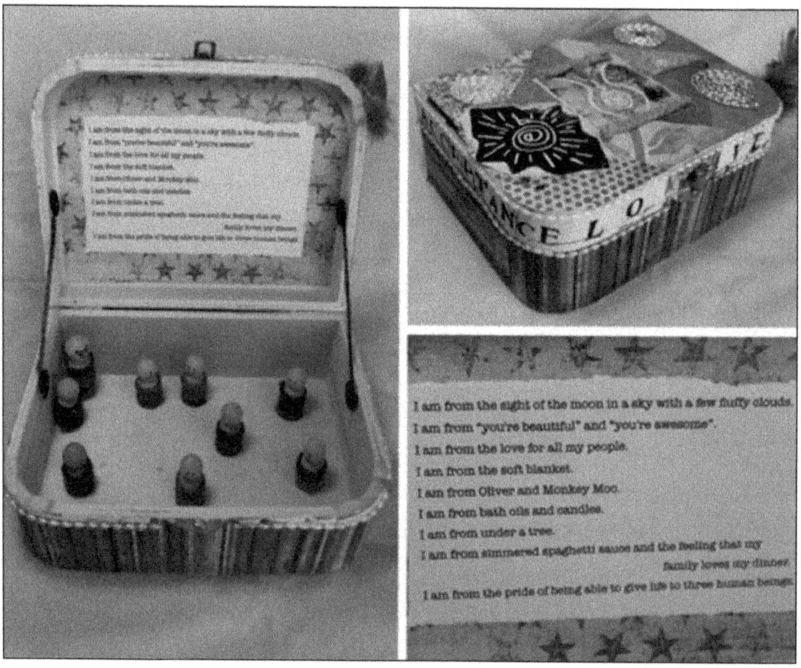

SWANS Story Box Project

This art work is part of a community project created in partnership with Sex Wokers Advisory Network Sudbury and Myths and Mirrors Community Arts. Guided by community artist, Sarah King Gold, women with lived experience in sex work, and their allies, committed to building safer and more inclusive communities for sex worker peers, and worked together and individually to artistically express aspects of themselves through "story boxes." The outside of the boxes represent the artists' public selves while the interior spaces represent their private worlds. This particular piece has been contributed to this anthology anonymously with permission by the artist. The poetic aspect of the project was inspired by Ella George Lyon's poem "Where I am from."

Excerpts from *The Maeve Chronicles*

ELIZABETH CUNNINGHAM

1.

Maeve and the one she knows as Esus meet at druid school. She is exiled after she saves him from becoming a human sacrifice. En route to find him again, she is captured by a slave dealer and sold into prostitution in Rome. Throughout her story, Maeve sometimes speaks to us, her twenty-first-century audience, directly. She does so here just after being led away from the slave block.

Maybe you are relieved to know that I was forced into prostitution. Sold. No choice. Some people insist there is no evidence that I was a whore at all; they are eager to save my reputation—which implies that they think there is something wrong with being a whore. It is true that his official chroniclers never called me a whore, just a crazy bitch or in polite language "a woman infested by seven demons." (We'll get to that part later.) Everyone seems to agree that I was saved, cleansed by his healing (asexual) touch and that I went on to become an important, if unacknowledged, disciple.

There is more to the story or I wouldn't be telling it. And I hope you will discover, if you don't already know, the difference between a stereotype and an archetype. Stereotypes are flat, one dimensional, like the donkey you blindly pin the tail on. Archetypes are rich, lush, juicy. Sometimes they go underground, submerged in mist and myth. But I am here to tell you:

You can't keep a good archetype down.

I didn't know any of that yet. As I said, I didn't even know what a whore was, but I must have had a premonition. I knew I was fucked.

Cunningham, Elizabeth. The Maeve Chronicles: The Passion of Mary Magdalen. *New York: Monkfish Publishing, 2006: 9. Print. Reprinted with kind permission.*

2.

Later that same day, Maeve meets her fellow whores while they all bathe before work.

"Here is the way how to think of it, *liebling*," said Berta.

We were all soaking together in the caldarium. I had grown up with springs and surf, but I had never been in hot water before (at least not literally). I was distressed to find myself enjoying the sensation; I was becoming Roman already. The big blonde, my fellow barbarian, had taken me under her wing, that is, she had a plump arm draped over my shoulder. The other whores sat across the pool, whispering and tittering as they eyed me and listened to Berta hold forth. Well, they could hardly help it. She had a voice as big as she was—the voice of someone who'd once lived in the open.

"You have been raped, yes? Who has not? I myself have been raped by a whole legion."

"Oh, not the legion again," said the little dark one. She caught my eye and winked at me.

"You know it's true, Succula," Berta scolded. "So. The Roman legion comes to my village. They burn the huts; they put the men to the sword, and they rape all the women. It is the same story everywhere. I was a virgin...."

"It is the eve of her wedding day," added a woman, who was blacker than anyone I'd ever seen with coil upon coil of snaky hair.

"She hears the thundering of many hooves," another woman continued.

I was shocked that they would mock such a terrible story. It took me awhile to understand. We all had terrible stories. Mockery kept the terror at bay.

"All right, all right," said Berta crossly. "I wasn't going to tell the whole story. I have a point to make."

"So make it already," the black woman said.

"If you would all shut up, maybe I could."

The others pantomimed sealed lips and made strangled noises.

"The point is," Berta ignored them, "we have all had it stolen from us. Now we make them pay. It's good. Yes?"

The lips came unsealed with general laughter and agreement.

I felt myself frowning. I was still tired and disoriented, but I knew something was faulty in their thinking.

"No," I said, "Domitia Tertia makes them pay."

They regarded me coldly, and I realized my mistake. I needed the good will of these women to survive.

"Well, at least she's a woman," I amended.

"And a whore," Succula added.

"And a hardnosed, tight-assed bitch," said the black woman.

"You got that right, Dido." Everyone chimed in; this description was apparently a compliment to the *domina*.

"As you say, Red," Dido added, addressing me directly for the first time. "She makes them pay. Does she ever. Nobody fools with her, and you won't either, Hot Twat, if you know what's good for you."

Apparently these women identified with Domitia Tertia. I found their admiration perplexing.

"So," said Dido, who shared a name with the fabled Queen of Carthage. "Are you really a *novica*? Never been a slave? Never done it for money?"

"I did it for passage on a ship."

Applause greeted this admission.

"But it didn't exactly work out," I understated.

In fact, that was when everything had gone wrong. Maybe I was being punished—an unfamiliar and disconcerting line of thought for me.

"Don't tell us." Dido held up her hand. "The bastard drugged your drink and you awoke trussed up and on your way to market."

"And on the way he sticks you every time he feels like it," added Berta. "Don't feel bad, *liebling*. It's not your fault. There is nothing you could have done to stop it."

Yet that's where the shame was, that it had happened to me at all. How could I have allowed it? How could I have been so stupid?

"Hey, none of us knows until it's too late: you gotta drug *their* drink first," Dido answered my thoughts.

"That's right, *liebling*," Berta patted me and made comforting clucking noises.

Suddenly I was undone. Their unexpected kindness loosed my tears. I covered my face, expecting my weakness to be met with contempt. Instead I found myself surrounded by female bodies. Breasts brushed against my cheeks, bellies against my breasts. I breathed in the sweet, salty scent of women, the scent of home and I cried even harder.

"I was born," I said when I could speak again, "on an island of women."

"Only women!"

"I had eight mothers."

"Sweet Isis!"

"And one old, old woman."

"My granny used to take care of me," someone sighed.

"And then the Romans came?" prompted Berta.

"No. No Romans. The Romans will never find my mothers' island. It is not in the same world."

"Then why did you leave there? Why would you ever leave?" Dido sounded angry and wistful at once.

Why? I knew, but I could not begin to say.

"It's all right," soothed Berta. "You will tell us your story when you're ready, yes? Listen now, *liebling*. Let me tell you how we do things here. You stick by us, we stick by you."

"Don't try to act like you're better than everybody else," Dido explained.

"Don't steal anyone's regulars," added Succula.

"And then we teach you everything we know. All the little tricks."

"How to spit it out without him knowing."

"The surefire hand job."

"How to keep your womb locked up tight."

I was a long way from druid school.

"Don't worry," said Succula. "Tonight everyone's gonna know you're new. Novelty will make up for lack of technique. You'll catch on."

"So, are you with us, Red?" Dido fixed me with a deep black gaze; she was gorgeous. "We're all foreigners here, except for Succula. She was raised in the house. What matters is we're all whores. You can be out for yourself or you can be one of us. How do you want to play it?"

I looked at the women surrounding me, their impulsive kindness now replaced with wariness. If I got close to them, would they hold me back or would they help me? Part of me wanted to say, I am not one of you; I will never be one of you. You are slaves to the Romans, and you accept it. Then I remembered my beloved, prophesying in a druid grove. "Rome is not a place," he said. "Rome is cruelty." And here, among these women, I had, for a moment, been back home on The Isle of Women.

"I'm with you," I said.

"Good. Now let's show her how we seal a deal."

And one of the women rose to her knees and dipped their forefingers into their vulvas. They waited until I did the same; then we all pressed our hands together, and each woman gave me a smacking kiss on the mouth.

"Now you're a whore, *liebling*!" exulted Berta.

Cunningham, Elizabeth. The Maeve Chronicles: The Passion of Mary Magdalen. *New York: Monkfish Publishing, 2006: 18-21. Print. Reprinted with kind permission.*

3.

A brief passage in which Maeve reflects on her first night as a whore.

As I look back on that night, I see choices I didn't recognize then. I could have disavowed my body. That's not me straddling the general. That's just my body. Or I could become my body, its opening and resistance, its capacity for cruelty or compassion. But there is another possibility, and I think I sensed it even then: that I—this fraught, ecstatic coupling of body and soul—could become the conduit of some wild force, the mediator of it, the priestess.

Cunningham, Elizabeth. The Maeve Chronicles: The Passion of Mary Magdalen. *New York: Monkfish Publishing, 2006: 27. Print. Reprinted with kind permission.*

4.

Months later, Maeve and her fellow whores are taken to a Senatorial banquet where they are to provide entertainment and sexual services. Maeve (to her surprise) has her first experience as a whore priestess.

When I came to myself again, I found I was in a chamber with a frightened boy who wanted to fuck his first whore and instead found himself face to face with some wild divinity. For a moment, I almost felt sorry for him as he cowered on the couch, unable to summon the contempt for a slave that should have protected him and kept him in control.

But then I made myself remember: His people had enslaved and maybe murdered my foster-father. I looked at the soft, pimpled flesh of this over-indulged Roman youth and felt a rage and revulsion I had never known before. I wanted to be sick again. No, I wanted more than that: I wanted to kill him. The hairs on my neck rose as it dawned on me that I could. There he was, alone and vulnerable. Here I was, full of power and fury. I could tear him to pieces.

I closed my eyes and clenched and unclenched my hands. If this is meant to be, I spoke to something I did not name, if I am meant to be an instrument of revenge, use me.

I waited, and my crown ignited as the fire of the stars rained down.

No, I protested silently, without knowing fully what I meant. Not for him.

Open your eyes, a voice inside me said.

Reluctantly, I obeyed. When the boy saw me staring at him, he began to whimper.

Find the god in him, the voice prompted.

No, I answered. I hate him. I hate what he will become.

Call forth the god.

The fire was burning in my hands and in my sex, but still I resisted.

Why bother? I challenged the voice. These people already think they're gods.

Look again. Look deeper. The voice was implacable.

The boy kept his gaze on me as if I were the goddess, death, fate, all in one. And I was. He saw the truth. So I looked at him again. I looked deeper, and I saw it: earth and grain, sun and rain in the form of this boy. In that instant I knew something I could never again forget: All flesh is innocent.

I let out a long breath I hadn't known I was holding, sat down at one end of the couch and took his feet in my hands, pampered feet, hardly calloused, bigger than the rest of him. I explored their shape, the tendons, the length of the toes. The fire flowed through my hands as I touched this humblest part of the body, the farthest from the head, the closest to the ground.

Then the boy started to cry.

"I don't know what I'm supposed to do," he said.

"You will." I released his feet and stretched out beside him.

"Don't tell anyone," he begged.

"I am the keeper of secrets. I am the temple of mysteries. Enter."

The voice that had spoken within me now spoke through me. All distinction was lost between myself and whatever power claimed me. I was the chasm and the stars. I was the riverbed; through me the source flowed relentlessly to the sea.

Afterwards the boy slept on my breast and drooled. I was alone again with my small self, the force that had filled me ebbing away.

"Who are you?" I whispered aloud. "What do you want from my life?"

I heard nothing but the boy's soft snores.

Cunningham, Elizabeth. The Maeve Chronicles: The Passion of Mary Magdalen. *New York: Monkfish Publishing, 2006: 62-63. Print. Reprinted with kind permission.*

5.

Many years later, Maeve and her sister whores, now freed from slavery, open their own temple of sacred prostitution in Magdala, Galilee (where Maeve still has not found her lost beloved).

When I think of those early days at Temple Magdalen, I see images of feet. Our feet, painted with henna, anklets jingling rhythmically as we dance ourselves into ecstatic trance. Our feet planted in the soft, new-turned earth of the gardens we made or cooling in the spring after a long day. Our feet climbing trees when we pruned the upper branches and our feet purple with crushing the grapes of our first harvest for wine.

I see the feet of the men, too, the suppliants who began to come, only a few at first, but as word spread more and more each evening. The pampered feet of Roman magistrates, the callused feet of soldiers and rebel hill fighters, the feet of peasants, the soil worked so deeply into their soles that the distinction between earth and feet is almost lost. And of course the feet of fishermen who stood among the fish guts and never seemed to be quite free of scales.

Picture all of these feet finding their way to our temple gate. No one is refused. Gold coins, a basket of fish, a loaf of bread, a morning's labor in the vineyard, all offerings are acceptable. Maybe it is because we are veiled, as we guide men through the honeycomb of passages in the temple, that I am so aware of the suppliant's feet. I hold the lantern low so he can only see enough to take one step and the next. At every turning we pause, and he must shed something, his cloak, his insignias of rank, tokens of piety, or good luck talisman, and finally, his tunic, his undergarments, and sandals.

Some rich and powerful men turn back. This is not their idea of a whorehouse where they are accustomed to paying for (the illusion of) control. To become the god-bearing stranger, the suppliant must surrender, forget who he is in the world, be naked as he was at birth. When he leaves everything behind but himself, the whore-priestess leads him to a hot spring. She bathes him from head to toe. She anoints him with warm, fragrant oils. And here is our mystery, our surrender: to know that each stranger is the beloved of Isis. Through us she will know him, love him, heal him. Always it is when I touch the stranger's feet that she becomes fully present in me; there is no more distinction between goddess and priestess.

And I know something more. For it is my own beloved's feet that I picture most clearly when I think of him. It is his feet that walk beside me in my dreams, his feet, brown as earth, beautiful as the flight of birds. In the feet of every god-bearing stranger I remember him whom my soul loves. When I open myself to the goddess, he is restored to me again in the stranger's embrace.

That is all I am going to tell you about the mysteries of sacred prostitution. Because in some deep part of yourself, whether from this life or another, I know you remember. The light flickering on the curved, mosaic walls, the sound of water, the scent of spices, oil and honey. The way age and beauty and rank are consumed like so much candle wax by living flame. If you don't remember yet, someday you will.

Cunningham, Elizabeth. The Maeve Chronicles: The Passion of Mary Magdalen. *New York: Monkfish Publishing, 2006: 341-2. Print. Reprinted with kind permission.*

6.

Many years later, after her reunion with Jesus and his subsequent death, Maeve returns to Temple Magdalen to give birth to Jesus's posthumous child. She has fled the disciples, who tolerated her as Jesus's eccentric wife, but who now consider her a most unfit mother for the Saviour's son. They have begun to mass outside the gates. (Reginus is also a freed Roman slave who has found true love with native Galilean Timothy.)

What we came to call the Siege of Temple Magdalen began on a small scale: Just Peter, James, Andrew, John, and a few of the other disciples who came from the area standing, almost politely, outside our gates. They might even have been mistaken for suppliants seeking our usual services—(Oh the shame of it! That's how determined they were)—except that they refused our invitation to come inside. To step foot in a pagan temple whorehouse would clearly render them instantly unclean. God only knows for how long and what they would have had to do to become clean again. Nor did they invite me to come out. According to the Law, a woman is unclean for forty days after the birth of a male child and for eighty days if the child is female. But clearly they wanted to know if I had given birth yet, and if so—to a son or a daughter? There was debate within the walls of Temple Magdalen as to what and how much to tell them.

"Personally, I don't see what's wrong with lying," said Reginus.

Everyone was having an indoor picnic in the inner chamber where Sarah and I remained tucked up.

"What do you mean by lying?" Berta wanted to know. "You can't mean—"

There was a flurry of gestures and utterances as all the women present warded away all evil from lovely, healthy Sarah, who had gone to sleep again for the time being. Infant mortality was all too real a specter. No one wanted to speak of it out loud.

"Nothing terrible. Just, well, how about *I* claim paternity? Or Timothy could. Or better yet, both of us could. We could stage a loud, public argument with name-calling and fist-fighting and everything. Couldn't we, Sweetie?" He appealed to his lover. "It would be fun."

"Honey, everyone on the lake knows we're together," pointed out Timothy.

"Well, we could get a few of the regulars to join in the brawl, just to add to the confusion."

"But what about Mary's reputation?" objected Judith. "She is or was a respectable, married woman. (At least for a time.) The widow of our beloved rabbi."

"Respectable might be a slight exaggeration," I said, gazing at Sarah, asleep with her perfect little mouth twitching now and then. "Haven't you heard that I was tried for adultery in Jerusalem? If I have a reputation, you may assume it's bad."

"Frankly, I have never heard of men fighting to *claim* paternity of a whore's daughter." Dido, as always, injected a note of reality. "Usually they fight to *deny* it."

"That has possibilities, too," Reginus persisted. "We could all point fingers at each other."

"Sarah is my son's daughter," Ma proclaimed. "No one will deny it. Look at her. Just look!"

You may be surprised to know that I myself was not struck by my daughter's resemblance to her father, expect for the intensity of her gaze. To me she was darker—and wilder. Though I come from the bright-haired Celts, Sarah reminded me of the older peoples who had lived in the Pretannic Isles from before anyone's memory. But I was not about to gainsay Ma.

"That is also what they *want* to believe," said Dido.

"They want Jesus's child," agreed Judith. "They want his heir."

"Perhaps they will not trouble with a daughter?" asked Berta hopefully.

"They will want me to marry James," I sighed. "So that I can have a son next time. They will want to enforce the levirate. But don't I have the right to refuse, Judith?"

"I don't know," she frowned. "I am not learned in the Law."

"I know what, honey," said Reginus. "I'll marry you."

"No, I'll marry you," said Timothy. "At least I'm Jewish."

"We'll both marry her," said Reginus, taking Timothy's hand.

"Is James really so bad, Mary?" Judith wanted to know. "I hate to say so, but marrying him is the obvious thing to do."

"I don't want to marry anyone," I insisted. "No offense, Reginus, Timothy. If I did, I'd definitely marry you two. As for James, he's longwinded and earnest. All he cares about is getting control of Jesus's lineage, creating a royal, priestly dynasty."

"She *is* a princess," Ma said.

"So what do we do?" asked Berta. "Ignore them and hope they'll go away?"

"We could tell the truth," I said.

"That'll never work," grumbled Reginus.

At that moment, Sarah woke up and started to whimper and root for my breast.

"Give the darling to me when you're done feeding her," said Judith. "I'll swaddle her clean and fresh."

"What *is* the truth?" Dido raised one of her perfectly shaped eyebrows, as Sarah latched on to my nipple and quieted again.

"I have given birth to a daughter. I will raise her myself." I looked at my friends gathered around me, standing ready to do anything to help me from changing her diapers to commit bigamy. All new mothers should be so lucky. "With help from all of you, I will raise her here at Temple Magdalen."

"If only that were so," Ma spoke in a tone that raised the hair on the back of my neck, and I sensed her angels around her. "Ah!"

"What do you mean?" I asked her. "Ma? Please! Tell me what you mean."

But she would not say more, and when Judith took Sarah from my arms to go and swaddle her, Ma followed her.

"Wait!" I called after them and started to get up. "Don't take her out of my sight."

"Red," Dido restrained me. "Sarah will be all right. You get some rest. Judith will bring her back to you when she's swaddled. You're safe here. Sarah is safe here."

But outside the crowd was growing.

Cunningham, Elizabeth. The Maeve Chronicles: The Passion of Mary Magdalen. *New York: Monkfish Publishing, 2006: 106-109. Print. Reprinted with kind permission.*

Love Called My Name

SHILOH SOPHIA

Dedicated to the Magdalene
inspired by greeting her Lord in the Garden.

Love
called my name.
I answered.
In that answering
I opened.
Before Love called me
I didn't know
what my true name was.
I couldn't hear it
through the all the other sounds
that called to me.
Without my name
in my own mouth I didn't know
what was mine to say.
Now that Love has called me
I know what I did not know.
I know that I am called.
From death and rejection
through lies and disbelief
I am called to beauty.
I am called to Love
as I have been loved.

My teacher told us
To Love One Another.
We don't have to know
how to do that.
The love that flows through us
will show the way.
Our job is to listen
for the Master's voice.
And I do.
Now I listen through you.
Love is calling you
by your true name.
Do you hear the call in you?
I do.

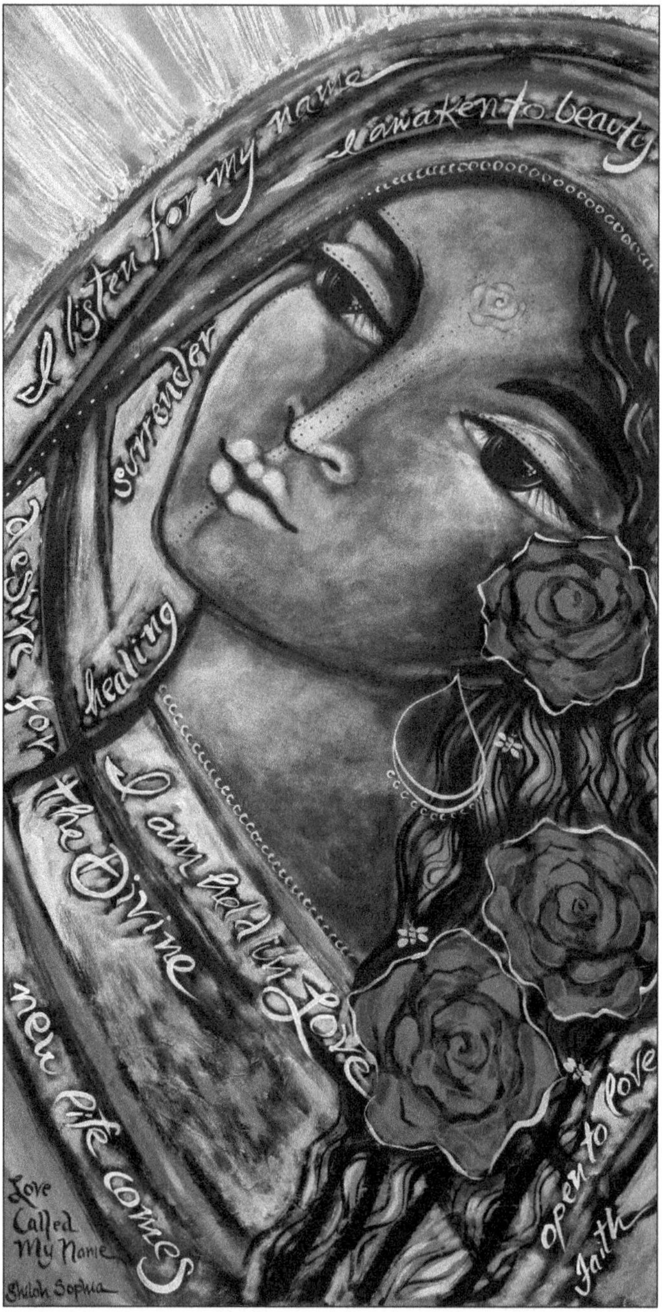

A piece of artwork created as a teaching instrument for the online presentation "Love Called My Name: In Honor of Mary Magdalene," acrylic on birch panel, 36 x 48 inches. <http://salon.shilohsophiastudios.com/love-called-my-name>.

Red Umbrella Babies

By Sex Worker Parents and Their Children

PJ STARR, JULIANA PICCILLO, MAMA B, AND GARY BULLOCK
ON BEHALF OF THE RED UMBRELLA BABIES COLLECTIVE

SEX WORKERS ARE USUALLY SILENCED. At best we are spoken for, or about. Sex workers are silenced, at times by people who purport to care about us, because we are thought to be "too marginalized" from the arenas in which our issues are being discussed or "too damaged" by our experiences to state our own minds. Some of us are silenced by people who wish to harm us, who lock us away in detention centers, rehabilitation centers, jails, and prisons. Many of us are silenced because we fear the consequences of our words (Aimee). We fear that by speaking up about who we are and what we do, we will be shunned in our communities or targeted by law enforcement. Those of us who are parents know that if our engagement in the sex trade becomes known—or even suspected—our children can be taken from us. Those of us who are the children of sex workers know that saying anything about our parents can have them taken from us, or we will be taken from them. In much of the literature children of sex workers are reduced to ciphers, silenced and harmed.

But that is what is imposed on us. Our experiences as sex worker parents and the children raised by sex workers are rich and diverse, filled with joy and love, loss and sadness. Just like anybody else's. Except we are not like "everybody else"; we defy the script as we will discuss more in this chapter.

In this chapter we share what we have learned, as we have taken steps to develop our own work to represent ourselves. The *Red Umbrella Babies* is a forthcoming anthology of writings, poetry, and artwork created by sex worker parents and the children raised by them. The anthology is edited by sex worker parents who are also writers, photographers, filmmakers, and artists. We are the Red Umbrella Babies collective. Our name, perhaps a little tongue in cheek, is a remixing of the ideas behind the phrase "red diaper babies," the moniker given to the children of communists or radical parents. The red umbrella has emerged in the last decade as the symbol of sex worker rights (McNeil), and although not all of us who have contributed to the *Red Umbrella Babies* anthology are activists, we cannot escape the fact that our writing and representation emerges at a time when the idea of sex worker rights is increasingly well established. The act of speaking up for sex workers and their families is its own rebellion against the silence.

STATING OUR TERMS

The term sex work was invented in the late 1970s by our most sacred mother figure, Carol Leigh AKA Scarlot Harlot, a San Francisco-based performance artist who needed a way to communicate that the prostitution and other forms of hustling she and her colleagues were involved in were economic activities. In the 1970s, feminists had been grappling with how to deal with the "problem of prostitution," and those who did not have experience in the work tended to gravitate to the notion that sexual commerce was inherently abusive and perhaps emblematic of men's power over women. Carol realized that just as "house work" was being redefined as "real work" in the 1970s, as part of "wages for house work" campaigns, so could prostitution be acknowledged as work, that is "sex work." Her insight changed debates over the meaning of prostitution forever, truly revolutionizing a generation of workers and bringing into sharp relief the disparate views of feminists, liberals, and radicals regarding the sexual lives of adults.

Many of us, but not all, who have contributed to *Red Umbrella Babies* call ourselves and/or our parents sex workers, and we use the term expansively. For us the term sex work can encompass the work of street walkers, exotic dancers, masseuses, pornographers, sugar babies, escorts, prostitutes, phone sex operators, cam girls and boys and queers, burlesque queens, rent boys, rent girls, and people doing what they have to do survive. But we are also very clear that many people do not feel that the term sex work describes what they do. Some of us reclaim the words "whore" and "prostitute," following in the footsteps of another mother, Brazil's most important *puta*, Gabriela Leite (Leite). Others in our group prefer to use the term "sex trade" because "sex work" may not encompass the experiences of people of colour. Collectively, we know that the term sex work has been important in terms of challenging oppression, but we are committed to naming our own experiences in whatever way works for us and other communities. We embrace, just like Carol Leigh does, the debates over the term sex work, the new terms, and social movements that are emerging.

Similarly, our use of the terms "parent," "children," and "family" is very open, inclusive, and perhaps surprising to outsiders who do not know our traditions. The relationship between sex-working women and their children is very often scrutinized both in research and practice (by social workers, the police and society at large). By definition, to be a whore and a mother is to be a failure. Culturally, the line between Madonna and Whore cannot be transgressed without punishment, so women who support themselves and their children by working in the sex trades are considered damaged victims who, also by definition, have "lost" their children or irresponsible sex pots who are unworthy of them. Some of the contributions to our collection are by cisgendered women who both challenge this simplistic framework and have been subjected to it, but many other works in our collection are by parents of other genders. Men in sex work transgress other cultural divides and are very likely to be constructed as "perverts" who need to be kept away from children at all costs. The experiences of sex working fathers shared in *Red Umbrella Babies* strip away these preconceptions. Transgender people who are sex workers and parents are perhaps the most invisibilized in our culture, and their stories are here. There is also a tradition in queer cultures of forming family, including the strong trans-mothers mentoring and supporting younger folks coming up in the gay community, and "all the 'house mothers,' 'gay mothers,' and other mommas defined by their nurturing rather than a title on a birth certificate"

(Hickey). All these forms of family are embraced in our collective. We are queer, we are trans, we are straight, we have found new parents and family in our community, we are family.

ACKNOWLEDGING OUR PARENTS, FORGING OUR PATH

The *Red Umbrella Babies* anthology primarily focuses on the experiences of people in North America and, for many of us, speaking collectively and publicly about sex work and parenting is something new. One contributor to the anthology noted, "As far as I know, this is the first honest book about sex workers as parents. This is a phenomenal thing. We exist and we wrote a book about it. You can read about us and you can see us. Hopefully a lot of books will follow" (Mama B). When we first started working on the idea of an anthology in 2011, other writers shared with us that our effort was not the first time parents have tried to come together to create an anthology, but previous efforts (years before) had fizzled because not enough people were prepared to be public with their experiences. We reminded ourselves that where ever oppression occurs, people organize for change, but often histories of resistance are lost to us who come in the next generation. Thus, the creation of the *Red Umbrella Babies* anthology includes pieces that link what we are doing in this century to the past. For example, a poem in the anthology, "How Your Mother Survived a Plague," is an act of remembering as the author wonders how she will explain to her newly born child what prostitution was like in the early 1990s, when acquiring HIV was a death sentence:

> Spinning straw, I pricked a finger, fell asleep for years,
> until today.
> Little one, in the future will I tell you? How can I tell you?
> This story that has yet to be noticed about your mother
> who erased
> the memory of all the days and nights she survived a plague.

We are also keenly aware that in many other places discourses on sex work and parenting are far more advanced than what we experience in the U.S. Some of the most important examples of sex workers organizing globally are located in South Asia, specifically in India. Our anthology emerges from our social context, but we have learned of publications from organizations such as *Brothel Born and Bred*, a collection of stories told primarily from the point of view of the children of sex workers, curated by SANGRAM in 2008. This collection focuses on how sex workers and their families heal the traumas associated with a dichotomy imposed on them by a discriminatory society. "The children of female sex workers inhabit two separate worlds," the editor explains. "'Your mother is bad. The company she keeps is bad. Her behaviour is bad': this is the child's first world; while the other is: 'My Mother.' When children step out of their home, one world begins; when they return home it is the other" (CASAM 1). Raju V. Naik had internalized negative ideas about his mother being a prostitute:

> I had a friend ... he too was the son of a prostitute. One day he told me that there was an organisation called Sangram. There, we were forced to think about issues like whether a prostitute is good or bad, moral or immoral, about patriarchy and matriarchy, and other similar matters.... Then I regretted my line of thinking. Now I feel that whether my mother is a prostitute or whatever else, to me she is my mother ... she has given me all that I need in life; I am proud of my mother. (CASAM 16)

Yellawwa Appanna Kenchkanawar, a schoolgirl and daughter of a Devadasi, grew up in poverty in Sangli yet understands how much her entire family unites to provide for her. "All these people in our small house have very big hearts. I am going to fulfill all their hopes," she notes, "I will become a great person. I will bring glory to their names" (CASAM 23). Many of the children of sex workers who have contributed to *Red Umbrella Babies* share conflicted feelings about growing up with a secret and at the same time *knowing* that their parents were taking care of them. The parents of one contributor kept the family afloat by sex work and drug dealing, and this allowed him to have the material support he needed to become the person he is today. But he had great trouble making friends. "I could not associate with other kids my age," he recalls, "I was the outcast dark child, full of secrets and hidden knowledge far beyond what my peers might know." Lila writes in her contribution "Sex Worker 2.0":

> Mom had very little education. She struggled to make ends meet, struggled to raise me. She engaged in a lot of strategies to make money and support us. One of those was prostitution. This she did on an ad hoc basis with friends she had, friends who were men who would pay her and back up if she needed money. My mom wasn't someone who kept many secrets from me. She knew I was a smart girl ... she would say, "Oh well, we are going to visit a friend. We will spend the weekend with him, I will have sex with him and he will pay me.... And buy you a new bike." Knowing all this made me wise beyond my years. I had to spend a lot of my childhood pretending I knew less about the world than I did.

The children of sex workers who have contributed to the *Red Umbrella Babies* anthology run the gamut of having seen their parents struggle (with arrest or with drug use or with violence or to make ends meet) to having lived stable, middle-class lives. Their narratives resist melodramatic tropes. Lila, for example, makes a decision to do sex work more successfully than her mother had done, using the money she earned to finance her higher education.

CONCLUSION

Despite the explosion of sex workers' coming-out stories in the last decade or so, parenting while working in the sex trade has remained a taboo subject. Coming out in this regard is bold and terrifying. The stakes are still very, very high in terms of the very real possibilities of custody issues and shaming of our children, but the stakes are also high because daring to embrace the personas "whore" and "mother" or "father" at once, daring to suggest that despite the risks we have no regrets, or perhaps, even harder, to say we do have regrets, is transgressive to the point of destabilizing to our most basic assumptions about who a parent must be to be worthy of caring for a child. It is an assumption many of us sex workers have barely examined in ourselves, so to do so on the page can be terrifying. Because of this, the process of reaching out and locating contributors has been daunting. And yet, our contributors, like us, have chosen not to turn away from the task. We've embarked on many journeys as editors, writers, and artists to understand why we have risked what we've risked, what we've gained, and what it means in the larger contexts of family, class and race.

These aren't just war stories full of gory details—they're stories of transcendence and courage. They're funny, poignant and they're so very important because they end the silence.

WORKS CITED

Aimee, Rachel. "Thoughts on Deciding whether or Not to Tell Your Kids You are a Sex Worker." *Offbeat Families*. 1 Oct 2012. Web. 1 Nov 2014.

Center for Advocacy on Stigma and Marginalization (CASAM). "Brothel Born and Bred: Children of Sex Workers Speak." *Paulo Longo Research Initiative*. 2008. Pdf. 21 April 2015.

Hickey, Darby. "Reflections on Motherhood." *Huffington Post*. 12 May 2012. Web. 1 Nov 2014

Leite, Gabriela. *Filha, Mãe, Avó e Puta*. Rio, Brazil: Objetiva, 2009.

Mama B. Personal communication. 1 Nov. 2014.

McNeil, Maggie. "The Red Umbrella." *The Honest Courtesan*. 17 Dec. 2010. Web. 1 Nov. 2014

REBECCA BROMWICH

All At Once

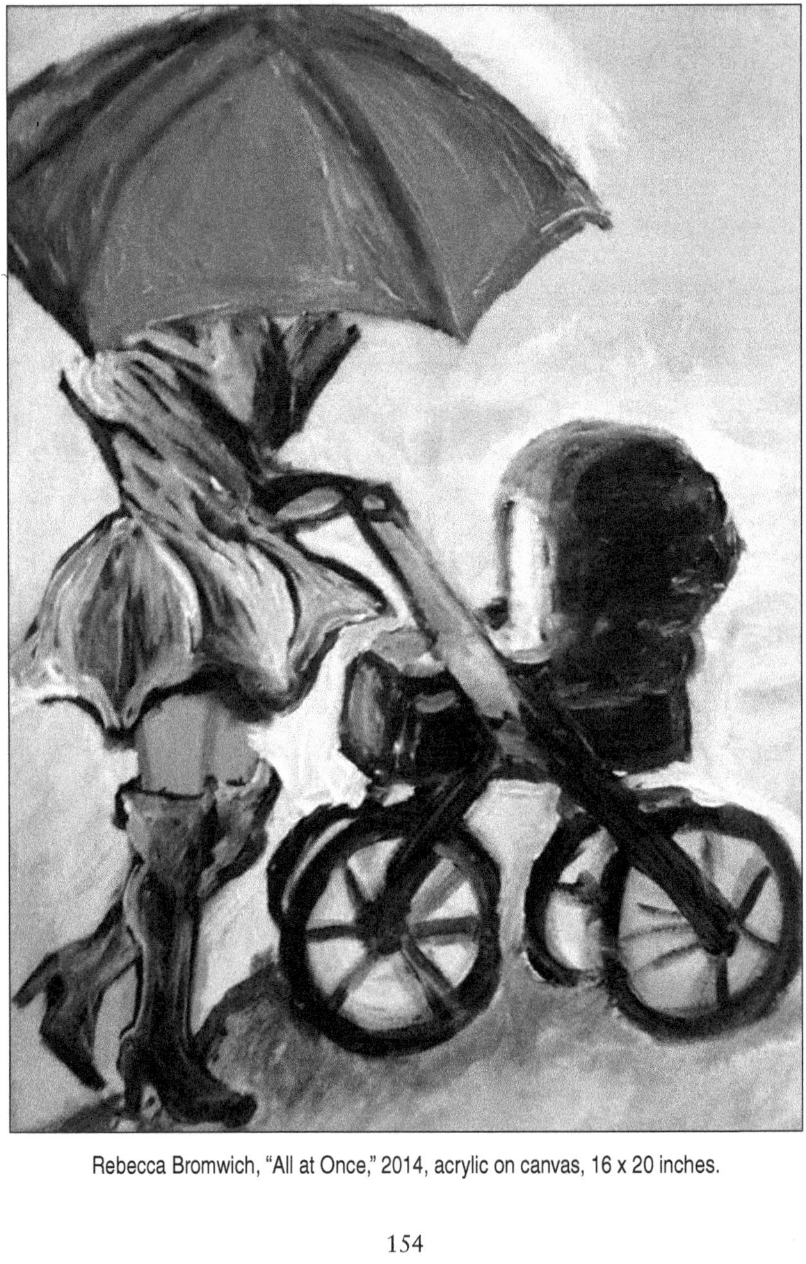

Rebecca Bromwich, "All at Once," 2014, acrylic on canvas, 16 x 20 inches.

For My Children

BESI BRILLIAN MUHONJA

CHARACTERS:

LADY/CASEY/ROSELINE: A 32-year-old African woman. Dishevelled and dressed in old jeans and an oversized T-shirt, too big for her skinny frame.

PATRICK: A 40-year-old white man. Well dressed.

DETECTIVE: A 32-year-old white, female detective in uniform.

PROSECUTOR: A 45-year-old white man. Well dressed.

TIME: Present day, mid-afternoon

SCENE: A well-lit interrogation room at a New York City police station. One table dominates the stage. There are three chairs around the table and another one in a corner. A one-way observation mirror dominates the wall upstage.

Lights come up to the DETECTIVE standing over the LADY who sits at the table, staring up at the DETECTIVE.

DETECTIVE You need to come clean with me....

LADY Haven't I?

DETECTIVE Have you? I don't think so.

LADY Are you calling me a liar?

DETECTIVE You are in an interrogation room, Lady. Don't sound so offended.

LADY So you *are* calling me a liar.

DETECTIVE All I said was that....

LADY I turned myself in, for heaven's sake?

DETECTIVE You did!

LADY Just so I could lie to you?

DETECTIVE Don't get testy with me, Lady.

LADY But you won't let me—

DETECTIVE Listen when I talk to you! Stop interrupting me!

LADY I'm listening....

DETECTIVE Did I ask a question? *I* am running this interview!

Silence. The LADY *doesn't speak.*

So?

LADY I'm waiting for you to ask a question.

DETECTIVE There you go again! That attitude will not help you.

LADY What are you going to do?

DETECTIVE Excuse me?

LADY What are you going to do? Put me in jail? Please do.

DETECTIVE What?

LADY You heard me! I'm through being threatened. You think I could live in a worse hell than I have been in?

DETECTIVE You are so cold.

LADY Sometimes you have to be.

DETECTIVE What do you mean?

LADY Just that. Sometimes you have to survive and you need to be icy cold for that to happen.

DETECTIVE So you have no remorse?

LADY I feel nothing.

DETECTIVE You don't care that you killed someone?

LADY That would require feeling.

DETECTIVE You feel nothing! You feel nothing? And what about your victim? What?

LADY Victim? Victim?

LADY laughs bitterly.

DETECTIVE Lady, I gotta tell you. I have never seen anyone as cold as you, and I have seen some bad people.

LADY Yay! I win something! Break out the champagne!

DETECTIVE I can't believe this. You are suppossibly—

LADY "Supposedly." I hate it when people mangle the English language. "Supposedly" is the right word. "Suppossibly" doesn't mean anything. It is not English.

DETECTIVE Wow! A hooker murderer is correcting my English. Now I've seen it all. You think you are so smart? You think you can outsmart us all? You are not so smart. And English is my first language.

LADY Why don't you just say what you really want to say: that I am an African. How could I possibly know English better than you?

DETECTIVE Do not lay that on me. You don't know me. I am talking about the English language and—

LADY You are the one misusing English words. Suppossibly? Victim?

DETECTIVE So he isn't a victim?

LADY Just like I'm not a hooker.

DETECTIVE But you—

LADY Sleep with strangers. So that makes me a hooker?

DETECTIVE Doesn't it? Don't you get paid?

LADY No, I don't. So go ahead and label me again. This time what have you got in your bag of language tricks? Slut?

DETECTIVE You said it.

LADY Sure I said it! I know what you are thinking. I'm used to that. I know what you are thinking. Might as well say it.

Everyone does.

DETECTIVE Will you just....

LADY You hate that I am in your mind. I see what you think. I know what you think of me. You hate that I can read you. So easy.

DETECTIVE Some African magic?

LADY See, I knew you would go there. I couldn't just be smart. It has to be Voodoo. If a white person had said what I just said, would you have thought of Voodoo? Careful, Detective, your prejudice is starting to blind me in its glare.

DETECTIVE Who do you think—

LADY I am? Nobody. Just another slut. Or a hooker. Dumb African? Take your pick.

DETECTIVE Casey....

LADY Don't call me that!

DETECTIVE Don't interrupt me again! Did you not hear me? I'm losing my patience with you. So, Casey....

LADY Again, stop calling me that! Lock me up now! Lock me up!

DETECTIVE Your type are always—

LADY And what's my type?

DETECTIVE Well....

LADY Do you realize that it has been four hours since I got here, and you haven't asked me a thing about myself?

DETECTIVE What are you talking about? I have done nothing but ask questions.

LADY To Casey, the hooker. Not me. You see only what you want to see. All you cops are the same. Women like you don't see women like me.

DETECTIVE Just answer my questions and everyone—

LADY Will be happy? Have you had your happily ever after, Detective Lady? Have you? Are you happy? Does everyone find happiness? You are talking crazy! Lock me up! Lock me up!

DETECTIVE Now you are getting out of hand. If you don't calm down and allow this process to continue, I will have to get help and put you away. I'm trying to help you.

LADY Another savior? Lock me up! Lock me up!

LADY stands up holding her arms out in fromt of her, wrists touching, inviting the DETECTIVE to handcuff her.

Lock me up!

DETECTIVE Calm down!

LADY I want to be locked up. I'm done here!

DETECTIVE Settle down or—

LADY Please do! Quit threatening and just do it.

DETECTIVE Sit down!

LADY Or what?

LADY walks to the window and bangs on it.

Somebody lock me up! I'm a bad prostitute! Lock me up!

The door opens and PATRICK walks in.

PATRICK Don't say another word! I represent this woman.

DETECTIVE And you are....

PATRICK Patrick Dumont. May I have—

DETECTIVE We were—

PATRICK Can my client and I have the room please, Detective.

DETECTIVE leaves.

PATRICK I like what you are doing. That's good.

LADY What are you talking about? Who are you?

PATRICK I'm your lawyer.

LADY That's okay. I can't afford a lawyer. Plus, they already know I did it.

PATRICK I'm doing this pro bono. You don't have to pay me.

LADY Who pays you?

PATRICK My company. So, let's talk.

LADY So, you will just represent me for free? Why? Why would your company do that?

PATRICK So we can look like good people. It's part of the system.

LADY So you don't really want to be here?

PATRICK Oh, I do! I do! This is a juicy case.

LADY This is my life.

PATRICK I'm sorry. I know. I just meant this will be a good case for me if it goes well.

LADY Do you even care about me?

PATRICK I am here, aren't I? Do you care to get out?

LADY I did it.

PATRICK You have to stop saying that.

LADY I already told them.

PATRICK Did you understand what was going on?

LADY What do you mean?

PATRICK Did they explain everything to you?

LADY You mean what was going on? No.

PATRICK Then we are okay. You have rights.

LADY In this country? Rights? You are a funny man. I'm not American.

PATRICK They told me. That's why I'm here.

LADY Because I'm not American?

PATRICK Because you say you were trafficked.

LADY You don't believe me? Rights for the illegal immigrant? You are a funny man.

PATRICK I'm not trying to be. I'm here to help you.

LADY Right! Another savior!

PATRICK What?

LADY You are here to save me too? I have many saviors.

PATRICK I have never been called that but I will do what I can.

LADY So many saviors. So why am I in this mess? It's almost funny. I'm a woman without a home but with so many saviors. So many saviors. I am so lucky.

PATRICK Are you doing that crazy thing again? That is good.

LADY Don't call me crazy.

PATRICK No, no. You misunderstand me. That is good. If you act crazy.

LADY I am not.

PATRICK I'm just saying that if you were, or ... or looked it, we could use that.

LADY And I'm just saying, I am not crazy.

PATRICK Look here, Lady, I'm trying to help. Help me understand you.

LADY You can't. Nobody can. What I say makes no sense to anyone. What I feel—

PATRICK See, that's what I was talking about. You keep playing crazy like that, and we have a defense. Insanity. Trauma from the trafficking....

LADY I'm not crazy. I'm not playing.

PATRICK Okay. Just help me understand.

LADY I couldn't take it any more. I just couldn't.

PATRICK Take what? Was the victim—

LADY Victim? Victim? You too?

PATRICK How do you know ...?

LADY The victim? Is that what we are calling him? Are you not my lawyer? Anyway, he was my savior, he might as well be a victim, too. What do words and meanings matter? He was my savior and now he is a victim.

PATRICK Okay, I'm at a loss. Would you prefer that I leave?

LADY I am just talking about words, naming, meanings. Victims, lost babies, suffering, depression....

PATRICK Are you depressed. Babies? Post-partum depression?

LADY Post-partum depression? Have I had a child? "Post" means after. "Partum" means—

PATRICK You are so smart!

LADY Does that surprise you? How could I be in your eyes. I'm just—

PATRICK I mean no disrespect. One doesn't just come across a woman this smart in your circumstances.

LADY That just shows how little you know.

PATRICK About what?

LADY About this issue of sex trafficking. About me. And you want to represent me? Another savior who knows little about me.

PATRICK So tell me.
LADY It's a waste of time.

PATRICK Time is all you've got at this moment.

LADY Is this funny to you?

PATRICK No.

LADY Then stop cracking jokes.

PATRICK Listen, Lady, I'm here to help you. But if you would rather waive your right to this help, free help might I add, then I will leave. I have too many other women in your situation to help. So, we are not going to waste time with this back and forth.

LADY I'm just....

PATRICK Do you want my help or not?

LADY I do.

PATRICK Then let's work. I do this every day. I help girls in your position every day. It is what I have dedicated my life to. So I know what I'm doing.

LADY What do you mean girls in my position?

PATRICK The problem of human trafficking in rampant in this city, this country. I don't mean to burst your bubble, but you are one of many women. I have done this before, many times before. Let me help you.

LADY If there are so many of us, why me?

PATRICK Why not?

LADY But why me?

PATRICK Because you are the first client I have had who actually murdered her pimp. You need me. Yours is a serious issue.

LADY You don't even know me. Do you get that? How can you defend me if you can't see me?

PATRICK What?

LADY Nobody sees me. Do you realize that you haven't asked me one thing about me, and yet you ask about my "victim"? Do you even know my name?

PATRICK It's on the file.

LADY Then why do you call me Lady? Do I look like a lady to you? How can I be a lady and have a victim? And pregnant with a child I don't want?

PATRICK Do you not like kids?

LADY What?

PATRICK Do you not want to be a mother?

LADY These are stupid questions.

PATRICK These are questions the cops and the prosecutor will ask. So, do you not like kids?

LADY I like kids. I love children.

PATRICK Then why—

LADY Because this is not my child! I did not choose this.

PATRICK But... this makes no sense.

LADY I just don't want this child.

PATRICK But you killed him over an abortion. He was going to give you one.

LADY An abortion or death?

PATRICK I'm sorry, I....

LADY Another time at that kitchen counter?

PATRICK Another time?

LADY The last time, it almost killed me.

PATRICK Okay, Casey, my apologies. Can we start over?

CASEY He said he would help me.... He was a savior. I guess I better take you to the beginning.

PATRICK Okay.

CASEY I thought I was coming to work in a hair salon. Things were not going well. I was in a bit of a fix.

PATRICK And he saved you.

CASEY It is not what I agreed to come to. It was not supposed to be like this. No. It should have been better. Good, somehow ... better.

PATRICK You mean better than Africa.

CASEY Africa is not a village. I mean better than my situation.

PATRICK Which was?

CASEY I had a good life. A good job. I was a high school English teacher in a nice school in a small town. Until my first savior came along, offering me the perfect lifestyle for me and my son.

PATRICK You have a son.

CASEY Two. I told you you do not know me. My son and I ate everyday. I saw him everyday. I saw my family. I had a degree in education. My savior whisked me off to a life of promised luxury as his wife in the big city. "You don't need to work," he said. He was going to take care of us. So I left my job as a teacher of a state school. That meant they would never hire me again, especially since I hadn't finished my probation period. But I loved my savior. I married my savior. I gave him a son. And then he turned into my tormenter. I have been beaten. I lost count of the bones that were broken. It was hopeless.... Just a sex slave. And I may have survived until I found somewhere to go, but then he turned his anger on my children, and I had to get out. And then he came. My second savior came along. He gave me a place to go. America. Beautiful America. The USA. New York. Streets paved in gold. Where there is easy money to be made.

PATRICK I wish I knew that America. When was this?

CASEY Almost five years now. I should have been back home by now with enough money to build a home for my children. But they are still hungry in my poor mother's house.

PATRICK I'm sorry. I know things can be tough there.

CASEY In Africa? Where all kids starve and have protruding

malaised bellies? Is that what you mean?

PATRICK No, I just meant in marriage separation cases. I have been there ... fights over chidren, property. You know, all that.

CASEY I was not separated. I escaped death. With my children. I got nothing. So no, I don't know all that. Nobody fought over my children, and I didn't get the chance to fight for anything.

PATRICK I'm sorry.

CASEY I would have managed eventually. I am a smart woman. I had my life. Me. They promised America would be great. That I would have a great job working at the salon. I would make good money. They said not many people could braid hair like I did in America. I have always been a good braider. I used to make my sisters' and friends' hair. But in Kenya, that is no big deal. Many people can do that. They said I would have many clients. Good money. My sons would be fed. That is what I came here for. I was ready to braid up to three heads a day. And I did. And for what? My old mother hasn't seen a penny from me. She struggles with my children still. I received from the salon just enough money to buy cheap food and my feminine products. I lived with nine other girls in a two-bedroom apartment. Everything else went to my savior. I was an indentured servant.

PATRICK Why didn't you leave?

CASEY You don't understand. I was sold off. The people who brought me here sold me along with all my legal papers to my employer. I am not legal. Leave and go where? I had no papers and no money. And I wanted so badly to have something to bring back to my children. My dear boys. But he took everything.

PATRICK So you killed him?

CASEY Not him. I killed my third savior.

PATRICK You do have a lot of saviors.

CASEY I told you so.

PATRICK So who was Cayuna?
CASEY What? I don't know. Someone else's savior?

PATRICK The vict... I mean, the dead man. Cayuna. It says here—

CASEY Kiuna. Kiuna. That's his name. He took me away from the salon. He was from my country. I trusted him. He came to cut his hair. And then he kept coming back. He said he would save me.

PATRICK Did you know him?

CASEY Kenya is not a village. I met him at the salon. He is from my ethnic community. He said he loved me. He said he would marry me. He said he would take me away and help me get back home. He would help me get new legal papers if I married him because he had a green card. He promised. So I ran away from the salon and left with him.

PATRICK And he didn't.

CASEY I killed him.

PATRICK Your savior?

CASEY I killed my savior. I just wanted to be safe. A chance to get back home to my family. Not him crawling into my bed at night. Forcing me. I was tied to a bed for a month. I needed permission to pee once a day. Once a day. He said I needed to learn self control, and he said it would help me be better at sex. I ate once a day.

PATRICK That's awful.

CASEY How can you know what that felt like? The man threatened to kill me and he said no one would miss me.

PATRICK So you killed him.

CASEY I might have survived him. I could have. Just him. It is the others whom he started to bring.

PATRICK What others?

CASEY Oh! They didn't tell you I was a hooker?

PATRICK Yes, but not like this.

CASEY Like what? Are there special ways of being a hooker? Nicer ways?

PATRICK You know what I mean.

CASEY Oh! You thought I was walking the streets? Perhaps it would have been better that way. At least I would have a say in whom I went with. Know what you mean? No. But I know how I was a hooker. It was just one every so often. I refused and he beat me up. He beat me up almost to death. I served them, he got paid. I was locked up in a room except when he let me out to clean or cook.

PATRICK That's slavery.

CASEY Thanks for the education. Like I didn't know. I was there.

PATRICK I'm sorry.

CASEY So am I. They started to come in larger numbers. Two three, sometimes four on some nights.

PATRICK I'm sorry.

CASEY He took everything from me, even myself. He gave me a new name. Said my name was not sexy.

PATRICK Casey is not your name?

CASEY I am whoever they want me to be. Who would know any better. I don't exist. I have no papers. Nobody cares.

PATRICK I do.

CASEY You didn't even ask who I was.

PATRICK Tell me. I am sorry. Tell me.

CASEY Now you feel sorry for me? You feel guilty? Why? Because your countrymen bought me and sold me off to each other? Don't worry, one of my countrymen did the worst damage.

PATRICK I just want to know the real you.

CASEY Why? Nobody remembers her. I'm sure my children have forgotten her, too.

PATRICK Please. Please. Don't make me call you Casey or anything else. I am not your savior. I just want to get to know you.

CASEY Roseline. Thirty-two years old. Mother of two. AKA whore, slut, bitch, piece of meat or any other name that feeds your fancy. I am whatever they want me to be. The customer is always right. After all, they are paying. Even if I don't pay for this free legal service, I still owe you. You say it is free, but I feel like I owe. My son is still hungry. So I will be whatever you want me to be.

PATRICK Stop. Stop now.

ROSELINE Why?

PATRICK Don't do this. Don't beat yourself down. I'm not one of them.

ROSELINE He said I couldn't be anything in this country without him. I want to be me. But I just got tired. I couldn't fight anymore. I was tired of the beatings and sleeping hungry and having no tampons. He said it didn't matter. Some men have fetishes and preferred me on my period. They even paid more, and I cleaned up the mess after. I cleaned them up too. I couldn't fight anymore. Nothing about me was sacred anymore. I was fully exposed. I was nothing. So I became Casey. I became anything, anyone. It was just easier. The resistance was not worth the abuse. But it was also easier to be there if I erased Roseline. So I was Casey, and I cooked his food on time just like he liked it. And I opened my legs anytime they asked me to. And my mouth and anything else they wanted me to. I opened it. And I was not Casey....

PATRICK It is nice to meet you Roseline.

ROSELINE Really? Is it?

PATRICK Not like this. But I'm glad I can help. I hope I can—

ROSELINE Save me?

PATRICK I don't want to ask you to relive this, but I need to.

ROSELINE I've already been to the bottom. It can't get worse. I can't feel worse.

PATRICK I'm sorry.

ROSELINE Ask anything. I'm used to giving and answering. All I asked was that they use a condom. Some of them wouldn't. I got beat-up a lot for asking that they use condoms. So I stopped. It was just easier. They couldn't hear me. They couldn't hear me cry when they hit me, and tore me up and tied me up. They never heard me.

ROSELINE yells.

NOBODY HEARS ME!

PATRICK I hear you!

ROSELINE NOBODY HEARS ME!

The DETECTIVE rushes into the room ready to restrain her. PATRICK steps in her path.

PATRICK Please don't do it. She is okay.

ROSELINE I'm okay. I'm okay.

DETECTIVE Ma'am, this is not acceptable. I heard you from outside. I'm not even supposed to be hearing your deliberations with your lawyer.

ROSELINE I'm okay. I'm okay.

PATRICK You heard her? What about her rights?

ROSELINE I have no rights. I am not American....

PATRICK What about her privacy? This is highly irregular, Detective. I will have you brought up on charges and—

DETECTIVE It's not me. It's the prosecutor. He is out there. They say she waived her right to that privacy.

PATRICK The prosecutor has been listening in? This is irregular.

DETECTIVE She waived the protection.... Didn't you?

ROSELINE I don't know what you mean. I don't know what all this means. I didn't know what I was doing when they asked.

DETECTIVE You seemed to understand and—

ROSELINE She is calling me a liar! Just take me in. Lock me up. Give me the lethal injection!
ROSELINE runs around the room, crazed and screaming.

PATRICK Calm down, Roseline. I will handle this. Calm down.

ROSELINE No, they will kill me anyway. They don't care. And I don't care. Do anything!

DETECTIVE Ms. Casey, out of respect to your lawyer—

ROSELINE (*Yells and bangs the table*) I am not Casey!

DETECTIVE That's it!

The DETECTIVE wrestles her to the ground and handcuffs her.

PATRICK Roseline! Please. Calm down.

ROSELINE I am not Casey! Wait, but to her, I am. I am a hooker. A nobody. A poor African. A murderer. I am anything she wants. I am anything they want. I am Casey. I'm okay. I'm okay. It's just handcuffs. I'm used to it.

DETECTIVE Do I need to get back up?

PATRICK No. She is okay. Really, Detective, she is harmless.

DETECTIVE She killed a man.

PATRICK It's just the name. Her real name is Roseline.

DETECTIVE But her file says... she said....

PATRICK It's not her name.

DETECTIVE Counsellor, your client is not okay. This is not normal.

PATRICK Would you be, Detective?

DETECTIVE What are you talking about?

PATRICK Just stop for a minute. Maybe even listen. She is handcuffed, isn't she?

ROSELINE She doesn't hear me. Nothing new. He didn't hear me when I said I did not want to die. He didn't. He wanted me to have an abortion. I wanted the abortion. I was carrying a stranger's child. I wanted it out of me. I wanted nothing more than to go to a hospital to get it out. I was not going to tell anyone about him. I just wanted it out. He said I should just take some tablets. Then he said they would knock me out for too long, and he wanted me there to work in the house and serve the customers. He said he would do it. He was a certified nurse's assistant. He would take it out himself. He asked me to boil water and then lie on the kitchen counter. I said I wouldn't do it. I couldn't. It almost killed me the first time he did it. I wanted to live. I couldn't do it. He hit me in the face with a skillet for talking back. See this huge bruise right here? It was a huge swelling a few hours ago. My head still hurts. He knocked me down. I was bleeding. I wanted to live. I don't remember how. I just wanted to live. I couldn't stop. It was the kitchen knife. I just kept stabbing. Or he would hurt me. I didn't want to die. I didn't want to die.

ROSELINE *breaks down crying.*

The DETECTIVE *touches her shoulder.*

I just wanted to live. Are you ready to lock me up now? I am tired of fighting. I just wanted him to hear me. I just wanted him to see me. To see me. I didn't want to die.

The Door opens and the PROSECUTOR *walks in.*

PROSECUTOR Counsellor, Ma'am. I am the prosecutor, and I have been listening in. Sorry but it was necessary, Counsellor. The detectives have been reviewing the information, and everything you say checks out. It appears you are in deed a victim of human trafficking and have been prostituted by someone we have been trying to apprehend for years. Mr. Cayuna has done this to other women. You were the lucky one to make it out alive, although I can see you have been mentally impaired by it. For all these reasons and especially because he is here illegally, you were acting in self-defense, also you do not appear mentally capable of handling a trial. We will enter a plea of self-defense and insanity and let you go. However you must leave the country immediately. Please sign these papers, and you are free to go.

ROSELINE Mr. Dumont, what does that mean? How do I go? Where do I go? You have to lock me up. I can't afford to live here. What will I do?

PATRICK No, no, Roseline. You don't understand. She means—

PROSECUTOR You will be deported back to your home country. Immediately. But you can never return to this country again.

ROSELINE I can go? I can go? Home? Home? And no one will ever charge me again?

ROSELINE breaks down crying as she signs the papers.

PROSECUTOR No one. Now that you are free, double jeopardy attaches. No one will ever charge you with this crime in this case again. That's how the American system works. Take the handcuffs off, Detective. These are your copies, Ma'am.

The DETECTIVE takes off the handcuffs as Roseline cries.

ROSELINE God bless you, Mr. Prosecutor. Thank you. Oh my God. My children. My children.

PROSECUTOR Good luck to you, Ma'am. You are free to go. I hope life is kinder to you than it has been so far. Detective, let's give her a private moment with her lawyer.

DETECTIVE Good luck, Ms. Roseline.

The DETECTIVE and PROSECUTOR leave.

ROSELINE Thank you, Mr. Dumont. Forgive me for everything. I never wanted to lie to anyone or hurt anyone. I just wanted to be free. I just wanted the suffering to stop. I had to do what I did. I am sorry.

PATRICK It will be okay, Roseline. I understand. Everyone does. I have to go now, but they will give you your travel details before you leave. They will have you back in your country within two days, I'm sure.

PATRICK walks to the door, opens it and then turns around.

What about the baby? What are you going to do about it?

ROSELINE What baby?

PATRICK looks back at her in shock.
ROSELINE gives a sly knowing look and smile to the audience.

LIGHTS FADE TO BLACK.

Intersections of Violence, Space, Motherhood, and Culture in the Sexual Assault of Sex Workers

KRISTINE VANDENBURG

Writing an essay about gender violence while working in a domestic violence shelter and taking hotline calls for a sexual assault and domestic violence hotline brings a whole new level of meaning to my work. My life for over five years has been a total immersion in the world of gender violence in San Diego with two-and-a-half years spent as a sexual assault victim advocate, two years on the hotline (before it was defunded by the city), six months as a domestic violence shelter advocate, and a brief stint in the U.S. Navy as a civilian sexual assault victim advocate, all the while blogging about gender violence on tumblr. In my years as an advocate I worked one-on-one with over 450 victims of sexual assault, which placed me in a somewhat unique position when it comes to academic explorations of sexual violence in the U.S. When reading Arjun Appadurai's "Dead Certainty: Ethnic Violence in the Era of Globalization," I became interested in his footnote:

> Several colleagues have suggested to me that in the United States and in the advanced industrial societies of Western Europe many of the features that I see in global ethnic violence are strikingly present in domestic abuse directed against women. This comparative insight opens up the wider question of the links between ethnic and sexual violence and of the structural relation between these forms of violence in more and less wealthy societies. In the current context, this link is a reminder that large-scale violence in

> the context of intimacy is not restricted to the non-European or less-developed countries of the world. (240)

It is this footnote that informs this essay's exploration of the intersections between violence, law, motherhood, and space using the sexual assault of sex workers in the U.S. as the point of exploration and a critical geographical frame to shape the analysis. Sex workers are marginalized by their social identities, status as illegal workers, the spatial dimensions of their social categorization, and the sexual assault of sex workers, as well as the cultural response to it, which exemplifies and promotes violence on individual and state levels.

It is important to begin any discussion of sex workers by acknowledging their varied circumstances. They have a variety of racial, economic, sexuality, and gender identities. Some are coerced into their work; others freely choose it; still others exist between those margins. Some enjoy what they do; others want to get out of the profession but may not have the means or power to do so. The category of "sex work" consists of people engaged in all types of work including strip clubs, peep shows, prostitution, escorts, etc. For my purposes I am focusing on those who engage in sexual acts with their clients, so when I say sex workers, I am referring to that specific group. In no way am I claiming that my arguments apply universally to all sex workers.

The classic narrative in feminist spaces (including the agency for which I worked) about rape is that it is about power, with sex as the weapon. However, Appadurai offers us a more nuanced view when he so eloquently describes ethnic violence (which often includes rape) as an "even more grotesque way of simultaneously inflicting deep pain, injury, and insult while imposing a brutal sort of intimacy between enemy bodies" (239). In the case of sexual assault, the terminology of "enemy bodies" is one that is rooted in patriarchal structures of women as other and one which certainly has relevance in cultural constructions of sex workers (with the word "whore" being commonly thrown around as an insult rooted in both sexism and discrimination/othering of sex workers). The concept of brutality through intimacy explores *why* sex is the weapon and serves as a central point of exploration in this paper. Through this exploration I am in no way removing the agency or responsibility from perpetrators of sexual violence. My goal is to explore some of the spatial, legal, and social factors that contribute to their decisions to sexually assault and the cultural aftermath of that decision (and the feedback loop created by the relationship between the two).

Sex workers occupy a marginalized space in US society. Many come from lower socio-economic backgrounds and depressed neighbourhoods, belong to racial minorities, and are female or female-identifying, and the work in which they engage has been classified as illegal in the U.S. in all states except for a few counties in Nevada. Obviously, all of these factors are part of much larger frames of exclusion: classism, racism, sexism, and gentrification, among others, as expressed through cultural attitudes, historical events, and state laws. All of these factors inform the social positioning of sex workers in the U.S. It is this unique set of spatial and cultural factors that leads me to choose this group as the focus of this paper. Additionally, in my experience as an advocate, some of the most brutal cases I encountered were those involving sex workers, the dynamics of which are consistent with the brutality discussed in Appadurai's article.

Violence is obviously a pervasive theme in any discussion of sexual assault. There are the more obvious forms that are demonstrated on the bodies of sex workers directly, but there are also more insidious forms of violence, like those perpetrated by the state, that impact sex workers and may contribute to their status as targets of sexual violence. One such state-sanctioned form of violence is the designation of sex work as illegal. Categorizing the work that sex workers do as illegal forces them to the literal and figurative margins of society. In his book *Operation Gatekeeper: The Rise of the Illegal Alien and the Remaking of the U.S. Mexico Boundary,* Joseph Nevins argues that categorizing undocumented immigrants as illegal does something similar (and it's important to remember that there are undocumented sex workers whose intersectional illegal identities make them especially vulnerable). Nevins argues, "Illegality—a form of extreme social marginalization—is part of a process of domination and subordination" (151). Through this argument, it is clear that the discursive power of labelling people and their actions as illegal not only serves to marginalize populations, but also establishes a power dynamic of control between the state and people whose bodies and actions have been declared illegal. For sex workers this kind of power dynamic may exist on multiple levels. The vulnerability created by the state determining their work to be illegal has the potential to lead to a similar process of domination and subordination in sex workers' interactions with pimps and customers, which may serve to illuminate their particular vulnerability as well as the brutality of the sex crimes perpetrated against them.

The way the sex work industry now operates is primarily through street work or through the Internet via websites like Craigslist or any number of more explicitly sex-related sites. Both forms make sex workers particularly vulnerable because they force them into geographical spaces that are less safe than they would be if sex work were legalized (or at least decriminalized). Imagine that sex work were legal in the U.S.: It would be regulated; sex workers would have more agency and power to define their own boundaries and limits as they would have particular physical spaces (brothels, etc.) that they could occupy. Regulation would put sex workers in control of some aspects of their working conditions. Rather than them getting into cars, going to customer's residences, or having customers come to their own residences, they could have regularized places of business. It's hard to imagine such a world given current cultural paradigms surrounding sex work and legal frameworks through which we understand it. The fact that this kind of sex work paradigm is so hard to imagine is paralleled by Nevins' invocation of Blomley's argument about the relationship between the state and violence:

> That such an option is not even considered reflects how the law occupies a powerfully ideological position in American society. The dominant view of the law sees it as rational, benign, and necessary, as well as independent of any specific social and/or geographical context as it supposedly rests on immutable principles. The effect of such a worldview is to put the law beyond question, and thus to normalize socio-spatial relations. Of course, as a social creation, the

> law embodies (in terms of its origin and effects) particular power relations. (Blomley qtd. in Nevins 176)

Clearly, the law is not absent a geographical context, and the physical space sex workers are required to occupy due to their illegal status reflects the normalization of socio-spatial relations dominated by a power paradigm that places sex workers as subordinate to state and individual power.

Cultural reactions to sexual assault and brutality against sex workers are also indicative of the intersection of violence, identity, and law. In my experience, cases in which sex workers are assaulted rarely go forward to prosecution unless there is an extreme amount of brutality or it is part of a series (as sex workers are frequently targeted by serial rapists precisely because of their social position and the cultural attitudes surrounding sex workers). A big part of the reason why so few cases go forward unless they exhibit those characteristics is because it is difficult to convince a jury that not only can sex workers be sexually assaulted, but also their sexual assault doesn't have to be brutal or a perpetrated by a serial rapist to be legitimate. These social attitudes are informed by myriad racial, gender, and sexual politics shaped by legal frameworks and manifested in geographical contexts. When a victim is asked questions such as *Why did you get in his car if it didn't seem safe*? or *Why did you go to a stranger's house*?, the answers are far more complex than, "Because that's my job." Victims get into cars that don't feel safe or go to strangers' homes because the spatial limitations established by the law don't give them any other options—not to mention other power dynamics that may be at play, like being under the control of a pimp, or in the case of transgender sex workers, not being able to find more "legitimate" work due to social, legal, and spatial constraints society has placed on their gender identity and gender non-conforming bodies (a topic which warrants deeper exploration in another essay).

Those cases involving sex workers that do go forward often result in sentences that are far lighter than cases I witnessed in which the victim was not a sex worker. I attribute this to the rape culture paradigm, wherein victims exist on a continuum of guilt and innocence. It's important to consider who we imagine a victim of rape to be in the cultural imagery. It's safe to say that the "stranger in the bushes" narrative is the most common. We think about an "innocent" (read: virginal, white) young woman minding her own business who is snatched by a stranger and raped. These are the stories that receive the most media coverage and the ones that are the easiest to prosecute because the issue of consent can't really be contested in a case in which the victim had never previously seen or spoken to the perpetrator. These are the cases that also receive the most support from people in our culture because it's clear that the victim wasn't doing anything "wrong" and therefore didn't "deserve" what happened to her. (To be clear, no one deserves to be sexually assaulted, hence the quotations marks.) While it's always hard to come forward and identify oneself as a rape victim, in these kinds of cases most people are on the victim's side (who is clearly read as an "innocent victim"). However, the vast majority of the cases involve perpetrators whom the victim knows (including those with whom they[1] were in a relationship), and over half of the cases involve alcohol. The more closely a victim knows the perpetrator and the more activities they participate in that complicate their status as "innocent" (e.g., drinking, using drugs, engaging in sex work or other illegal activity, previous consensual sex, belonging to a racial group that is stereotyped as hypersexual), the less likely society or court will believe them.

Sex workers in particular face multiple stigmas associated with their illegal work: the perception that any sex they engage in is consensual; the geographical limitations their illegality imposes on their physical movements in space which is read as consent; and a number of other stigmas associated with their personal identities. The role motherhood plays is an interesting role in this dynamic. In sexual assault cases in which the victim is not a sex worker, her status as a mother would most likely make her more sympathetic to a jury and judge. Cultural stereotypes about mothers would place her closer toward the "innocence" side on the continuum of victim responsibility in the cultural imagination. I have seen prosecutors play up a victim's status as a mom in order to win empathy from a jury. If the social identities of a sex worker and mom are added to the equation, cultural empathy can go in a number of directions. When motherhood and sex work is reviewed in sexual assault cases, motherhood is often used to soften the image of the stigmatized sex worker. This is particularly true if she is read as a "good" mom who is doing everything she can to care for her children and part of that only happens to be an illegal and stigmatized job. The reverse is true if she is read as a "bad" mom who is engaged in sex work for reasons counter to popular culture ideas of how women can be good moms: she's drug addicted, involved with dangerous people, etc. In that case, her status as a mother negatively impacts the way she is read as a victim of sexual assault.

Together, the legal, social, and spatial frameworks outlined in this paper construct a cultural stigma about sex work. In turn, this stigma intersects with the cultural stigma associated with sexual assault in general, motherhood stands out as one of the only identity/behaviour factors that affect cultural attitudes in such vastly different ways depending on intersecting identity markers. If someone is not a sex worker and uses drugs when they are assaulted, they move further away from "innocence" on the rape culture paradigm of victim responsibility. Similarly, a sex worker would move further away from "innocence" if they were using drugs when assaulted. The same can be said for someone who is raped by someone with whom they've previously had consensual sexual encounters; they bear more "responsibility" for their assault whether they are a sex worker or not. Motherhood is a factor, however, that is unpredictable in its impact and is largely dependent on the other factors present to determine where it places a victim within the "innocence" and "guilt" rape culture paradigm.

The depths of this spatial power dynamic as it relates to sex workers and motherhood is illustrated powerfully by Sherene Razack's article "Gendered Racial Violence and Spatialized Justice: The Murder of Pamela George" in which she analyzes the sexual assault and murder of First Nations sex worker Pamela George by two white men who picked her up in the red light district of Regina, Canada. The perpetrators, Steven Kummerfield and Alexander Ternowetsky, lured her into the car while one of them hid in the trunk (as other sex workers had refused to get in the car with two of them), took her to a remote area, sexually assaulted her and then beat her to death. They were found guilty of manslaughter rather than murder and were sentenced to 6.5 years in prison, of which they served four. This case received a lot of attention at the time because of the racial dynamics of the assault and the larger legal and cultural exploitation of indigenous populations in Canada.

As is common in most representations of sexual assault and brutality against sex workers, Razack illustrates the way that spatial scales make George responsible for her own victimhood by simultaneously identifying George's body as that of a sex worker and placing her geographic location in the red light district. These scales remove responsibility from the perpetrators whose own bodies as white men are imbued with social capital and whose location in the red light district is assumed to be anomalous. Razack illustrates the connection between colonial practices of displacing and marginalizing indigenous populations with the murder of Pamela George. Not only does the murder and subsequent minimal sentence for the perpetrators demonstrate a colonialist narrative of white exploitation of indigenous populations, but also it is precisely because of colonialism that many aboriginal populations were forced into "the urban margins" (Blomley 133). In other words, the sexual assault and murder of Pamela George needs to be contextualized within a framework of colonialism, racism, and poverty that all stem from issues surrounding property both historically and presently, and which feed on and reinforce one another. Pamela George inhabits a corporeal space (sex worker) and geographic space (red light district) that is understood to make her responsible for the violence against her. But it is precisely because of her corporeal space (aborigine) and her geographic space (urban margins) due to colonialism that other dimensions of her social location exist.

George was also a single mother, and many of the news reports surrounding the case highlighted this fact. There is a lot to consider when examining this characterization. First, by emphasizing that she was not only a mother, but also a single mother, news outlets were subtly invoking thoughts of her children who now have no parents to care for them. The news outlets also emphasized that she only engaged in sex work a couple times a month as a means of helping to support her two daughters. Through this framing, it is clear that her motherhood is being used to "excuse" her sex work (since popular cultural attitudes view sex work as something that needs excusing and explaining). Media outlets were using her motherhood as a means of justifying her sex work, which served to build compassion and empathy for George and the injustice wrought in her trial. This use of her motherhood aligns with this paper's earlier argument that sometimes sex workers' status as mothers is used to highlight their "goodness" despite cultural stigmas against sex workers. Had George been involved in sex work for reasons less explicitly related to her status as a mom, cultural sympathy may have gone in a different direction. Several articles also highlighted the fact that when she was a teenage mom, her two-year-old son died in a tragic drowning accident. George's status as a mother became an incredibly important part of the narrative about her and moved her more toward the innocence side of the continuum. Despite this, the verdict and sentencing followed typical patterns, so her status as a mother, while a prevalent part of the narrative about her, ultimately did not impact the jury in a significant or meaningful way.

Brutality directed toward sex workers is common in my experience. Generally, sexual assault cases do not involve a lot of explicit violence (which is not to downplay those that do nor to imply that the very act of sexual assault is not a violent one, which it is). But in my experience, many cases involving sex workers involved weapons and great bodily injury, and incorporated other crimes like robbery, which are generally rarer in sexual assault cases. It is this brutality that I would like to focus on, as it is one thing to explore the ways that space, identity, and power intersect, yet it is another to explore why those particular manifestations take the forms they do. While Appadurai focuses specifically on brutality in ethnic violence as it occurs between social intimates, my exploration is focused more on the expressions of brutality between persons engaging in physically intimate acts. Appadurai's footnote is certainly worth exploring in the broader context of sexual assault between acquaintances and social intimates, as that accounts for the vast majority of assaults; however, for the purposes of this limited paper, my focus on sex workers enables an exploration of the brutality he describes as it intersects with power and space.

Appadurai's central theme is that vivisectionist violence carried out in practices of ethnic violence is rooted in shifting, unstable senses of identity as a result of globalization. This leads to such horrifically brutal expressions of violence because it is the perpetrator's attempt to both know himself through intimate knowledge of the other as well as to establish a macabre sense of intimacy between enemies. As I have already established the social positioning of sex workers as marginalized by numerous legal, spatial, and cultural factors, it is important to examine the specific manifestations of sexual violence using Appadurai's article as my frame.

Sex workers are arguably perceived as the "other" in U.S. culture. They engage in intimate acts for profit, acts that people who are not sex workers are understood to engage in for physical pleasure and/or love (which is not to say these reasons cannot be present for sex workers as well). They thus establish an intimate relationship with the purchaser of their services, but it is simultaneously an intimacy characterized by an economic exchange that potentially creates distance and promotes othering. Indeed, the service being purchased is directly tied to the body of the sex worker, thus commodifying and potentially dehumanizing her body in a way that might make extreme brutality more likely due to a perpetrator's decreased sense of her humanity or a sense of temporary ownership that comes from the act of purchasing. Social attitudes toward sex workers are also informed by media portrayals that often criminalize their profession and downplay violence perpetrated against them. This discursive power of the media is explored by Appadurai when he says, "Political labels become powerful bearers of affect, and ... verbal propaganda and mass-mediated images can literally turn ordinary faces into abominations that must be destroyed" (238). Given that frame, sexual assault can be understood, much like ethnic violence, as a rational "solution" for disciplining and exploring bodies that have been othered and turned into abominations by patriarchal cultural forces like media, law enforcement, and the state.

Gender is a significant component in both sexual assault generally and that which is specifically directed toward sex workers. While there are certainly male sex workers, the majority are female or female-identified. Rape is a particularly gender-based form of violence, and Appadurai explains its use in ethnic violence as "additionally the most violent form of penetration, investigation, and exploration of the body of the enemy ... the penis in ethnocidal rape is simultaneously an instrument of degradation, of purification, and of a grotesque form of intimacy with the ethnic other" (239). And while his argument is about the ethnic other, which certainly applies in some cases in which sex workers are assaulted, their othering through legal frameworks, identity categories, and economically driven intimacy creates a similar connection to the use of rape in ethnic violence. Gender is also implicated by Blomley as he talks about sexual assault of sex workers: "This sexual and racial violence is perhaps also predicated upon phallocentric claims to the ownership of women's bodies ... and reliant in addition upon gendered codings of property and public and private space" (134). Thus, deeply engrained patriarchal claims over women's bodies combined with factors of othering, result in sexual assault of sex workers that not only serves to reinforce those claims over women's bodies but also implicates gender in the coding of space and underlines the role of gender in rape as a tool for exploration of the other.

A central part of Appadurai's argument is the role of globalization in creating shifting identities and instability, which, he argues, causes people to turn to violent conflicts as a stabilizing mechanism to know themselves and the other. The effects of globalization in "third world" locations of ethnic conflict are potentially more obvious as groups fight for control of valuable resources, for example. Potentially less obvious are the impacts of globalization in so-called "first world" nations, a point that Appadurai's footnote calls into question. To explore all of the ways globalization impacts people in the U.S. is a book unto itself. For this paper's purpose, I am taking it as a given that globalization has caused a rupture in people's identities in the U.S. One could point to de-industrialization that leads to industrial sector job loss, porous borders and an influx of immigrants from a variety of countries, as well as the recent recession with accompanying financial crises it brought to millions of Americans. In the case of sex work, transnational and intra-national flows of people have created an environment of sex workers moving (or being moved) around to different cities, thus potentially destabilizing their support networks and sense of spatial belonging. I have attended several trainings that discussed how pimps move sex workers from city to city around a West Coast ring as a means of keeping them transient and unable to set down more permanent roots. Geography is thus implicated again as a form of power some pimps use to maintain control.

Undoubtedly, globalization has impacts that cause instability in identity for millions of Americans. Using Appadurai's framing in terms of ethnic violence, it provides a potential starting point for investigating sexual assault against sex workers in the U.S. It is important to note that that does not excuse sexual assault of any kind, as there are plenty of people who live under similarly destabilized conditions and are not choosing to sexually assault others as a way to understand themselves, others, and the world around them (just as I am sure there are people who live in situations in which ethnic violence is present and do not participate in it). As Appadurai argues:

> It is precisely in situations where endemic doubts and pressures become intolerable that ordinary people begin to see masks instead of faces. In this perspective, extreme bodily violence may be seen as a degenerate technology for the reproduction of intimacy where it is seen to have been violated by secrecy and treachery. (241)

Given the already marginalized space occupied by sex workers due to social, legal, and spatial factors combined with people's increasingly destabilized sense of identity in the U.S., sexual assault of sex workers is a clear manifestation of precisely what Appadurai argues: that shifting, unstable identities in a globalized world promote violence that manifests in intimate ways influenced by sexuality, motherhood, and space, such that people can define themselves through intimate knowledge of the other.

[1]The gender-neutral pronoun "they" is employed to allow space for victims of all gender identities to be part of this discussion.

WORKS CITED

Appadurai, Arjun. "Dead Certainty: Ethnic Violence in an Era of Globalization." *Public Culture* 10.2 (1998): 225-247. Print.

Blomley, Nicholas. "Law, Property and the Geography of Violence." *Annals of the Association of American Geographers* 93.1 (2003): 121-141. Print.

Nevins, Joseph. *Operation Gatekeeper: The Rise of the Illegal Alien and the Remaking of the U.S. Mexico Boundary*. New York: Routledge, 2010. Print.

Razack, Sherene H. "Gendered Racial Violence and Spatialized Justice." *Race, Space, and the Law*. Toronto: Between the Lines, 2002. 121-156. Print.

Eden Sleeps Next to Her Cell Phone

ALICIA VERA

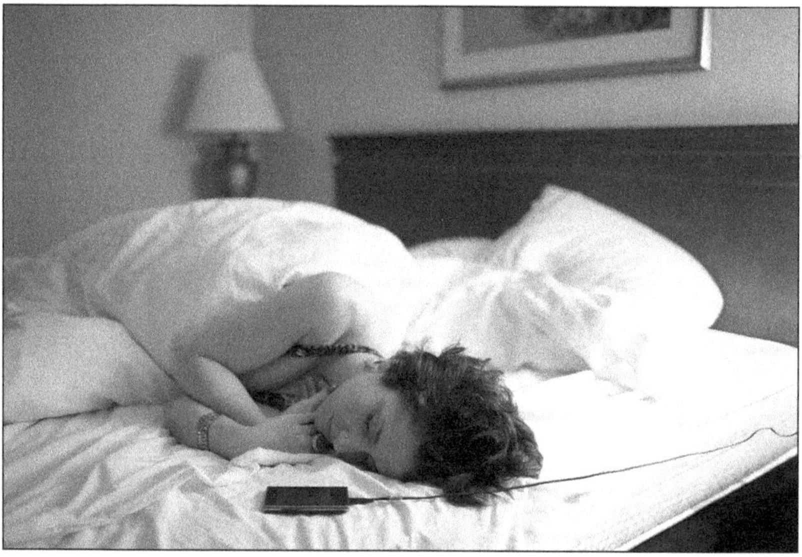

Because of Eden's unconventional work schedule, she takes frequent naps throughout the day. Her cell phone is always within reach so she doesn't miss a client's call.

How Could I?

A Personal and Political Contemplation of Entering the Sex Trade

LILITH BRIDGES

Without stories there is no articulation of experience. Without stories a woman is lost when she comes to make the important decisions of her life. She does not learn to value her struggles, to celebrate her strengths, to comprehend her pain. Without stories she cannot understand herself.... She is closed in silence.

—Carol P. Christ

PART ONE: IDENTIFYING AND CHALLENGING STIGMATIZING IDEAS

I AM A MIDDLE-CLASS, IRISH/ENGLISH descendant of Turtle Island colonizers. Married ten years, I am mother to a daughter and a son. My mother is a sexual abuse survivor. My father is a Jewish survivor of the Second World War. Their stories of survival have shaped who I am. Healers and writers, their work has also shaped who I have become.

I contribute to my family's living through my work as an artist and social artist.[1] My husband is a musician with a day job that he enjoys. We are blessed.

For the past year and a half, I have offered my art facilitation skills to a group of sex workers[2] who have formed a collective to support each other and their peers. We have created two bodies of artwork together. Soon, we will begin a project to explore sexuality through art making, story sharing, and personal and cultural teachings. The project is an invitation for us to heal through sharing our stories, developing our voices, and supporting one another by building an inclusive, accepting community.

To prepare myself for my work with this group as a participant and facilitator, I have challenged myself, and have allowed myself the luxury, to explore an area of personal interest in an intensive and intimate way. I have been actively exploring how I might enter the sex trade. At various points in my life I have had fleeting moments of contemplating selling sex for money. Those momentary thoughts were quickly abandoned by prohibiting messages and the lack of financial necessity. The prohibiting messages remain and the financial benefits are appealing but are still not urgent. Yet, I still feel drawn to contemplate this work now. With my contemplations come many questions.

WHAT, WHERE, WHEN, HOW AND WHY?

An entangled mass of questions exists beneath the surface of the initial, "I think I might like to be a sex worker." The deeper I delve into this occupational inquiry, the more questions emerge. The questions are personal, social, and political—with no easy answers.

What kinds of sex work options are there? In which would I be interested? What are the laws around sex work? What are the risks? What are the benefits? What are the harms? Where am I situated in this work? What are my privileges and disadvantages, and are they helping me or hindering me? How might I construct a positive experience in this work? How can I keep myself safe and protected? What are the rules? What are my rules? Why am I doing this? How could I? What the fuck am I thinking?

Moving through the cyclical exploration of seeking answers to my how, what, where, when, and with whom I might do this work, I find myself coming back to why.

WHY DO I CONTEMPLATE THIS WORK?

I have a right to consider being a sex worker, even though my culture shows me otherwise. I do this to better understand the world in which I live and how I might be a catalyst for change and an ally in a compassionate, empathetic and respectful way.

I do this careful contemplation seriously, ironically aware that I am being far more careful than I would be in contemplating any other profession. I seek conscious, educated decision-making. I seek wisdom and freedom of choice. Why not?

WHAT *IS* THE PROBLEM WITH ME DOING THIS WORK?

Sex work is unthinkable for a "good" girl[3] in a culture that shames female promiscuity. Only a fallen "bad" girl enables a destructive lifestyle by it and struggles through it. Forced into it by internal desperation or external exploitation, one must be rescued from it. No rational person *chooses* sex work. In fact, the sex worker position is not seen to be a choice; it is an abject position devoid of agency. The "good" are irrevocably tainted by it and must be protected from it. The abolitionist position permeates our Western culture and consciousness, presenting the sex worker as a victim of her pimp or her own false consciousness (Parent et al.). A woman claiming to choose the work is seen as an unfit member of society. If discovered, she risks losing community respect, other employment, friends, family, and even her children.

Through my contemplation of the work, I challenge these stigmatizing ideas and attempt to dislodge the firmly established notions of "good girl," "good wife," "good mother," and "good citizen" that are threatened by the notion of "the sex worker" (Rubin). I delve into the facets of my own identity as a "non-sex worker" and resist the idea that they would be tainted by a choice to do sex work (POWER). I embrace the sex work positive position of sex work as "legitimate and fulfilling work making an important contribution to society" (POWER). Drawn to stories of sex workers who are activists within their work, who fight for the right to do this work, and who write and speak with bold, brave, and poetic honesty about their work and lives, I seek to learn from them. With a shared responsibility to speak out against injustice, I write my story and share my discoveries. This work is about developing my own subjectivity; it is about clarifying my subject position and becoming aware of constraints upon my agency. I do this first by sharing my stories: the facets of my identity that contextualize my desire to do this work. I then articulate and push against the prohibiting messages I face. I explore safe routes. I develop my voice toward what my father calls "active participation in the process of self-construction, or the lifelong task of identity formation" (personal communication published with permission).

WHO AM I IN THIS CONTEMPLATION?

I am a daughter: resisting silencing and shaming

My strong, courageous mother grew up with a father who abused her and a mother who sacrificed her daughter to maintain her marriage and social standing. Upon their sixtieth wedding anniversary they asked for "tributes" to their "wonderful union." My mother made her tribute that day at the closest police station to her childhood home. I make mine every time I write about her story. My mother's story poured into my and my sister's stories. Poured into our sex. The pain. The cellular memory of violence. Of betrayal. It poured into my consciousness at year five, well before coming of age, just after I could think of such things. To protect me and my sister. To save us from his touch, her story rang in my ears, vibrated through my body. For a long time it was a forbidden story. Do not say, do not speak, do not question. There is shame there. But shame for whom, I was not sure. He (father) was free, she (mother) was free and my mother (daughter) was trapped. We (daughter's daughters) were trapped, gagged. They celebrated. We shamed. So much confusion. Who is shameful? Then came the public disclosure, the truthful accusation. She spoke out! This time to protect us in a different way. She responded to my confessions of my damaged and damaging sexuality. I had shared my incapacity of positive sexual experience. My fantasies of rape, oppression. My sexuality came with trauma and left shame. She saw... she heard the continued torment of her children, keeping her secret. She, who loves us, her children, wants us to be safe, protected. She spoke to protect us. To rightfully place the shame. Return it to its owner. Shame keeper no more. She lifted it from our backs that day in the courtroom as her story, her truth, her courage filled the room, making it lighter. That day light shone in all the dark places in the courtroom, in my mind and body. That night

I looked out to the points of light in the dark sky. I looked into that vastness from the quiet patio, hugged by the curious family celebratory sounds within the restaurant, and felt free from the heaviness of darkness and held by its goodness. I became light. A point of light born from a point of light, surrounded by points of light, illuminating our truths.

With my mother's voice heard and validated, I could move more freely, *my* story could come into being. I could begin to understand how her story was part of mine and I could begin to see mine as separate from hers. This story work continues with thinking about sex work as a potential profession for myself. I am allowing myself to push the boundaries of what has been deemed okay for me by others. I continue to work against the silencing, the shaming, and the violence. I do this for me, for her, for my sister(s), and for my daughter and son.

I am a wife and mother: seeking relational and financial security

I married for love. Patrick and I married within a year of our meeting and had our first child just before our one-year anniversary. Through my privilege I was naïve about financial realities of life. We married with debt and together we built upon that debt.

We moved through our life together with careless abandon and willful ignorance to our real situation. Through the years, we clung to that sense of love and freedom we found in the beginning when we felt alive and free, when we brought out the childlike beauty in one another. Really, we were children: adult children. We made the conventional sacrifices. We sacrificed our sexual freedoms to be with each other exclusively. I was drawn at the time to explore my bisexuality. But he was enticing enough for me to let that go, at first. His music seduced me, his tenderness humbled me. Both twenty-five and living through our art. We joined and melded together. We dreamed of our life.

We lost each other in the process of building our dream upon a shaky foundation. The house needed new flooring, the children needed good organic food, the bills pilled up, and on and on. We needed and wanted to be artists, parents, and lovers. It was all too much too soon.

Resentments seeped into our foundational cracks. Anger, frustration. You don't know me. You want me to be different. You are afraid of me. I can't stand you. You don't want this life. You want what feels good to you. Your mistress music. I turned my back on my lovers. My art. Men. Women. Those parts of me, swallowed. By you, by the children.

Your mistress of sound turned into flesh and blood. A woman with whom you could make music and connect, be accepted by, wholly. She listened to you, gave you new life. You became like children together. You offered me half-truths for protection. You spent precious time with her. I consoled you when you cried for her. I tried to be open to it all.

For me, there was a seed of freedom exposed within this upheaval. But my deep pain was for the love. You gave her your heart. Denied me your affection. Suddenly. Violently. Survival was my constant fear. Financial. Emotional.

How could I raise the kids on my own? Could we afford two homes? I didn't know how to live without you, but living with you was killing me. I couldn't eat, couldn't sleep.

I had survived well before you. But now the stakes were higher. Babies. Motherhood. Debt. I struggled to keep from drowning. I began to take back my financial power. Started tracking our money. It was the only thing I could control. Your lies were exposed in the expenditures. Money you spent on her. Our money. Our children's money.

Finally, I asked you to leave. After I had unearthed the truth. One after the other, I pulled the lies from their hiding places. The lies were what almost killed me. I understood it. What you needed. I tried to tell you what I needed to feel safe. You ignored me. My sense of security was gone. My trust in you was gone.

I resolved to build my own security. On my own. I chose to make the sacrifices needed for my survival. I'd figure it out.

It was at this point that you finally saw me … at what might have been the end, skinny, drawn out, dying. You saw that I was not the fearsome monster you imagined and from whom you hid. I was not an indestructible person. I was destructing in my humanness. I was breaking. I was not perfect, either. But we had made a contract, a commitment founded on trust and security in love. I made babies with you and needed security. I deserved the respect and fulfillment of your contract. Our children did, too.

Work was the mortar needed to repair our cracks. We began to fill them again. Slowly, gradually turning them to gold.

He stayed. He cut all ties to her. Since then, we have been working together to repair our foundation financially, emotionally, and intimately. He told me of his fear of hurt, of my betrayal. He was afraid of my desires. The ones I told him in my attempts to stay true to myself. He would shut down, hide from me and his fears. Fearing rejection, loss, and pain, he was unable to speak his truth. It was the silencing kind of fear. I know about that one.

This experience opened us both. It was the most difficult time of my life and the most revealing and empowering. Through this, I discovered how much love I was capable of giving. I discovered I could love and accept *myself*. When he took his love from me, I looked to my self and found a well. Love was always something I sought outside myself. Now, I overflowed. At times I felt love and compassion for her, the woman with whom he fell in love. My heart broke open.

I discovered what was deeply important to me: honesty, truth, openness, understanding, support, and *security*. I also discovered my vulnerability in this world, as a woman with children. We discovered ways to begin stepping out of marital conventions prescribed for us. We had to break the moulds of silence and deceit to do so. To seek what we desire, we must dislodge imposed notions of "husband" and "wife."

I am in training: developing skills, boundaries, and ethical practices

My sex work contemplation is part of exploring my desires, and Patrick and I are breaking the mould to explore this together openly. He is supporting me in my quest for safe experience in the work. Twice, we have practiced exchanging sexual services for money. The first time was convoluted, the boundaries unclear. I had been drinking and did not keep to our initial agreement: a hand job for the forty dollars he had in his wallet.[4] During the session, I became aroused and used intercourse to tease and toy with him. If he wanted more, he had to pay more. Later conferring with my friends, Ivy and Lola, I was told this is a common tactic to get more money. They call it "up selling." After, though, I felt I had been unprofessional.

Before the second attempt, my husband shared with me that although he had enjoyed our exchange, if he were to purchase the services of a sex worker, he would not want intercourse. This is very intimate for him and not something he would feel comfortable buying.[5]

Sober and better informed about protocols of selling and buying sex, we had a clear negotiation of the desired exchange and our personal boundaries and safety considerations. We agreed upon a topless and slow hand pleasure session and fellatio for $85. He handed me the money. Had we crossed the threshold from sanctioned marital sex to sexual criminality? If caught, could we be charged? As a married couple?[6]

I got into my "uniform," prepared my tools (lubrication) and safety gear (condom). I stroked and kissed his chest, arms, and belly. My hands moved around his body, incorporating massage. I gave him exclusive attention, taking my role seriously. I did, however, have some internal questioning: Was I performing my idea of "the sex worker?" Because I was getting paid, did it have to be a chore? Could I enjoy my work?

When I decided the time was right for fellatio, I tried putting the condom on with my mouth. That was fun, and I did it pretty smoothly. However, giving head with a condom is something I didn't enjoy. I did my best to recreate my moves with it on but soon realized that he was not as responsive as usual. We decided to return to the erotic massage. Taking my time and checking in, I built the energy and drew out the experience.

When it was all over and he had received his session, he was satisfied. I was satisfied with a job very well done. I made some money and the transaction was complete.

This was a very revealing experience for us. It opened a space within which we could: ask for what we want; give fully with purpose and a sense of professional duty and pride; and find voice and strength in getting our needs met. Through this exchange we are questioning what it is to be in a partnership in terms of exchanges, how exchanges can be clarified, and how we move in and out of these arrangements and roles to get what we want. We are exploring our sexualities in new ways, intellectually and physically.

I am a sexual being: healing through deep listening and voicing desire

Part of this practice, with the guidance of my friend Ivy, is Tantric massage exploration. With the framework of offering a service and fully receiving, my husband and I have begun to explore this powerful area of sexual experience, expression and healing. Through this Tantric practice I am beginning to listen to my body and allow Her to speak through feeling and sensation.

For a long time She was silenced. She now calls to me. Asking to be heard. She wants to show me what She can do ... if only memory could shut up. Don't beat yourself, She says. Always gentle. Never pushy, berating or aggressive, She loves me. She wants the best for me. She might need to become a little pushier. But that's not Her way. She is Earth. She invites my seed, for me to enter Her, to feel and find something receptive. I am ready to plant. I ran away and hid from Her but She beckoned me back. Now faced with fire, I look to her for guidance. She says, "This is your home. Gone so long, I know you fear the return, the pain, but home is your place of nurturing. It is safe to you and you will grow, you will pass the stones blocking your path, seek the water you need, the nourishment I offer. Once you begin, you will find your way. I will be there to guide you and you will begin again."

Through this process of sexual healing, listening, and voicing, I am beginning to heal and shift my cellular memory of pain, shame, and violence. This shift is sending shock waves into another area of my self, as a woman mothering a girl.

I am a mother: striving to nurture budding sexualities

My daughter's articulated feelings about sex are conflicted, as were my own unarticulated feelings around sex at that age. I now see her feelings reflective, in part, of where I am as a sexual being. My mother's abuse and inability to talk about sex is reflected in the subtle and overt messages I have given my daughter about sex as forbidden, hidden, and shameful.

This way of communicating is changing through this process.

I am shifting my learned behaviour. Shedding shame allows me to speak about my body and about sex. She helps me to see myself as a little girl. I was curious and confused with little way to gain understanding about sex except through images and stories, most of which were violent and shaming. She and I have begun to exchange open and real conversations about bodies and sex, relationships and love. When she asks me challenging questions, she no longer squirms or recoils. Nor do I. I now continue the work my mother did to break the cycle of generational shame transfer. We are becoming strong girls, strong women, together.

I am an ally: learning from knowledge keepers

A goal of this work is to become a better ally to my sex worker sisters, my friends, my fellow local and global community members. I seek their guidance on how best to support them toward positive social and political change. As sex positive and sex worker feminists encourage one to become more comfortable with their own sexualities as a way to become a better ally, this is part of my work here.

Through this experience I have had many humbling moments of fear and have been in awe of the amount of strength and courage one must possess to work in this industry, let alone speak out about the conditions. Those who speak are the only voices we can hear. Silenced, oppressed, and shamed voices must be bold and brave to speak. We must listen to their authentic vulnerability and power. As an interconnected community of human beings, equally responsible for and affected by their oppression and liberation, we must include our voices toward changing the circumstances that oppress (Young). In my personal exploration of sex work and my defence of my own right to do the work, I defend their rights as well.

PART TWO: THE PERSONAL AND SOCIAL POLITICS OF ENTERING SEX WORK

"SOCIAL" POLITICS

I would be vulnerable to violence, stigmatization, and victimization

Through this serious contemplation the stigma and fear associated with sex work are becoming palpable to me. Since my mother used her voice to resist her and her daughters' oppression, I have developed an outspoken way of living. However, as I move deeper into this professional exploration, I feel the building up of repressive blocks, censoring residue in my throat. Lately, when I'm at my children's schools, on the street, in my work, I look at people and wonder what might they think if they knew what I was thinking? Would they judge me? When I unconsciously speak out and openly contemplate the work with a friend or acquaintance, I feel regret and fear soon after.

WHAT the hell am I thinking? I tell myself, stop. Be normal. Be safe. Be "good." Stop thinking about all this. Just be a good mom, a good citizen, a good woman. Be safe!

Here are the prohibiting messages at work. And the risks are real, the fear is justified. For sex workers the fear is constant. Endless decisions must be made about with whom to talk openly, what to say, how to say it. Even when they are vigilantly careful, there is always a risk.

> How would you like to be on your way to a meeting ... anxiously hoping you'll make a good impression, and also clenched up with the raw, primal fear that you might get deceived and arrested? ... I wonder whether people who aren't sex workers – can begin to imagine that terror. It's gut wrenching, routine, and faced all alone. Protectors of the public are what we *fear.* (Phoenix, *Are They Bad Girls or Brilliant?* 30)

Although it is not illegal to sell sex in Canada, the work is criminalized. It is illegal to buy sex, so the client is criminalized and so are third-party beneficiaries in the sale of sexual services. Therefore, few protections exist for people in the industry. The criminality and lack of protections for these "fallen women and men" hold me in suspense, looking down, fearfully, contemplating the plunge. It angers me, enrages me that this work is disrespected. As I expand upon later, I agree with the position that sex work is a social service, even an important part of the healthcare and justice systems.[7] The same systems to which sex workers could contribute vilify this work, criminalizing, stigmatizing, and infantilizing "fallen" women and men who are deemed unfit, undeserving, and disposable.

A MESSAGE FROM THE DEPARTMENT OF INJUSTICE

"*She is a whore. She is not to be trusted. Don't believe her. Don't believe her when she says, 'He raped me.' She liked it. She must have consented. Look what she was doing. She was putting herself out there. She asked for it. Look at the way she behaves. Her sex hanging out there. Well, she deserved it.*"

Sex workers and non-sex workers alike are sent chilling messages by the stories of injustice against sex workers, messages which rattle my core: *"Don't do this work! You will not be protected by us if you cross over to the other side. Like them, you will become disposable, your life devalued. Your voice will be discredited."*

My mother's parents discredited her voice by telling everyone who asked why she had left home at sixteen that she had gone to sell her body on the streets. The commonly held perception of "prostitution" was used to discredit her and deflect the attention from the abuse they inflicted upon her. She, an insane whore, was not to be believed, whatever she may say.

"AND DON'T believe her when she says, 'I like my work.' She is not to be trusted when she says this. She is a victim. How could she possibly like that work? She is brain-washed, exploited, desperate."

So, with these pervasive messages, I am fearful. But I am still safe. I am only thinking about the work. I am still a "non-sex worker." Furthermore, as a white, middle-class, (mostly) heterosexual, able-bodied person, I would have privileged protections if I chose this profession. Olive Seraphim, a sex worker activist, challenges non-sex workers in her blog, *How to be a Feminist Ally to Sex Workers*, to "place privilege theory as a corner stone [sic] to understanding sex work." To explore this profession consciously, I need to recognize that the work environment I would step into would be like everywhere else in this world for me: easier and safer *because* of my privilege. Sex workers who are also marginalized by class, race, sexual orientation, gender, or ability have multiple stigmas to contend with and more to fear (Bruckert and Parent).

I would be a worker doing precarious labour

As discussed above, the messages about sex work are shrouded in danger, shame, and desperation. How might I even enter this profession, let alone do it safely? From where would I work? How would I stay safe? A large part of my exploration has been to find what my friend Ivy calls a safe point of entry. The experiments my husband and I conducted are what my friend Lola calls "practicing," and I see it as one of my safe points of entry.

Ivy told me about this concept when she and I discussed a commonly asked question: "Would you want your daughter to do this work?" She contends that if there were a safe entry point and a safe exit point for her daughter and if she were safe and respected in the work and she wanted to explore the work, then yes. I fully agree. In part, I am doing this work of exploring this area and writing about it to help transform the terrain from violent, disrespectful, and stigmatized to respectful and safe. Although it is not an easy thing to think of our children as sexual beings, if they really wanted to do this kind of work as adults, we would want to know that it was safe, that they were respected for their contribution to society, and that they were given the same basic human rights as everyone else.

Just as all people require equal access to protection, services, information, and support that help them to be safe in their work, so do sex workers. They require freedom to report harassment and violence without fear of being criminalized, stigmatized, or victimized. They need acknowledgment for the safe work practices they adhere to and support to reduce their vulnerability to pressures that compromise their safety. They need to freely determine their work and require respectful assistance to leave exploitive situations. They need to be respected as valued members of society.

Because of the social and safety risks associated with sex work, finding a fully suitable point of entry is challenging. My friend Lola has offered me an opportunity to accompany her on a "double" with one of her regulars. I know her and trust her, and she trusts him. This is a point where the offer of actually doing the work is close to home in more than one way. I could do the work tomorrow in a fun, supportive, and relatively safe way. However, the fear of potential consequences stops me in my tracks. My identity shift from non-sex worker to sex worker could occur rapidly. And with that rapid shift my social identity would alter. I would fear being exposed; my social standing would become precarious. What if people in my community found out? If I worked close to home, it would be easier for my family with respect to time and money, and it may be physically safer for me. However, I feel if I am going to explore this work in a way that is *socially* safe for my family and me, I need to go away.[8]

Through my friends I have made connections with a group of sex workers in a large Canadian city. These workers have formed an alliance to survive and thrive in their work. I am contemplating a trip this summer to learn how they work and support each other. In the meantime, I will continue my research, and develop my knowledge and skills, with the help of my husband and friends. Patrick and I will continue to talk to ensure that this is a risk we are willing to take.

"PERSONAL" POLITICS

I would still be a wife

I now feel respected in my marriage. We got through the storm. We grew as individuals and in our partnership. We now see Patrick's affair as an opportunity to break down walls and begin talking about what we need and want out of our partnership. With trust, respect and a lot of checking in, we are moving through this exploratory journey together. I share my contemplations with him. He tells me how he feels about each new discovery, each new idea I have. We discuss together the risks and the benefits and how it might or might not work for us. In fact, this whole experience has opened us to a new way of being with each other. He respects what I am doing and no longer sees my desires, my curiosities, as a threat to the security of our partnership or to my love for him. He no longer sees me as a possession to lose. He is, however, deeply concerned about my physical, emotional, and social safety and that of our family. It remains to be seen how the actual work might affect our emotional and sexual relationship. It is one thing to think about the work of fulfilling the sexual and emotional needs and desires of other men and women, but it is another to actually do the work. I am pushing and grappling with the conflicting notion of the "good" wife with the inclusion of this type of work. If I do the work, he and I will have to remain fully honest about our feelings as we go.

I would still be a mother

As a married woman, I have a greater sense of security than single mothers. If my husband and I had separated, I would have had to face financial insecurity. Sex work might have been presented at that time as an option. Vulnerable in many ways, that time may not have been a good place of entry for me. It is, however, the point of entry for many. Aphrodite Phoenix began her path as a sex worker as a "dangerously poor single mother" ("Are They Bad" 130). Among the benefits she found in the work were financial security and more time with her children. For some single moms, sex work is a way to be autonomous and successful in the caring for their children.

> In just two or three hours a day, I earn even more than what had taken me sixty hours a week to earn before. Overnight, I had plenty of money. And time? So much that I couldn't believe it. Time for the real job: my family. (Phoenix, "Are They Bad" 161)

Phoenix promotes sex work as an ideal profession for a single mother or an artist. Cosi Fabian writes that as a single, childless, and parentless woman, she was in an ideal situation to enter into the profession, as no one would be shamed by association. As an artist married with children, I find these perspectives equally conflicting and resonating. Although the work can offer sex workers financial security and flexibility of time, it can also be a source of tension among family members. Keeping the work a secret can be a very difficult way to live:

> The only wrong thing was the lying I did. I was forced to be untruthful to my children. I had to become a prostitute. In our culture, one can't tell her children that. ... What would they do with the knowledge that their mother had

> turned into a whore? They were living in a world that would teach them that I had become something vile. (Phoenix, "Are They Bad" 163)

There is much social shaming experienced by mothers who are sex workers. The shame is sticky and can, as Fabian suggests, cling to everyone who is involved with a sex worker. Many keep their sex worker identities hidden from family and friends. Phoenix describes how her identity could be distorted by others. Her children's view of her as a mother could easily be warped by the narrative of the "whore." With her entrance into the work she is "turned into," she "becomes something" other than a good mother. She is now vile and unfit, even though the work allowed her more time with her children and she could provide for them well as a single mother. As Gail Pheterson writes, the prostitute identity disqualifies the mother status.

If I were to do this work, I wonder how my children might be impacted. Would it take me away from them or bring me closer to them? Would I have more time with them? Might it negatively affect them socially? Would I be able to talk to them about my work? Internally, I may feel okay with the work and my ability to be a good mother and provide for them, but outwardly there would be struggles to integrate the two identities.

The greatest thing I question with regard to my ability to be a good mother as a sex worker is in my ability to continue to be alive and well. Is doing this work putting myself at risk? How is this work any more dangerous than being a fire fighter or a police officer? As I have noted previously, the risks are increased by the stigmatization and criminalization; they are not inherent to the work (Abel and Fitzgerald). How might the work and the lives of those who do it be different if the work were respected in the same ways as fire fighting, police work, or healthcare?

"RADICAL" POLITICS

Using the erotic to nurture and heal

Aphrodite Phoenix describes herself and role models in the industry—Cosi Fabian, Delores French, and Norma Jean Almodavar—as all sharing a sense of their work as a nurturing and healing service:

> Most of all, Sheila improved their self-worth. She made men feel worthy in bed ... most of them, no matter how young or how old, needed to feel worthy in bed. (Phoenix "Breaks")

> I do enjoy my work very, very much. I like to make people feel good, and it gives me joy to see someone who normally wouldn't have any sexual release be able to have a healthy sex life.... I service men and women from ages 20-70, all of whom are lonely individuals who just want some comfort that I am willing to give. (Olga)

Sex work is related to emotional work, as much of the work involves listening to clients needs and desires, sexual or otherwise. Laura Agustin writes that "the emotional labour performed in listening to clients' stories" bolsters their egos, teaches them sexual techniques, and provides them with emotional advice. Men and women of varying abilities and walks of life seek non-judgmental intimacy, to feel physically desired and to express their desires. The services that sex workers offer can be a loving way for all people to access these basic human needs.

My nurturing, loving, and healing nature is deeply attracted to the emotional aspects of the work. I see the work as a means to feed my desire to help people, provide opportunities for healing, and make the world a more loving place. Recently, I have been looking at men and women of all sizes, abilities, and levels of attractiveness, imagining myself providing them sexual services, imagining what intimacies they might desire. I feel open to and excited by these imaginings.

SEX WORK ACTIVISM: VOICING, DREAMING, SHARING AND CREATING

I am an artist: exploring resistance through dreaming

A sex worker's life and work are precarious. One must face serious risks in order to choose this work. But one who wishes to do the work can imagine an ideal within which to live and work. She can seek out and work for better circumstances for her chosen profession. The world I dream of values sex workers for what they offer to society. In this world, people are not shamed for seeking intimate companionship from professionals. In my dream, overall wellbeing includes sex, not just as a luxury but as a necessity. In my dream the healthcare professions embrace and include the intimate labours. In my dream, women and men are respected, honoured, and appreciated for their choice to work as sex workers.

My contemplation is not over. It has just begun. I will continue to explore my desires, write about them, and explore this profession. I will continue to expand my sexual expressions and strengthen my voice and knowledge as an ally. I am still ignorant, but I feel I am moving toward understanding.

I will continue to offer my services as an artist to sex workers to strive for their voices to be heard, for their rights to be validated, for them to be respected as healers, helpers, and valuable members of society. I will continue to work toward the collective dream of sex workers to determine their work, to work in safety, to be respected, and to have sufficient access to information and health care.

This *is* a profession that I would like to experience. I believe I would be good at it and that I would offer a valuable service not only to individuals but also to society as a whole. But must I put my self at risk to do it? Must I sacrifice my safety, my social status, my marriage, my children, and my professional life? Must I trade respect for disrespect? What choices are these? What must be dislodged from our collective notions of "good" in order for people to move from non-sex worker/wife/mother/citizen to sex worker/erotic nurturer/wife/partner/mother without damaging any facet of identity? Must these identities be mutually exclusive? How can we reconstruct a society that not only tolerates such work but also supports people to do it if they wish? How might the whole of society and the individuals in it benefit if sex workers were celebrated rather than stigmatized, criminalised, and victimized? Well now, that is a thought and another question for another piece of writing.

[1]Social artists use creative skills to work with people or organizations in their community toward social change.
[2]I, like others, use the terms "sex work" and "sex worker." This is a conscious choice to emphasize them as workers doing work. I reject the terms "prostitute" and "prostitution" as they perpetuate stigmatization and the devaluation of the work and the individuals.
[3]I acknowledge that sex workers are not only women. However, for this paper I am exploring the female sex worker position.
[4]In reality this money belongs to both of us. But it was money that he had made playing music. All the money we make belongs to both of us and we decide on our spending together.
[5]We decided that he would do the same for me for a monetary exchange. This kind of exchange has been an opportunity to safely practice this work and make clear sexual exchanges with no guilt and no obligation. But what if we continued with this practice? What do we do with the money? I thought initially that I'd spend it on myself. However, as ours is a shared income, we would have to budget for this increased spending on ourselves. What do sex workers who are parents spend the money on? It is most likely spent on the basics of living.
[6]But our marriage itself could protect us from criminalization. This might be seen as sex play between a consenting married couple. But really I don't know. The rules about non-normative sexuality are vague, the legalities of sex work shift continually.
[7]Norma Jean Almodovar, founder of International Sex Worker Foundation for Art, Culture and Education, states in the documentary *American Courtesans* that sex workers could be a great ally to the police in stopping trafficking if they would only partner with them. According to Louise Toupin, sex worker groups "have become leaders in the fight against forced labour, debt bondage and minors working in the sex work industry" (128).
[8]This is an instant where my privilege of not (yet) being known as a sex worker allows me to retract to protect my identity.

WORKS CITED

Abel, Gillian, and Lisa Fitzgerald. "Risk and Risk Management in Sex Work Post-Prostitution Reform Act: A Public Health Perspective." *Taking the Crime Out of Sex Work*. 2010. 217-237. Web. 28 May 2015.

Agustín, Laura María. "Sex as Work and Sex Work." *Jacobin*. 16 May 2012. Web. 25 May 2015.

American Courtesans. Dir. James Johnson. Perf. Kristen DiAngelo, Norma Jean Almodovar, Pearl Callahan. Cenetex Enterprises, 2013. Film.

Christ, Carol and Spretnak, Charlene "Introduction" in Spretnak, Charlene, ed. *The Politics of Women's Spirituality*. New York: Anchor Books, 1981. Print.

Fabian, Cosi. "The Holy Whore: A Woman's Gateway to Power." *Whores and Other Feminists*. Ed. Jill Nagle. New York: Routledge, 1997. 44-55. Web. 25 May 2015.

Olga. "Confessions of a Sex Worker." *The Working Girls Blog*. Tumblr. July 2011. Web. 18 April 2015.

Parent, Colette, et al. *Sex Work: Rethinking the Job, Respecting the Workers*. Vancouver: UBC Press, 2013. Print.

Pheterson, Gail. *The Prostitution Prism*. Amsterdam: Amsterdam University Press, 1996. Print.

Prostitutes of Ottawa/Gatineau Work, Educate and Resist (POWER). *Power Ottawa*. n.d. Web. 25 May 2015.

Phoenix, Aphrodite. *Are They Bad Girls or Brilliant?* CreateSpace Independent Publishing Platform, 2013. Print.

Phoenix, Aphrodite. "Breaks." *And the Point of All This Agony Is?: A Collection of Short Stories*. Amazon Createspace, 2014. Web 25 May 2015.

Rubin, G. "Thinking Sex: Notes for a Radical Theory of the Politics of Sexuality." *Pleasure and Danger: Exploring Female Sexuality*. Ed. C. S. Vance. London: Routledge, 1984. Web. 25 May 2015.

Seraphim, Olive. "How to Be a Feminist Ally to Sex Workers." *Olive Seraphim*. 24 March 2014. Web. 10 April 2015.

Toupin, Louise. "Clandestine Migrations by Women and the Risk of Trafficking." *Sex Work: Rethinking the Job, Respecting the Workers*. Ed. Colette Parent, et al. Vancouver: UBC Press, 2013. Print.

Young, Iris Marion. "Responsibility and Global Justice: A Social Connection Model." *Social Philosophy and Policy* 23.1 (2006): 102-130. Web. 25 May 2015.

Protective and Proactive Mothering

Prostituted African American Mothers' Use of Intergenerational Family Networks

VALANDRA

AN AFRICAN AMERICAN STANDPOINT ON mothering and motherhood provides a cultural context for understanding the legacy of mothering in African American communities (Collins; hooks; McAdoo; Waites). Within the African American cultural context, many scholars note that mothering is critically important to the nurturance, survival, and empowerment of African American children, families, and communities. For example, drawing on Black Feminist scholarship, Andrea O'Reilly notes that:

> African American culture, understanding the importance of mothering for individual and cultural well-being and empowerment, gives power to mothers and prominence to the work of mothering.... Black mothers require power to do the important work of mothering and are accorded power because of the importance of mothering. (100)

The mothering practices of many African American families are rooted in and structured around an intergenerational, extended family, and kinship network of care (Collins; McAdoo; Sudarkasa). To adequately care for, protect, and empower children, mothering requires the negotiation of a complex array of individual, family, community, and societal conditions presenting both opportunities and adversities for Black families in the US (Billingsley; Collins; McAdoo). Extended and kinship family networks of intergenerational care have served the needs of African American families for centuries (Waites). Within the context of African American mothering, extended family and kinship network structures of care are relevant in assessing intergenerational dynamics with respect to mothering among prostituted African American mothers. However, the literature on the mothering experiences of prostituted African American women largely ignores the influence of intergenerational or extended family networks and how they shape women's perceptions, responses, and experiences as mothers navigating the complexities and intersections of prostitution, poverty, and parenting. The women in this study experienced prostitution as a form of "modern-day slavery" (Valandra, *Reclaiming* 195). More often than not, they were involved in street-level prostitution, were controlled by a pimp/boyfriend, and experienced incarceration as well as physical, sexual, and emotional abuse by pimps, boyfriends, and men who buy sex (Valandra, *Can I Get a Witness*). Poverty, violence, abuse, and past trauma create conditions akin to enslavement by circumstance. Within this world of prostitution, women's agency and resilience, while limited, are acknowledged in surviving, resisting, and adapting to the environmental conditions in which mothering occurred.

HISTORICAL ORIGINS OF EXTENDED FAMILY CARE

African Americans are a diverse group with a shared history that serves as a common thread in understanding the complexity of the extended and kinship family system and its intersections with individual, family, community, and societal life patterns. Some scholars trace the historical origins of the extended family and kinship model to the institution of slavery while others locate this family structure within the traditions of African culture prior to the enslavement of Africans in the U.S. (Gibson; Nobles; Staples). Both starting points are relevant in recognizing the innate and adaptive resilience of Black family life and the value of extended families and kinship networks in what is often described by social scientists as a hostile social, political, and economic environment (Billingsley; Manns; McAdoo; Staples).

Scholars have offered several theoretical frameworks, classification schemes, and definitions to describe the structure, functions, and effects of the extended family and kinship model of Black family life. Recognizing the diversity of the Black experience, many scholars often framed African American families as entities within a larger nested social system or network of mutually interdependent and dynamic interpersonal relationships encompassing individuals, communities, and the wider mainstream European-dominant society (Billingsley; Logan, Denby, and Gibson; McAdoo; Staples). This ecological-cultural perspective provides for a better understanding of the demographic, economic, and geographic diversity that can exist within an extended family and kinship network. Additionally, the economic, social, and political circumstances, cultural patterns, and socialization practices and experiences African American families face living with the duality of navigating the expectations of their own cultural norms and those of a White-dominant society are more apparent (Norton). It is within this nexus that the mothering experiences of prostituted African American mothers are located.

MOTHERING AMONG PROSTITUTION-INVOLVED MOTHERS

The mothering experiences of prostituted women with their children are gaining significance in the literature. Overwhelmingly, research indicates that mothering among street-level prostituted women is fraught with difficulties and stressors that impede parenting (Dalla, "When the Bough Breaks"; Sloss, Harper, and Budd). Stressors identified include poverty, substance abuse, homelessness, health issues, early childhood and adult trauma, stigmatization, police harassment, and incarceration (Dalla, "When the Bough Breaks"; Perdue, et al.; Sloss, Harper, and Budd). Scholars also note the direct and indirect effects of biopsychosocial, cultural, socioeconomic, and political contexts in shaping mothering activities (Collins).

Previous research has recognized high rates of pregnancy and mothering among prostitution-involved mothers (Dalla, "I Fell Off"; Sloss, Harper, and Budd). Early family of origin dynamics, particularly parent-child relationships are purported to be a significant predictor of intergenerational parenting practices among street-level prostitute-involved mothers and their own children (Dalla, "When the Bough Breaks"). Examining intergenerational parent-child relational patterns among street-level sex workers,

Dalla ("When the Bough Breaks") found intergenerational trends of abuse and abandonment prevalent among the experiences of study participants (n=38) and their children.

For many African American mothers involved in prostitution, early childhood development often occurs within an intergenerational or extended family system, a fact which significantly shapes the patterns and practices by which those mothers parent their own children (Valandra, *Can I Get A Witness*). Family studies within African American communities have traditionally focused on assessing the benefits and risks of extended family support in low-income, single, and teenage mothers, and grandmothers assuming the role of parent with their grandchildren (Gibson and Lum; Gibson). The term "single-mother" in African American families, however, does not often equate to mothering alone (Sterrett et al.). A study on parenting in single mother-headed African American families found that 95 percent of single mothers identified a family member or another adult who assists them with parenting, including grandparents, aunties, cousins, siblings, friends, and the child's biological father (Jones et al.). A growing body of empirical literature demonstrates that kin support and extended family parenting can be linked to positive health-related outcomes for African American women living with children in poverty (Taylor, Seaton, and Dominguez; Taylor). Positive child outcomes attributed to extended family care in these populations include improved educational achievement, enhanced parenting, and educational and emotional well-being in youth (McAdoo).

Studies examining the extended family and kinship structure and mothering among prostituted African American mothers are limited. However, prostituted African American mothers acknowledged the extended family system as an influencing factor regarding their experiences in the sex industry (Valandra *Reclaiming*). African American women identified kinship support as a protective factor in their decisions to leave, and remain free of the grip of prostitution, but they also named extended family members as a risk factor in their entry to the commercial sex industry (Valandra *Reclaiming*).

The current investigation expands previous work on the mothering experiences of prostituted mothers by exploring the perceptions of African American mothering within the context of intergenerational family networks. Specifically, mothers' perceptions of and lived experiences with intergenerational family dynamics that influenced their child rearing decisions and practices are the focus of this paper. The afrocentric intergenerational solidarity (AIS) perspective guided this investigation.

THEORETICAL ORIENTATION

The AIS perspective (Waites) provides the theoretical foundation for examining intergenerational familial dynamics and specifically the mothering experiences of prostituted African American mothers. Key assumptions of AIS are derived from family life cycle theory (Carter and McGoldrick), multigenerational relationships (Bengtson), life course perspective (Bengtson and Allen; Elder), intergenerational family dynamics (Bengtson and Roberts), and the afrocentric perspective (Schiele). The integration of these frameworks provides a more comprehensive and multidimensional approach for understanding the transactional nature of extended family dynamics and interactions in the lives of prostituted mothers and their children across a time and place continuum.

Three key assumptions underlie the AIS perspective. First, historical and contemporary social, economic, and political elements intersect in ways that shape the life course trajectories and transitions through which families move across generations (Carter and McGoldrick). Another assumption of the AIS perspective emphasizes the legacy of African-centered values and diversity among African descendants of the diaspora, including a holistic, interdependent, spiritually based worldview that recognizes and promotes cultural assets and intergenerational networks (Asante; Schiele). A third assumption of the AIS perspective centers on the interconnectedness of individuals, families, extended families, and communities. This concept acknowledges generational interdependence, strengths, resilience, and roles as well as supports, collaborations, and conflicts (Waites).

Six domains of intergenerational family networks are recognized as relevant in research and practice with African American families. They include family norms and traditions and adaptive behaviours; roles and responsibilities; communication dynamics; shared values, beliefs, and traditions; emotional sentiments expressed and reciprocated across generations; patterns of resource sharing and help-seeking behaviours across generations; and the geographical opportunities and barriers that influence intergenerational interactions and access to technology and transportation for maintaining contact (Waites). These sensitizing concepts offered a comprehensive and multidimensional framework for understanding mothers' perceptions of their lived experiences of prostitution-involved mothering within the context of intergenerational or extended family networks.

METHODS

The data from this study are a subset taken from a larger study originally conducted to meet the requirements of a doctorate in social work. The purpose of the study was to understand how African American mothers' experiences of sexual violence influenced their parenting practices within the context of extended family and kinship networks. To be eligible, participants had to be adults who were currently parenting, self-identified as African American, and survivors of sexual violence. The study received Institutional Review Board approval and data were collected from January through May 2011. When no new information emerged during data collection, recruitment ceased. Participants were recruited from the public and agencies providing services for prostitution recovery, substance misuse treatment, emergency shelter, and parenting in an urban city in the Midwest. Flyers were posted at various venues around the city and emailed through the local chapters of professional social work organizations and social service agencies. Participating agencies made flyers available to clients, informed agency staff of the study, and spoke with clients about the study, and two agencies provided private space for conducting participant interviews. All participants were voluntary and expressed an interest in the research through direct contact with the researcher by phone, e-mail, or in person at an agency participating in the study. Each participant read and signed an informed consent and confidentiality statement prior to being interviewed.

PARTICIPANTS

This study included 13 participants of the 21 women who volunteered for the original study. The mean age of mothers in this study was 44 years with a range of 38-57 years. Approximately two thirds (n=9) of the women were also grandmothers. On average, mothers had 4 children (range, 2 - 5) and 2 grandchildren (range, 0 - 7). The mean age of mothers' male children (n=20) was 22.5 years (range, 4 - 35), and the mean age of their female children (n=21) was 21.2 years (range, 5 - 39). Over half (n=8) of the mothers earned a high school diploma or attended but did not graduate from college, while less than half (n=5) either did not finish high school or did not disclose their educational background. Five of the mothers reported being employed or unemployed; one participant reported receiving disability income, and two women did not disclose their employment status. All of the participants reported an extensive history of substance use beginning in adolescence, and, in two instances, during childhood; however the majority of mothers started using drugs or alcohol as teenagers and continued the use well into adulthood. All of the participants stated that they were sober during the time of the interview and reported varying lengths of sobriety from two and a half months to a couple of years. Five participants reported experiences of domestic violence and eight of the mothers reported having been incarcerated, on parole, or on probation as adults. All but one of the participants reported that they were sexually abused during their formative years by fathers, stepfathers, brothers, uncles, male cousins, grandfathers, or male family friends. One mother reported being raped as a teenager by two strangers. Ten mothers had a son or daughter (n= 4) or other female family relatives (n=6) who also experienced intrafamilial sexual abuse.

DATA COLLECTION PROCEDURES

One in-depth, semi-structured, audiotaped, face-to-face interview lasting between 60-180 minutes was conducted with each participant. Interviews took place in a location comfortable for each participant, including private rooms in agencies or the participant's home. Women were invited to share as much or as little as they felt comfortable discussing. All participants were informed that the interview would be stopped if visible signs of distress were observed during the interview. All participants received a list of mental health resources at the end of the interview. Participants received ten to twenty dollars in cash and the music CD *Rhythms of My Heart: Healing from Within* (Valandra, *Rhythms*) upon completion of the interview. Field notes were completed after each interview and used to note nonverbal communication occurring during the interview.

DATA ANALYSIS

Interviews were transcribed verbatim and used to construct descriptive first person case narratives based on multiple readings of the verbatim transcripts to preserve the style and manner in which each woman shared her story. Coding and analysis were based on the sensitizing concepts from the conceptual framework, emic codes from repeated readings of the transcripts, and negative case analysis—looking for cases that did not fit within patterns or trends anticipated (Denzin; Patton). A cross-case analysis was conducted using a process described by Creswell as the "data analysis spiral" or "moving in analytic circles" (150)—comparing constructed cases with existing codes for similar and divergent patterns and themes, and rereading constructed cases to integrate and refine themes based on the reinterpretation of initial codes. Pseudonyms were used for each mother and any members of her intergenerational network whom she identified.

RESULTS

Mothers' perceptions of their prostitution-involved mothering experiences are presented. The results are organized by mothers' experiences with intergenerational mothering regarding (1) communication, (2) adaptive mothering roles (3) intergenerational mothering conflicts, (4) intergenerational trust, and (5) intergenerational forgiveness and spirituality. There is some overlap in the organizational themes as mothers' retrospective accounts of their mothering experiences occurred across their life span and do not fit neatly into analytically constructed and mutually exclusive categories and themes.

Intergenerational Communication

Mothers' overall perceptions of mothering while involved in prostitution suggest a strong reliance on family members and kin for mothering support. In several instances, the intersection of prostitution and drug addiction shaped mothering experiences and the use of extended family in raising children. For example, Angela describes how her communication with her children evolved around her life of drugs and prostitution:

> *I shaved 12 years off my life in and out of jails, workhouses and prisons. Now, that's not what's up. Sometimes when I was traveling to sell product or prostitution, I would call my mom, say, "Mom, what you doing, what the kids doing?" She'll be like, "When are you coming home?" "I'll be home tomorrow," or something or she'll say, "Well, your boys want to talk to you. They want to see you, so, I'll be...." You know, if my mom said the boys want to see me, I was on the next thing smoking coming home.* (Angela, age 44)

Mahalia, on the other hand, feeling conflicted about her family values, role, and responsibilities as a mother, relinquished her children to their father and chose not to communicate with them for an extended period:

> *I had the kids with me and my drug addiction just started getting crazy. I started just, you know, using all the time and I wasn't taking good care of myself or the children at that point like keeping food and stuff, and the electricity was still on, just barely [chuckles]. So at that point it was like, um, I'm getting drunk, they can't be proud of me. You know, I honestly wasn't thinking, you know, being responsible. Well, he [husband] came and got my kids... you know, I met someone else [pimp/boyfriend] and that relationship was like, stayed pretty much a user relation-*

ship. I had lost contact. Well, I could contact my kids but I just didn't feel worthy, you know, and I wasn't living properly, so what could I bring them to? So I kind of just shut myself down for a minute. I stopped really contacting them a lot. I was, oh gosh, eight, nine, ten months without talking to them. (Mahalia, age 44)

Adaptive Mothering Roles

Reflecting on her experiences mothering her children, Maya acknowledged the meaningfulness of kinship and extended family mothering in her children's lives and her attempts to continually maintain her role and responsibilities as a mother despite the limitations of her involvement in prostitution and prison. She stated:

My relationship with my children, it's getting better. I didn't have one at one point. We're working on building trust with each other. They're working on allowing me to parent them again, due to my drug use, my past drug use, and getting into prostitution, all the stuff I was involved in. So it's gotten a lot better. I'm still learning how to, change the roles, so they can stop being a parent, and now I'm the parent. I think that's the stage that we're in right now, reversing roles [chuckles]. I've been parenting my children the whole entire time. I just haven't been parenting them either, I was parenting them, trying to parent them while I was still in the streets and using drugs, and then I was still parenting them in prison, by means of using parenting classes and I tried to, you know, I tried to do some, um, like they were trying to do some intervention stuff though. So I've always tried to reach out from prison in parenting them, as much as I could over the phone, through letters. I, like I never stopped trying to be a parent and it was hard, so, a lot of the kids' trust have now been broken. Yeah, my mom was there for me, a big impact in their life. My family was a big impact on their life. Main—mainly my mom and like their family, like their dad's side, their dad. You know, and so they also pitched in and so everybody kind of helped and volunteers in the street from other programs, did their best to help my children. So I don't know, there were a lot of people that were parenting my children. The children's father pitched in, churches, extended family members. A lot of people helped with parenting my children. (Maya, age 42)

Some mothers emphasized their drug addiction as impairment to their mothering more than their prostitution experiences. Diane reported:

My second boy, he holds grudges forever. Yeah. That one there, he just, oh, my God. He's still mad at me. And this is something that happened over [chuckles] 15 years ago. He's still mad [nervous laughter]. I told him I wasn't going to start smoking crack no more and I did and to top it all off, [what] I basically did is I chose being a drug addict over being a mom and I told him exactly that's what I was doing, out of my mouth, so it wasn't no misunderstanding and he got very pissed off about it. So, oh, shucks. He was about 16 or 17, something like that at the time. It was 2003. The other kids reacted basically the same way. Child protection let my sister have temporary custody [of] my kids and I was supposed to do what I was supposed to do to get them back and I just decided to let her have, um, legal custody. I kept my parental rights but she basically had them physically, um, 'til they all became of age. (Diane, age 44)

Nina shared the "back and forth" experiences her children had living between her and their grandmother as she struggled with years of addiction:

I parented my children off and on due to my addiction. I was caught in addiction for over 20 years so my kids were mainly with my mom. They were back and forth from me to my mom. I've been in recovery six months this round. I had two years before this and I relapsed for eleven months and now I'm clean again. (Nina, age 41)

Intergenerational Mothering Conflicts

Mothering within intergenerational family networks did not always serve the best interest of mothers as Harriet found out the hard way when, after overcoming her addiction, she tried to get her children back from the informal arrangement she made with her mother to care for them. Harriet explained:

> *You know, smoking crack was the ultimate slap in the face to my mom. But I think she really liked me being sick, because as long as I stayed sick, she knew she'd have control of the children. You know, and I'm just now coming to the realization of the dynamics of that. You know, since I've been clean, I've been clean 14 months; my mom does not accept any of my calls, none of them. It's like, "How dare you get clean and want to be responsible. You know, I need this money for these kids" [laughs], basically, you know. But I thought I was loving them more by giving them away because she does provide stability, even though, that emotional stuff wasn't there. You know, I had been very unstable. She's their guardian and gets money for them through the state so my being clean threatens that.* (Harriett, age 39)

Similarly, Octavia's family members cared for her children until they were teens before they were returned to her and she was not prepared to be a parent because she lacked the necessary parenting skills, lifestyle, and sobriety to do so. Octavia had this to say about her experience:

> *When they was little kids, um, they was like spread around. It was good for me. I was good with them but they was spread around because my sisters didn't have any kids and they wanted this one, one wanted that one and then my mom wanted my oldest. You know, my oldest was sick. He was born sick and she [mom] was like, "Let me keep him for a week." Then a week turned into a month. The month turned into a year, then years. I moved around the corner from her, and had got married.*

> *Then I had a girl and my sisters, they had her most of the time then my third child, um, my mom had and then my last child, I did, 'til he got to the age of 11. He, um, stayed with his grandmother on his father's side 'til he was grown. I got three sisters and three brothers by my mom. They stayed with everybody else until they got in their teens and then everybody wanted to give them back to me. I didn't know what to do with them because I was drinking and in the street [prostitution] and I really wasn't being a parent. I was wanting to be drunk, or I be trying to put them on punishments or trying to tell them what to do. It was too late. My girl, my oldest one, when she got eighteen, she left; really when she was sixteen. She came back at eighteen and then she left again and then my younger one, she was just I think some part of a gang or something. Then my oldest son, he was with my mom and his other grandmother, back and forth. He's my youngest one. When he was eleven he went to Gary, Indiana.* (Octavia, age 50)

Intergenerational family networks were not always embracing systems serving the emotional and financial needs of its members. Although Mary's oldest child stayed with her mother and her youngest three with their dad while Mary was "getting high and turning tricks," she did not feel she could otherwise trust or communicate with her extended family beyond their care for her children:

> *I don't talk to no one in my family because all they do is run back and tell your business. I can't trust them so I don't get financial or emotional support from nobody except the state. I use to go to sober clubs and parties. You know, and to be honest with you, I had a few tricks [men who buy sex] there that turned out to be a friend of mine for over 20 years and we're still friends to this day and I call to just talk to them, that's how close I stayed in contact with them. You know, people like that, a couple of them.* (Mary, age 42)

Intergenerational Trust

In addition to the availability of extended family members, mothers' trust issues also influenced their decisions regarding where children were left while mothers were involved in prostitution and illicit drug use and distribution. Michelle, had this to say:

> *I have four sons and one daughter ... I believe that [we] were so close coming up, even though I was away from home working [prostituting] sometimes two weeks at time I'll be out of town but the kids always believed we were close and I always believed we were so close that we sat down and ate together. I studied with them and gave each one of them an hour of study, so that no one will feel left out or shunted but as I am older now, I see that, uh, my kids still try to have that connection where we're together. I had two babysitters throughout their whole life and one was their great-grandmother and another was her housekeeper, whom I had befriended. So, I didn't trust nobody.* (Michelle, age 56)

Maya also voiced trust concerns regarding her decisions about with whom to leave her children:

> *When my kids were little, I didn't let nobody watch them. Didn't care who you were. If you weren't my mom or real close family member, my kids would not be watched. Matter of fact, when I started selling drugs, I was on welfare and my kids had a nanny. I paid a nanny [close family friend]. I was so terrified of something bad happening to them as kids, people molesting them, um, that if you weren't my mom and them, you weren't touching my kids. You weren't watching my kids. A stranger never watched my kids and then I finally hired a nanny. My kids was young and had a nanny for all four of them and she had a really clean house. I would give her food stamps, food, and everything needed to really take care of my sons. So, I just didn't trust people with my kids. Like I didn't care, like to this day I'm like that. Like to*

> *this day, like when older women try to come at them, I used to step in, like, "No, you ain't fittin' to be molesting my kid." Like I still had that mentality. Like, "You're not going to molest my son. You're not going to rape him of his childhood. You're not..." I was getting real indignant.* (Maya, age 42)

Intergenerational Forgiveness and Spirituality

The intergenerational family value of forgiveness emerged more often through mother's reported efforts at reconciliation and reunification with their children and other family members. However, several mothers also acknowledged that it was critically important for them to forgive themselves and the male family members who sexually abused them as children.

Cicely parented her children for about six years before they were removed from her home by child protection services based on an allegation that she physically abused her oldest daughter. She acknowledged that her drug use kept her children from being reunited with her sooner. She supported her drug habit through prostitution until she met a man on the "ho stroll" willing to support her and her addiction. Seventeen years later she was reunited with her children and described their reconciliation:

> *My daughter, my oldest daughter, she claimed, she says that she forgives me and that she loves me, but it's ... deep down inside I don't feel like she really understands, you know what I'm saying? Because we have a problem communicating. Now, as for my baby, she's, ah, she's good as gold, and, you know, I would think she would have the most problem with it but she told me that she forgave me a long time ago and now she's pregnant. She's fittin' to have a baby this month. This is my first grandchild. She told me I could be a part of her and her baby's life, so I'm happy with that. You know, I didn't know how the outcome would be once we saw each other after 17 years, but it went pretty well.* (Cicely, age 49)

Remembering how her mother raised her, Diane reported:

If I am wrong, I'll always admit it. I let them [children] know that I messed up and ask for forgiveness and that's a humble pie that's very hard to swallow. Um, you know, I always ask God for forgiveness but if I specifically do something to them, I have to ask them for forgiveness. You know, and they don't always give me their [laughter] forgiveness either. You know, "Mom, you said you wasn't going to do that." "Okay. You know, I'm wrong, whatever." (Diane, age 44)

Nina expressed her pride for her children, attributing the family values with which they were raised to the role her mother played in their life as well as her own mothering efforts during the times she was sober and available to her children.

I'm just proud of my kids period whether they are right or wrong. I love my kids and I'm proud of the fact that my kids are so forgiving and respectful. They're very respectful kids and nonjudgmental. I'm just proud of the way my kids turned out, period. I think the way my kids are has a lot to do with my mom. She treated my kids different from the way she treated me. She wasn't abusive to my kids the way she was with me. I worried about that because I know what misery I grew up in but she wasn't abusive to my kids. I also contributed to the way they turned out because when I was around, I was very nurturing to my children. (Nina, age 41)

Reflecting on the values instilled by her grandmother, Harriet recognized the importance of believing in herself and self-forgiveness. She also shared this about her mother's boyfriend who sexually abused and impregnated her as a thirteen-year-old child:

I've got to forgive this man, so that I can move on. Otherwise I'm going to stay sick, you know. I didn't do it [forgiveness] for him; I did it for me. I think he realizes the turmoil that has cause everybody, you know, the heartache. You can just see the sorrow in his face.

Mary had a different perspective about forgiveness and spirituality in relation to her experiences of ongoing child sexual abuse by an uncle at age 11, being pimped out by her mother at age 13. She mothered a child fathered by the man who prostituted her in the streets at night along with other girls and made sure she attended school during the day to minimize suspicions. Mary also mothered three children fathered by a man who bought sex and impregnated her. She had this to say:

> *Not forgiving helps me continue ... Remembering use to keep me sad a lot, it doesn't do that no more for me. I will never forget and I try to forget. I don't know why I have to keep remembering. Maybe I keep remembering for a reason. I just can't explain it [chuckles]. Remembering keeps me alive. It keeps me going. You know, it makes me to where if I'm ever in a situation like that again, I can remember, "Is this where I want to be?" before I get that far, get there again, you know. I know the feeling of when a person's fittin' to do that to me because I remember how it started, you know, just the remembering I guess. What it means to be a survivor to me is that I went through it. I'm still here. It didn't tear me down. It didn't break me apart. It didn't kill me. You know, I survived through it all. What keeps me going is reading my bible, reading my daily words. Church. I don't go every Sunday but I go and talk to God. My faith.*

Eight of the mothers participating in this study made specific references to God and or spirituality as a source of comfort for themselves and a family value they hoped they instilled in their children.

CONCLUSION

Intergenerational mothering among prostitution-involved mothers has a limited presence in the literature. More often when present, scholarship tends to focus almost exclusively on intergenerational dysfunction transmitted to future generations (Dalla, "I Fell Off").

The above themes expand that paradigm using an Afrocentric intergenerational perspective that recognizes conflicts and challenges but also strengths and resilience. As such, the agency with which prostitution-involved African American mothers navigate their lives and mothering roles reflects a rich cultural legacy cultivated and adapted throughout history in addressing harsh environmental realities while mothering thc next generation. Refocusing the intergenerational mothering lens to recognize the strengths and resilience of prostitution-involved African American mothers is critical to developing culturally responsive prevention and intervention programs and policies that meet the needs of African American families and communities and support an agenda of social, economic, and political justice.

WORKS CITED

Asante, Molefi Kete. *Afrocentricity*. Trenton, NJ: Africa World Press Inc., 1998.Print.

Bengtson, Vern L. "Beyond the Nuclear Family: The Increasing Importance of Multigenerational Relationships in American Society. 1998 Burgess Award Lecture." *Journal of Marriage and the Family* 63.1(2001):1-16. Print.

Bengston, Vern L. and Katherine R. Allen. "The Life Course Perspective Applied to Families Over Time." *Sourcebook of Family Theories and Methods: A Contextual Approach*. Ed. Pauline Boss. New York: Plenum Press, 1993. 469-498. Print.

Bengston, Vern L. and Robert E. Roberts. "Intergenerational Solidarity in Aging Families: An Example of Formal Theory Construction." *Journal of Marriage and the Family* 53(1991): 856-870. Print.

Billingsley, Andrew. *Black Families in White America*. Englewood Cliffs: New Jersey: Prentice Hall, 1968. Print.

Carter, Betty and Monica McGoldrick. *The Expanded Family Life*. 3rd ed. Boston, MA: Allyn & Bacon, 2004. Print.

Collins, Patricia Hill. *Black Feminist Thought: Knowledge, Consciousness, and the Politics of Empowerment*. New York: Routledge, 2000. Print.

Creswell, John W. *Qualitative Inquiry & Research Design: Choosing Among Five Approaches*. 2nd ed. Thousand Oaks, CA: Sage, 2007. Print.

Dalla, Rochelle. "'I Fell Off [The Mothering] Track': Barriers to 'Effective Mothering' among Prostituted Women." *Family Relations* 53.2 (2004):190-200. Print.

Dalla, Rochelle. "When the Bough Breaks...: Examining Intergenerational Parent-Child Relational Patterns among Street-Level Sex Workers and Their Parents and Children." *Applied Developmental Science* 7.4 (2003): 216-228. Print.

Denzin, Norman. *The Research Act: A Theoretical Introduction to Sociological Methods*. 3rd ed. Englewood Cliffs, NJ: Prentice Hall,1989. Print.

Elder, Glen H. "The Life Course as Developmental Theory." Child Development 69 (1998):1-12. Print.

Gibson, Priscilla A. "Intergenerational Parenting from the Perspective of African American Grandmothers. *Family Relations* 54.2 (2005): 280-297. Print.

Gibson, Priscilla A. and Terry Y. Lum. "Informal Kinship Care in Minnesota: A Pilot Study." *Final Report to the Minnesota Kinship Caregivers Association*. University of Minnesota School of Social Work, St. Paul, MN. 2003. Print.

hooks, bell. "Homeplace: A Site of Resistance." *Yearning: Race, Gender, and Cultural Politics*. Boston: South End, 1990. 41-49. Print.

Jones, Deborah J., et al. "Coparent Conflict in Single Mother-Headed African American families: Do Parenting Skills Serve as a Mediator or Moderator of Child Psychosocial Adjustment?." *Behavior Therapy* 34.2 (2003): 259-272. Print.

Logan, Sadye M., Ramona W. Denby, and Priscilla A. Gibson. *Mental Health Care in the African American Community*. New York: The Haworth Press, 2007. Print.

Manns, Wilhelmina "The Significant Other: Type and Mode of Influence in the Lives of Black Families." *Black Families*. Ed. Harriette Pipes McAdoo. Thousand Oaks, CA: Sage, 2007, 184-200. Print.

McAdoo, Harrietta Pipes. Ed. *Black Families*. 4th ed. Thousand Oaks, CA: Sage, 2007. Print.

Nobles, Wade W. "African American Family Life: An Instrument of Culture." *Black Families*. Ed. Harriette Pipes McAdoo. Thousand Oaks, CA: Sage, 2007. 69-78. Print.

Norton, Delores, ed. *The Dual Perspective: Inclusion of Ethnic Minority Content in the Social Work Curriculum*. New York: Council on Social Work Education, 1978. Print.

O'Reilly, Andrea. "African American Mothering - 'Home is Where the Revolution Is.'" *Mothers, Mothering and Motherhood across Cultural Differences: A Reader*. Bradford, ON: Demeter Press, 2014. 91-117. Print.

Patton, Michael Q. *Qualitative Research & Evaluation Methods*. 3rd ed. Thousand Oaks, CA: Sage. 2002. Print.

Perdue, Tasha R. et al. "Offenders Who Are Mothers with and without Experience in Prostitution: Differences in Historical Trauma, Current Stressors, and Physical and Mental Health Differences." *Women's Health Issues* 22.2 (2012): e195-e200. Web. 25 May 2015.

Schiele, Jerome H. *Human Services and the Afrocentric Paradigm*. Binghamton, NY: The Haworth Press, 2000. Print.

Sloss, Christine M., Gary W. Harper, and Karen S. Budd. "Street Sex Work and Mothering." *Journal of the Association for Research on Mothering* 6.2 (2004):102-115. Print.

Staples, Robert. *The Black Family: Essays and Studies*. 5th ed. Belmont, CA: Wadsworth, 1994. Print.

Sterrett, Emma, et al. "Predictors of Coparenting Relationship Quality in African American Single Mother Families: An Ecological Model." *Journal of Black Psychology* 36.3 (2010): 277-302. Print.

Sudarkasa, Niara. "African and Afro-American Family Structure: A Comparison." *Black Scholar* 11 (1980): 37-60. Print.

Taylor, Robert D. "Kin Support and Parenting Practices among Low-Income African American Mothers: Moderating Effects of Mothers' Psychological Adjustment." *Journal of Black Psychology* 37.1 (2010): 3-23. Print.

Taylor, Ronald D., Eleanor Seaton, and Antonio Dominguez. "Kinship Support, Family Relations, and Psychological Adjustment among Low-Income African American Mothers and Adolescents." *Journal of Research on Adolescence* 18.1 (2008): 1-22. Print.

Valandra. *Rhythms of My Heart: Healing from Within*. Key of V! Productions. 2002.

Valandra. "Reclaiming Their Lives and Breaking Free: An Afrocentric Approach to Recovery from Prostitution." *Affilia: Journal of Women and Social Work*. 22.2 (Summer 2007): 195- 208. Print.

Valandra. *Can I Get a Witness: African American Mothers, Parenting Networks, and Attachment*. Diss. University of Minnesota, 2012. Minneapolis. Print.

Waites, Cheryl, ed. *Social Work Practice with African-American Families: An Intergenerational Perspective*. New York: Routledge, 2008. Print.

JESSE MALEY

Chained Heart

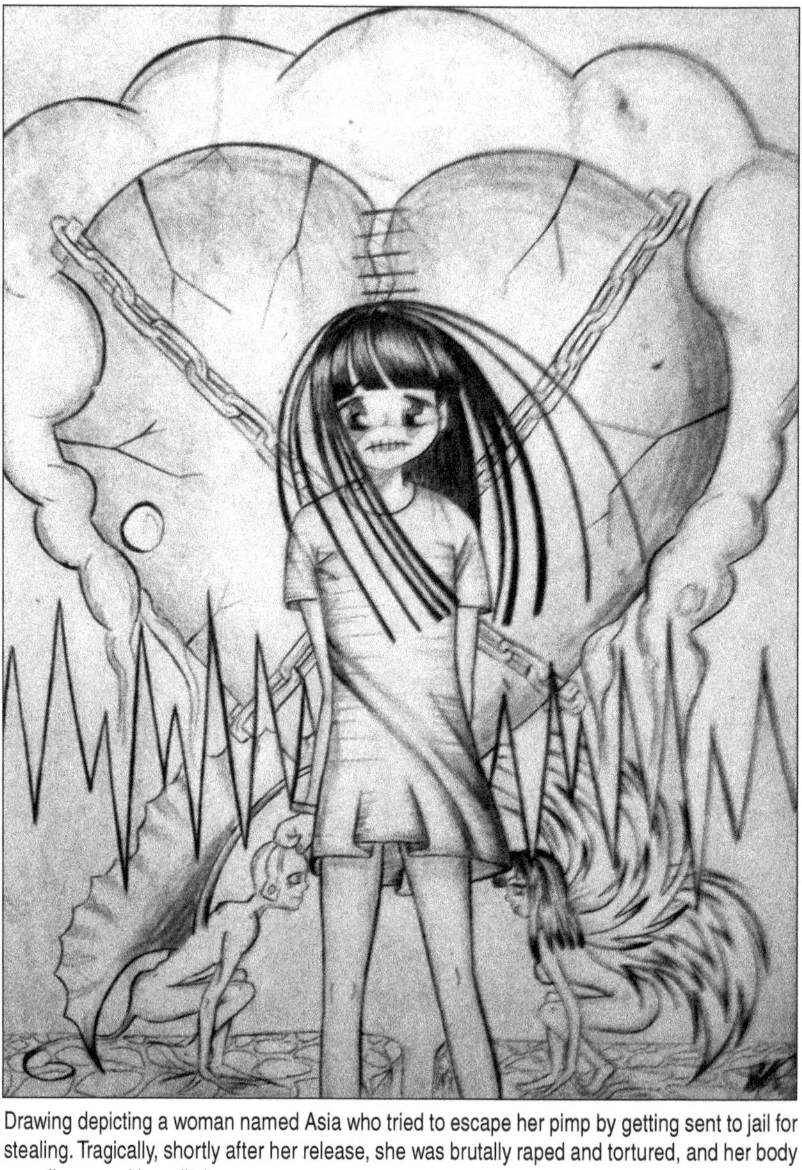

Drawing depicting a woman named Asia who tried to escape her pimp by getting sent to jail for stealing. Tragically, shortly after her release, she was brutally raped and tortured, and her body was discovered in a ditch.

Breaks

APHRODITE PHOENIX

SHEILA WAS A SEX WORKER. An escort. Her work was illegal, but she liked it. She had started while in her late thirties, and it was her own decision. She had never been pimped or forced.

In her thirties she'd understood things that she never would have at twenty. Now forty, she thrived on compassion.

She looked into the faces and bodies of men, no matter how handsome or ugly, and she understood the need and the soul there. She took care of men as a nurse would, yet in ways that a nurse wouldn't ever, got paid six times more than the nurse would, and left them all stress-free and happy.

Sheila understood that sex work was the peeling back of layers, and enjoyment of the sweetness underneath. The first layer was always the hardest.

She'd arrive at a guy's house or hotel room, or he'd come to a room she provided, and if she didn't know him she'd be frightened, with a dread the guy felt just as much.

It was the terror of getting arrested. Both of them had to get past it. It was like pulling the inedible rind off an orange, to get to the succulent juice.

"How about a hug?" Sheila always asked a new guy. Actually, she hugged everybody. The regulars always responded with a hi-great-to-see-yuh squeeze, but the new ones hugged back more intensely. They revealed all their gut-clenching fear of arrest with embraces as needy as mourners.

That kind of hug was her cue. Whenever their grip was that ardent, she knew all was well, she was safe. She figured a detective wouldn't do that. Would an undercover cop hold her desperately? A cold hunter paid to arrest her?

Not a chance.

Once, she had gotten set up. On the phone the guy sounded harmless, but there had been two red flags. They were small ones, but still, she should have known. The first one was that he kept calling. He persisted like a hound, and that was different. Normally, whenever she kept putting a guy off, he'd give up and find someone else.

The second red flag was his over-the-top sweetness. There was such a thing as *too* nice. He kept calling her "honey" and "sweetie," just as if he'd known her forever. His tone was like slathered-on syrup, not a trace of caution or shyness, even though he didn't know her, and she could be a cop or a rip-off.

And then, when she got to his motel room, she found the place horrendously trashed. It looked like he'd been partying for days there without any housekeepers' cleanings. The trash bucket brimmed over with beer cans. There were rumpled clothes strewn all over. There were ashtrays piled high with butts.

Afterwards, Sheila would be asking herself: *What do cops think clients are? Do they think they're all addicts or alkies, shacked up in that kind of mess?*

The cops just got it so wrong. They just got so much so wrong.

As soon as she entered that pigsty, she should have turned around and taken right off. It was actually a third red flag.

But once you made a commitment, and the guy himself looked okay...

...and the bastard was sitting there rolling a blunt, knowing that would work like a hug...

Now she knew how to walk out.

"Sheila! I just read the paper! Jeez, are you *okay*? Is there anything I can *do*?" There were twenty-some emails and texts like that, the day after she got arrested. Two of the messages were from her best friends who lived in the town where they nabbed her, who had read the area news. Neither of them were escorts.

They were simply her most loyal of girlfriends from way back in the day, with liberal mindsets and master's degrees and somewhat rewarding jobs, but incomes way less than six figures. They knew that their Sheila had found something lucrative that they would never take up, but that hadn't changed how they cared; they were faithfully rallying round her.

The other reach-outs were from clients. She liked their concern, that made her feel good, but she knew she'd be waiting for quite a long while before any of them would make new appointments. A busted escort had the cooties.

She also knew their fears were ridiculous. Getting arrested for selling oneself was only a misdemeanor. The madams and pimps were the people who got tapped and stalked and stuff confiscated. They were the felons in the biz.

But try telling paranoid clients all that.

"Is there anything I can *do*, say they," she mimicked them to herself. "Yes, you can do something," she pretended to reply. "Make an appointment, goddamit! Call me and see me and help me pay my bills, just like you always do!"

None of them called her for weeks. To cover her bills and the thousand or so that she had to dredge up for a lawyer, she was forced to meet with new clients who didn't know she'd been caught.

New clients, who could all be cops. When one of them tried to hand her the money, her hands clasped the sides of her head, and she looked like the face in *The Scream*. This guy was an old hand at escorts, and he kindly understood. He turned and put the money on a dresser, and said not another word about it. She reached out to him for the hug then, and he held her, and finally, she began to breathe easy.

Finally her heartbeat began to calm down, and then came sweet touching relief.

The cop who set her up, the blunt-roller, liked to strut and puff out his chest. After his partners got hold of her, he acted so proud of himself. It had taken some effort to get her to trust him, to trust him enough to go see him. Four or five phone conversations.

He had finally reeled her in.

He had kept the motel room door open. He'd been sitting in there, and he'd beckoned. She'd gone in and shut the door after herself, and then she'd sat down on the untidy bed across from the bed where he sat.

A clear plastic bag, a bag full of weed, had been wide open on his lap.

"Are you a cop?" the cop asked her.

Sheila responded: "Not!" And after a second she added: "I asked *you* that over and over, on the phone. So I won't put *you* through that again!"

"Thank you."

He made like a pothead, tonguing rolling paper, gluing two sheets together with spit. Watching this made her momentarily forget that he sat too far away, and that the hug couldn't happen with his lap so encumbered. She continued to watch as he dropped weed on paper and expertly made a blunt with his fingers and mouth.

All her life, starting in high school, she had seen so many guys do that.

Now he offered it to her. "No, thanks," she smiled in response. Sheila didn't get high a lot, and she never got high with a stranger.

He put the blunt down on the stand between the beds. And then, from somewhere in the clutter, he produced a handful of cash. He looked her right in the eye then, making sure that she saw the money, and he set it on her side of the stand.

She still couldn't go to him and hug him. The weed bag was still on him, still open, still precariously balanced by his knees; she didn't want to jostle his stash. So she stayed where she was, unable to touch him, and wondering what to do next.

Finally she felt the uncomfortable chill of knowing she couldn't take charge.

He said: "My wife doesn't care about sex. That's why I wanted to see you."

And there it was again: something different. Clients were seldom that straightforward at first. They wanted her to control things, so usually, their words fell away. Talk about wives happened later. A banner so small she didn't see it unfurled. It took off in her sky, just a dot, like a blazing red flare too far up, and she missed it. Sheila had decided that this guy was a stoner, a slightly aloof, roaming spirit. She figured he was being what people turned into whenever they got really high: distracted, and watching inner films of themselves, and speaking of the scenes flicking through them.

"No problem," she responded, and she started to take off her boots.

His partners came in then and cuffed her.

The cops led her into the room next door. The beds had been removed to alter the room into some kind of makeshift command post. Sheila was in shock but she managed to recall that when she'd first got here and parked, she'd noticed two mattresses and box springs outside.

So if ever again she were to pull up to a motel to meet with a brand-new client, and she saw tossed-out beds near his door, it wouldn't make any difference how much she needed the money; she'd get out of there burning some rubber.

There were eight or so wall-to-wall cops in there. She would never understand why so many. Perhaps this sting op was instruction for them, as it went in a teaching hospital? One of them pointed to a cheap straight-backed chair that they wanted her to sit down on. When she did, they all stood over her, staring.

Her handcuffed wrists behind her were uncomfortable, mashed into metal and the chair. Someone took the cuffs off her and put her hands in front of her and then put the cuffs back on. She responded with a genuine thank-you.

They asked her a bunch of questions. She was careful to say very little. But she did speak up when they wanted to know whether anyone pandered her.

"No, I'm not trafficked. I've never been coerced. And I don't have a pimp or an agent, never did."

The cops looked a little bit puzzled. The people they'd been programmed to flush out were the monsters forcing under-aged girls. They had fished for a shark and had landed something else, and they didn't quite know what to make of it.

She could see that these were nice people, habitually polite. Suburban cops, used to the soft life, used to arresting soft people. Well, Sheila was a softie, herself. Just a nice college-educated sex worker, helping guys stay out of trouble. She relaxed men, she made men so beautifully *released*, that they were less likely to abandon their families or get blitzed and kill someone, driving. They were less likely to be tense and pissed off, at work or at home or on the road. Oh how she wanted to explain that, that in truth she was every cop's ally, her job was peacekeeping like theirs ...but of course she just sat there in silence, because every single word was being recorded on that bleeping thing in the corner.

Suddenly the blunt-roller showed up. And he didn't just appear; it was more like, he *arrived*. He had a shit-eating grin and a swagger. He paraded around in this room full of his peers, and it was all about Sheila, his catch.

One of the other cops had started a lecture about all the dangers of sex work, all the chances of her getting hurt. Sheila got hugs and caresses and other nice things from her clients, but she'd never once gotten hurt.

The blunt-roller put in his two cents.

"Yeah, we arrest you to protect you! There's a lot of bad dudes out there!"

His lower-class traits were now obvious. Compared to these others, he was slummy. Later, when she read the arrest report, she would learn that this show-off was a setup artist pro who'd been borrowed from a much rougher county.

He enthroned himself on a chair close to hers. He was vigourously nodding his head. He was acting so sure of the shit he'd just done to her, acting like he'd done her a favour.

Sheila looked down and away from him. She had questions on fire inside her. *They want to PROTECT me? Then why don't they GUARD me?*

It was all she could do not to scream them.

After that, whenever Sheila got with a client, it felt like a break from persecution. Her known and trusted regulars and the just-peeled brand-new ones killed her fear, for the moment, of more cops, and so did the beautiful money. These people were always so grateful, and then they went one even better: as soon as they sensed her sweet attitude, they became just as sweet. Their ways were precisely the opposite of the police and the lawmakers and the religious and the feminists, the people who wanted to net her and cuff her and tell her she needed protection from the people who gave her a break.

She kept thinking about a girl from her teen years, someone she had lost track of, who got raised in an intensely Catholic home. Her parents had never used birth control, and they'd pushed out eleven kids.

They lived in a house built for three. There were beds in the upstairs hallway, and even in the corners downstairs. There were several more beds in the unheated, unairconditioned attic.

Her friend was neurotic. She had serious issues. She was just like a terrified puppy. She was easily depressed and insanely claustrophobic; on crammed elevators, she wet herself. She got nauseous at the high school assemblies, and she never went to even one game, and she even stayed away from the lunchroom.

In any jam-packed situation, it seemed like her brain was exploding.

Sheila took her under her wing.

But the mother of this girl was the creature who scandalized Sheila the most. She appeared as beatific as Mother Theresa, and she even looked a lot like her. Every time Sheila went to visit, this skinny little thing with a wrinkled face and shining eyes would be planted on the couch folding laundry from a cloth mountain high as her head, and even though her husband was an overworked prick, and all of her children were messes, she was always lit up, always cheerful.

And she always got around to her mantra.

"If I didn't have my faith, I couldn't get through one day!"

Sheila would keep herself quiet. That was hard, because she wanted to shriek:

"Can't you see that your *faith* is what got you into this *hell?* What good is a faith like *that?*"

And now, over two decades later, here she was herself, in a hell. Escorting wasn't religion, but Sheila was in the same fix. She liked being an escort almost as much as that woman had liked the Church, and each of them had paid a big price. Eleven squashed kids and a half-crazy husband were not the result of her choices, but because of what she had chosen, she was forced to live in fear of arrest.

My lifestyle is good, though. It makes sense. It's not just some crazy blind faith.

As the regulars started returning, Sheila knew not all of them would. Some had been frightened enough by her busting to never call her again.

No problem! Not a big deal. Those she'd lost were all getting replaced. Prince Charming was multitudinous. Kaleidoscopically plural. Initially, when she'd got herself into this work, she'd discovered that men and their affections were as duplicable as fresh loaves of bread. She'd also learned this did no harm. Not in this situation.

This find was like peering into one of those little tubes that amaze with their glorious secret. What pleasant surprises the world had to offer, if you just took the time to peek! If you just found the guts to say: *No. I'm not keeping my eyes on the ground. I'm not doing whatever I'm told. I'm going to pick up this kaleidoscope and find out what's inside.*

And then, when she deeply gazed into it, and happily twisted its front, the brilliant gyrations of patterns went in her, and she became twisted, herself. Delightfully. Colourfully. Illegally.

She morphed to a female iconoclast.

She came to understand that she'd taken her place beside all of the people who have ever been born who have rebelled against the status quo, not because they've been bad people, but because the world gets some things wrong.

Sheila understood she was a healer. And that healers take care of the masses.

"How are you doing?" she asked every client, after her ministrations.

"Oh, I'm doing fine, *now!*"

"How're things at home?"

"Oh, the usual. Okay. It's like, you know, she's my best friend. But it's like, you know ... we're just roommates. We're not even in the same bed."

Sometimes, with somebody else, the response might be a lot darker. Like: "Ah, I'm hanging in there. It sucks, but what can you do? Gotta wait till the kids are grown. She feels the same way. Gotta keep it going for the kids ... for now."

Or it could be even worse. "We hardly even speak to each other. It's been that way for years. But I'm not about to lose my ass in a divorce. I've worked too hard for that."

And then there were the lonely single guys.

"So...." They might begin shyly, after she'd let them talk overtime and lounge in Edenish bliss, "Do you ever go out on dates? Do you think we could go out, sometime? Like, you know ... on a real date?"

And Sheila would carefully think of an answer that was totally gentle and kind, but not any less of a no.

Most of them, married or single, eventually understood. After they fell a little or a lot in love with her, with Sheila's help, they got past it. They got it that she was a therapist, but the kind that guys dream about. Sheila was like having a stripper who consummates the tease. She was also like a sympathetic sister, wanting to be all helpful ears. But most of all, Sheila improved their self-worth. She made men feel worthy in bed. The married ones whose delusional wives thought their husbands were fine without sex, and the single ones tired of their hands ... most of them, no matter how young or how old, needed to feel worthy in bed.

She did that for them, and they loved that, and sometimes that made them love her. Then she would put them through a weaning, just like shrinks always did with their patients.

What she did for them had to be valuable to them, because they paid her so much. Like most of her peers, she charged like a shrink—as much as the elite ones, the MDs. Could be she charged even more. And she didn't earn the cash as the pitiful hole that her "protectors" thought she got used as. She did it by relaxing and letting men blossom as the sweet, giving lovers they were.

To be sure, there was the twenty-five percent or so who just laid back for her service. But all the rest paid her great money to let them feel they did it for *her*. She had never felt so appreciated, so rewarded for being herself, and often, the money didn't feel like a fee. Often, it felt like a gift.

Sheila hid, in that warm cozy place, from the law.

"I don't feel like it!" her daughter was griping. She was fifteen now, and impossible. Every single conversation became an argument. Every single one of Sheila's requests became an exhausting war.

Today, her bedroom was the problem. It looked like Katrina'd gone through it. Melanie wanted to meet with her friends, and

Sheila had told her to clean it up first, and of course, that had started a spat.

"Why do you always bug me when I want to go somewhere!" her woman-child demanded to know.

"I've been talking about your room for a week. It's *your* fault it's not done. Now *do* it."

Her daughter went rigid and glowered, looking totally able to kill. Then she turned and stalked off to her mess. She slammed her door rudely behind herself, and Sheila heard her furious clicking.

She was asking her friends to wait.

Is she obeying me because she respects me? Or just because I'm her ride? With a teen, you simply couldn't tell.

Sheila was the quintessential stressed out single mom. She got almost no help from the father. He sent minimal child support payments, if he sent them at all. The court was slow to get after him, and he never saw his child.

Sometimes her clients were her only breaks from bearing parenthood all alone.

It was hard, but she knew she had a lot to be glad for, like the money she made for her child. She had it like a two-paycheck family, and perhaps even better than that. Making two hundred an hour, she didn't have to work a lot. Ten or less hours a week as an escort was plenty to pay all the bills, and plenty for equipping her daughter with everything to help her succeed.

So Sheila got to park herself mostly at home, almost like a stay-at-home wife, being an available mother, and building herself as a writer.

She was also glad—mightily, desperately—that her daughter hadn't been *told*. And that most likely, her daughter never would. The arrest notice had appeared in only one paper, the one in the town she'd been caught in. It was thirty-some miles away. Sheila had never worked right where she lived, because she had thought of all that.

And the best thing was, no social service hawks had swooped down. Her child hadn't been dragged away. If they'd come for her, Melanie would have learned things too early, and not from the person who loved her. Not from the person who would tell it to her *right*.

This had been Sheila's first offense. Was that why the hawks hadn't come? Or was it the big budget cuts? The children of sex workers were getting snatched less, because less and less money was laying around to pay for the foster care?

Or maybe, just maybe—could she dare hope this?—someone out there was being savvy. Perhaps someone got it that she was a good single mother, because they knew that an escort had the time and the money to flourish as one of the best.

Whatever the case, she was deep in relief, because her kid was still with her, and knew nothing.

Someday she'd have to tell Melanie something about where she got all her money. She'd face a more scrutinizing daughter. But for now, her young lady was so self-absorbed that funding from Mom was her mission, and not caring much where it came from.

After some twenty minutes went by, the teen marched out of her room. "It's done," she announced. "Can we go now?" Her question oozed out as a groan. Giving in to her mother was like punching herself in the face.

But Sheila was missing the triumph of this rare acquiescence in her kid. She was riveted to the TV. CNN was reporting about another sex trafficking bust. Several young girls, all Melanie's age, had been forced into escort prostitution. Right here in the States, and only two states away. They'd been rescued by getting arrested.

"Mom."

The girl was talking to a mannequin.

"*MOM!*"

"*Wha…?*" Sheila's head turned. "Wait a sec."

The teenager ferociously grabbed herself. She got that murderous look again, and then she started to pace. The news segment finally ended, and only then did Sheila get up.

Melanie's girlfriends were waiting for her outside of the main mall entrance. After her child got out of the car, Sheila did not pull away. She made the cars behind her go around her.

She needed to linger and study the girls as they sauntered into the vast building. There were four of them, the season was summer, and there was a lot of bare skin. Two were a little bit chunky, but Melanie and the other one were perfect. Their flesh was as tight as a drum. Their curves and lush hair were commanding yet fragile, like exquisitely painted eggs.

Such girls drew the whole world unto themselves, without even knowing yet why. Sheila imagined men talking to them, and getting them into a car. Maybe it wouldn't be that hard to do. Not if they won the girls' trust. Melanie had been taught to not ever talk to strangers, but did that make sense anymore? It had made sense so many eons ago, when she was so small and compliant.

Now she was built to meet men.

How did you keep a girl safe from her nature, attracted to the opposite sex? How did you help her stay safe from the bad guys, when all she ever did was walk away? The media and law enforcement were proving that there were indeed bad guys out there, and they could be close to home. The media blew it up to the point where it seemed like there weren't any good guys, and Sheila knew that was pure bullshit, she knew that far better than anyone.

But there were a few bad guys out there, and they preyed on the weakest of women. Could one of them spellbind her fatherless baby, right here at the neighbourhood mall? Could he woo her and whisk her off to motels, and turn her into big bucks? Sheila imagined being forced to do what she had chosen to do, and imagined being her child, as well.

It was almost as bad as those three a.m. moments when she suddenly saw her child dead.

Yeah, we arrest you to protect you! The blunt-roller liar had said.

If the liar were ever to catch and bring home her hostage-turned-hooker baby, Sheila would kiss his feet. But then she remembered her activist buddy, and the things *she* always said.

"They need to see *all of us as children.* That's why they net us *all.* They think we're all damaged or ruined, and we have to be saved from ourselves.

"That's how they hide from the truth they can't face, which is: we're the strongest, smartest, ballsiest women the world has ever known!"

Sheila had been idling by the mall for too long. If Melanie came out and saw her, she'd think she was spying on her. She shifted into drive and began to take off, but she didn't get very far. She coasted to a parking spot way in the back, behind a million cars.

Wouldn't the bastards approve of me now, the ones who pull people over? I'm refusing to drive when upset.

She knew so much more than she wanted to know about the hunters sent to snare her by the people in power who "cared." She knew both the feeling of handcuffs and the feeling of being misunderstood, and she was growing more into her truth.

She was ready to stash Melanie at one of her friend's and go to a meeting for sex workers' rights, all the way in the city.

Her activist girlfriend had been bugging her to do that. Even more since her arrest.

Sheila wouldn't get with the media there, no, she could never do that; her buddy had done that, she wasn't a mom, she didn't have to worry that someone might see her who knew she was somebody's mother, and take it out on her child.

So she'd just go and sit in the back.

What a world, where you had to go to meetings in secret, and work in secret, as well. This, in a country where women were free? Every whore chuckled at that one. In the seventies women took their bras off and burned them, and everyone understood. But letting a man take off your bra for great money could get you thrown in jail?

"*MIND YOUR OWN TWAT!*" another pal yelled, whenever they drove past a clinic besieged by the pro-life fanatics.

Mind your own twat, indeed.

She hadn't aborted her baby. And she hadn't got food stamps, didn't need them. But now she had a record, they had made her unemployable. Not that it mattered, she liked who she was. But she couldn't get a straight job now if she wanted to.

She wanted to help cops catch the bad guys. She wanted to help them keep young girls safe. She had read about how in Brazil, where escorting was accepted, the sex workers and the nurses passed out condoms *together*. Sheila imagined herself tight with the blunt-roller, taking down traffickers with him. She figured she could somehow be useful for that, being so established in the business. In a country with the courage to face a whore's wisdom, and let a whore be who she was, she and the cops could get so much accomplished, they could stop so much evil, *together.*

Suddenly her Go-phone was chirping. This was the phone for her work. She checked it and saw it was a regular. He wanted to see her ASAP.

She had already taken her shower. All she had to do was get back to the house, put on some secret lace and satin, and freshen her face up a bit. She'd drive out to see him and be back in time to return here and pick up her daughter.

Sheila sighed, a breath that felt cleansing. She blew her nose and wiped her eyes and thought about how happy this nice guy would be, the second she texted him back.

Then she began to feel better.

The Border Brothels

Untangling Maternalist Media Discourses of Trafficked Women from a Sex Work Frame

ARIANA OCHOA CAMACHO

IN AUGUST OF 2014, THE SAN DIEGO County District Attorney's office formed a new task force to combat human trafficking (District Attorney). Resembling other anti-trafficking efforts in the United States, such as a federal effort led by Janet Napolitano in the Department of Homeland Security called the Blue Campaign, this task force is distinguished as a local initiative started by law enforcement at the city level. The definitions of trafficking deployed in these frameworks blend human trafficking, sexual exploitation of minors, and forced labour into one larger category of trafficking.

The blending of these categories is reflected in U.S. law and is emphasized by a number of state and local laws, such as the San Diego District Attorney's task force (District Attorney). Specifically, the passage of the *Victims of Trafficking and Violence Protection Act* (VTVPA) in 2000/2003 brought an unusual mix of politicians and feminists in convergence on one issue. Even so, the debates on the global sex trade split quickly apart between sex-positive feminists who emphasize occupational health or harm-reduction framings and, on the other hand, anti-prostitution activists. As Elizabeth Bernstein notes, "Evangelical and feminist anti-trafficking activism has been fuelled by a shared commitment to carceral paradigms" (Bernstein 1). As such, many of the local laws further ingrain a more conservative approach to the issue, ignoring labour as a major incentive in the international concerns for human trafficking, and work to criminalize migrant men connected with the border brothels. Discourses of secrecy, sex, and corruption are interlaced throughout the salacious media reports on sex trafficking. Feminist media producers, such as journalists, generate news reports and exposés in mainstream media to compel viewers into action to save border brothel workers from their monstrous "johns," or in Spanish "juans."

In such portrayals the newscasters who report on these camps are most often women from Western nations. Sex trafficking media coverage and exposés as genre of feminist journalism materialize a key paradox of Western maternalism in the contemporary era. Through their advocacy for trafficked women at the border, feminist journalists are transformed into heroines who save "innocent" women and children from animal-like johns and their illicit activities. Maternalists reject the idea of female dependency while they simultaneously "articulate their role as one of protector to dependent 'other' women" (Jacobs 89). In this process they act in a motherly manner toward women they see as in need of rescue and uplift. In doing so, maternalists fortify the border and defend the national borders from menacing sexual corruption. At the same time, reporters' efforts to speak as independent women and advocate for political reform or change exacerbate the domination of conditions many "other" women experience. The paradox of these feminist efforts is that they treat "other" women as voiceless and *in need* of rescuing.

The outdoor sex camps or "border brothels" in Northern San Diego County summon a moral panic to save the women of the border brothels, creating victims and heroines through media coverage of sex trafficking. Notably, this chapter does not make any claims about the occurrence of forced sexual servitude or sex work activities but addresses the narration of a broader category of "sex trafficking" activities treated similarly in the media. A discursive analysis of media coverage of sex trafficking reveals a set of interlocking narratives that (re)draw and cement the gendered and racialized hierarchies of US society while simultaneously obscuring the very social machinery that generates the border (Brady) and the conditions of migration. Gendered violence and sexual exploitation in the case of Latina immigrant women should be contextualized within the greater dynamics of a militarized border and the overall exploitation of migrants in the US (Chuang). In the context of a militarized border, certainly sexual violence, forced sexual servitude, and trafficking in persons can and do occur, but a careful examination to parse apart the concepts of slavery, sex work, and gendered violence reveal these as different kinds of practices. These categories are entangled in scandalized representations of the commodification and exploitation of women's bodies on the border by maternalist media reports that tacitly compel viewers to save brown women.

This chapter teases apart human trafficking, sex slavery, and sex work as a group of terms conflated in the media coverage through an analysis of two investigative sex trafficking exposé reports by prioritizing questions of consent, agency, and sexual emancipation. Many of these anti-trafficking discourses assert the innocence of "women and children" and, in conflating these two groups, evacuate women of their agency. A close look at the border brothel media discourses reveals the ways in which women involved in sex work and trafficking are "innocent victims" for the purposes of producing particular maternalist agendas. Problematically, this innocence model invariably leads to certain victims not being innocent enough. Finally, this chapter asks, "What do the sex slave discourses obscure?" and "How are the easy slippages between the sex slavery, prostitution, forced labour, and human smuggling productive in the context of the U.S.-Mexico border?" The media coverage facilitates the criminalization of Mexican migrant men as the "johns" in many reports. Paradoxically, this feminist media coverage implicitly participates in a discourse of migrant criminalization that makes Latinas vulnerable to both state interventions and other forms of violence. Concomitantly, the border brothel scandals also produce a feminist heroine, a maternalist who deploys the power of motherhood to save "innocent" women and speak for them.

Maternalists of our moment have recycled previous anti-trafficking structures and programs in ways that combine contemporary racial anxieties with the middle-class norms of sexual restraint generally applied to white women. By combining the innocence associated with the age of consent (indicating sexual inexperience) and a preoccupation over corrupting social environments, today's anti-trafficking campaigns recycle a genealogy of sexual morality in new ways. Their efforts require a rhetorical refiguring of innocence to make it available for sex workers usually presumed to be sexually experienced and lacking sexual restraint. The anti-trafficking campaigns are notable in that they combine concerns about innocence generally reserved for white women with racial anxieties surrounding migration from south of the border to create innocent victims in need of rescue. In doing so, maternalist feminists reinforce ethnocentric notions of women of colour by infantilizing them to make them passive victims of savage men (Mohanty) through which they evacuate them of sexual agency.

LEGAL FRAMEWORKS OF SEX TRAFFICKING'S SPECIAL EVILS

According to the Chamber of Commerce, Oceanside, California, can be imagined as a sunny paradise with its beautiful beaches, warm weather, and wealthy enclaves. With half-million-dollar houses lining its "small town" streets with Spanish-style, red-tiled roofs, and colourful adobe exteriors surrounded by assorted palm trees, this area of sunny Southern California serves as an escape from the crowded cities and completes the picture of a classic upper-class Southern California normalcy (Chamber of Commerce). Complete with historic wooden piers stretching west into the sunset while surfers play on waves, it is depicted as a paradise in the U.S. and is located just ninety miles south of Los Angeles and 35 miles north of San Diego. The cultural geography of Oceanside is intensely segregated and marked by the presence of a large military community. Even so, the border brothels menace conceptions of Oceanside as a paradise. The reports of these brothels resonate with rumours and ideas of racial taint of the "dirty" scandals (and people) leaking through the U.S.-Mexico border. This nexus of sexual scandal, smuggling, and criminality have been drawing the attention of journalists, policy makers, law enforcement, and community groups over the last decade.

The global sex trade as a form of transnational, organized crime has attracted attention from policy makers internationally alongside a broader alarm sounded on human rights. "There's a special evil in the abuse and exploitation of the most innocent and vulnerable," the U.S. President announced at an address to the United Nations (UN) General Assembly (Bush). In the same year the UN created an instrument directed at this group titled, "The Protocol to Prevent, Suppress and Punish Trafficking in Persons especially Women and Children," which offered an agreed-upon legal definition for trafficking.

The UN Protocol highlights consent and prostitution within its definition of trafficking (U.S. Department of State "Recent Developments"). The UN Protocol definition is:

> the recruitment, transportation, transfer, harboring or receipt of persons, by means of threat or use of force or other forms of coercion, of abduction, of fraud, of deception, of the abuse of power or of a position of vulnerability or of the giving or receiving of payments or benefits to achieve the *consent* of a person having control over another person, for the purpose of exploitation. Exploitation shall include, at a minimum, the exploitation of the *prostitution* of others or other forms of sexual exploitation, forced labour or services, slavery or practices similar to slavery, servitude or the removal of organs. (U.S. Department of State "Trafficking" [my emphasis])

In addition to physical force, the UN definition presumes that an individual cannot consent to sell sexual services. Notably, sex work is placed in a spectrum alongside forced labour, slavery, and even organ theft. Labour, though, is explicitly named in the international framework to expand the legal definition of human trafficking beyond the more restricted category of sex trafficking to account for the non-sex trafficking that makes up the majority of the trafficking activities (Chuang).

In a parallel process, the U.S. VTVPA was created in 2000 and reauthorized in 2003. This law punishes traffickers with severe penalties of up to thirty years for participating in trafficking (U.S. Department of State "Recent Developments"). Building on the provided UN framework, the U.S. act defines a special category designated as "severe forms of trafficking" in two parts—sexual and labour exploitations (U.S. Department of State "Trafficking"). The U.S. definition shifts the focus in the legal definition of human trafficking towards sexual exploitation. Despite labour being explicitly named in the U.S. act, the public motivation for the act's passage is to curtail the transportation of women and children across borders for the purposes of sexual servitude.

MEDIA DISCOURSES OF SEX TRAFFICKING

In a CBS News exposé, one reporter leads us from Tijuana's border where "young girls and boys are bought and sold [into prostitution] on dirty streets in front of nameless bordellos and moved North." In a secretive voice the reporter lures the viewer in with: "Now follow me into those fields. We travel across the border and into a corner of *America* rarely seen. It is known as the city of reeds, an outdoor brothel in Vista, California just North of San Diego" (*Invisible Chains* [my emphasis]). Even celebrity Ricky Martin was outraged and expressed the protective impulse that melds women with children in discussing trafficking and sex work: ". . . and we are talking about raping children. It is so frustrating and it gives me so much anger. The governments, they need to do something. They need to change laws!" he stammered on *The Oprah Winfrey Show*. A cluster of media reports emerged around 2003, a time of international focus on trafficking. These were followed more recently by a set of reports connected with efforts in 2013 and 2014 to pass new laws in California relating to trafficking (Sb 473 Human Trafficking; Sb 939 Criminal Jurisdiction). These reports demonstrate the tight relationship between the work of media and legislative efforts focused on human trafficking as a container that fails to distinguish sex work from forced sexual servitude.

Passed by the California Legislature in August 2014, SB 473 amends Proposition 21 focused on criminal activities by gangs and adds human trafficking as an offense that can be used to establish the pattern of criminal activity. Adding trafficking to the list of qualified felonies via this proposition increases punishments for any convictions for trafficking activities "by a group of three or more persons, whether formal or informal" (a definition that Prop. 21 provides for "gang") having one of its primary activities involved in one or more of the enumerated crimes. SB 473 adds human trafficking to this list of thirty-five qualifying crimes that carry additional penalties. In addition, Prop. 21 requires that certain crimes committed by juveniles, including sex offenses, be charged in adult courts without the review of the juvenile court system. At the time of its passage in 2001, Prop. 21 was decried by many communities of colour as targetting and criminalizing young men of colour. As Daniel HoSang notes, this recent political history of Californian ballot initiatives is characterized by "unchanging and undifferentiated racial domination, with rhetorical shifts simply masking an enduring racial animus" accompanied by a thin veneer of progress (2). The anti-trafficking SB 473 is a law that builds on this legacy and accomplishes a similar kind of rhetorical shift by masking its racial animosity and grounding itself in the more noble anti-trafficking discourses that appear to address the exploitation of women and children.

SEX WORK FRAMEWORK AND THE LIMITS OF A HUMAN TRAFFICKING AGENDA

Our understandings of human trafficking are not systemic, and there is little agreement from policy makers regarding a definition for trafficking itself (Parreñas). Policy debates on trafficking mix ideas of exploitation with the movement of persons in ways that do not address the greater context of sex trafficking as produced through the inequalities of global capital, which have deepened poverty and disenfranchisement as well as intensified extraction or wealth (Kara). These global dynamics have created variegated forms of citizenship, which produce different kinds of subjects who act and have agency within constrained circumstances (Parreñas; Ong). Despite the diversity of interpretations for trafficking, many policy discussions of trafficking configure consent and selling sex as mutually exclusive in both the UN and U.S. definitions. In the framework offered by both these laws a person cannot consent to selling their bodily services. Sex work activists, echoing feminist assertions about self-determination and body rights, contend that women have the right to consent to sell their sexual services should they decide it is their best choice (Alexander; Delacoste and Alexander; Kempadoo and Doezema; Pheterson). Current approaches offered by the UN or U.S. frameworks evacuate sex workers of their agency and mask the greater social contexts in which sex work takes place, including immigration regimes (Parreñas). Trafficking and prostitution can be teased apart and understood separately through concepts such as consent, agency, and labour. As sociologist Rachel Parreñas notes, "recognizing trafficked persons as labour migrants would force us to rethink not only our understanding of the vulnerability of migrant workers to abuse, including enslavement, but also our solutions" (46). By understanding sex work and sex trafficking as forms of labour (Parreñas), we are instead pressed to conceptualize the degradation of prostitution in terms of safety and work conditions rather focus on rescue or salvation. In such a frame human rights concerns regarding prostitution shift from a protectionist one on behalf of women as victims to include sex workers voices in self-determination (Pheterson).

Although news reports and popular media use these terms interchangeably, there are great differences in the terms "prostitution," "trafficking," and "sex work." Before moving on, here I examine these differences more carefully. Paternalistic notions, or rather maternalistic notions, about "other" women are embedded within the legislation in ways that conflate women and children as nearly indistinguishable (Chapkis). This conflation is mirrored in the cultural discourses, often grouping women and children without regard to sexual agency, innocence, and consent. Importantly, this grouping indicates an easy slide from woman to child that is propelled by maternalism—that is, as defining adults with the same need for protection from sexual exploitation as children. Importantly, this slide occurs from children to "other women" but never compromises the independence of the heroine journalist. Instead, it bolsters her independence by contrasting her heroic efforts to protect with the defenseless "other women" in need of saving.

OUTDOOR SEX CAMP SCANDAL REPORTS

Overwhelmingly, reports on human trafficking reference Asian countries, sex tourism, and women of Eastern European origins. Lifetime TV's "Human Trafficking" from the fall of 2005 is one such example (Duguay). While different forms of human trafficking from Latin America and greater Asia are often connected by media reports, this examination of human trafficking focuses on the accounts that are connected with the U.S. southern border.[1] The merging of children and women is notable throughout the cultural discourses on trafficking. In particular, adolescent women pose a difficulty for this sort of uniform categorization.

Young women or "girls" are invoked in the opening sequence for one shorter news report, "Fields of Shame." Their virginity is offered against the natural backdrop of the lush fields and forests, a clear metaphor for virginal lands. However, these lands surrounding Oceanside contain a "secret," NBC's investigative reporter tells us in a whispered voice: "Darting across the field of weeds, NBC4 found a group of what looked like students coming home from school ... but these young women don't have school books in their backpacks, and the men they are about to meet aren't their high school sweethearts," she ominously warns the viewer.

Invoking a youthful innocence of high school crushes and virginal land, the narrative in this report clearly juxtaposes the innocent girls with the men they are about to meet, mainly migrant workers. In the *Invisible Chains* series, the viewer hears about young women, some looking as young as thirteen on the streets of Tijuana, Mexico (*Invisible Chains*). Age of consent laws also vary from state to state across the U.S. and have a contested history correlated with racial anxieties of the late nineteenth century (Odem). These laws defined appropriate codes of morality for female youth based on more bourgeois definitions of girlhood and innocence.

MATERNALISM, CONSENT, AND VIRGINITY

Today's anti-trafficking discourses echo reformers' turn-of-the-century preoccupations with sexual slavery in ways that evacuate women of colour of sexual agency. They communicate a special "horror endured by hundreds of little girls aged 9-18" where customers will "pay a premium to take the virginity of a little girl" (Crouse). The innocence of the child is intentionally invoked in this rhetoric to create moral alarm without more careful attention to the legal concept of consent. Certainly, a nine-year-old girl has a very different capacity for consent or sexual agency than an 18-year-old woman. Even so, in the early twenty-first century contemporary anti-trafficking rhetoric draws no distinction between the youngest of girls and adult women. This easy shift between little girls as "virgins" and women engaged in sex work indicates that the concept of virginity that undergirds this slide in these discourses is conspicuously productive.

The virgin in need of rescue offers women up as a prize to their heroes: "The virgin is a charismatic figure within patriarchal discourse, the star of a sensational narrative that asserts and confirms male heterosexual hierarchical prerogatives while attempting to suppress alternative narratives, both of female autonomy and of homosexual desire" (Coyne Kelly 138). In this sense, the rescue of the virgin is an act that reinforces patriarchal sex/gender and racial hierarchies.

Virginity itself interlinks ideas of innocence, vulnerability, experience, knowledge, morality, and purity. As a social construct of Western European culture, virginity has marked the loss of sexual innocence ending with initiation into sexual experience with its accompanying, presumed responsibilities. The extensive literature on virginity, including medical understandings, identifies virginity as both a very powerful and malleable concept. Virginity shifts according to ideas about female sexuality and morality within the broader social context. Despite many efforts to develop a definition of virginity, including extensive "hymenology," there is no way to verify virginity (Coyne Kelly). This conspicuous preoccupation with virginity is based on middle-class codes of morality (Odem).

In the U.S., shifts in age of consent and sexual agency created a legal system and institutional structure aimed at working-class girls to enforce ideals of sexual restraint and modesty that these codes entailed (Odem; Walkowitz). Age of consent laws and programs through the twentieth century were distinctively concerned with white sexual slavery as a product of white women's moral corruption; their advocacy seldom addressed the concerns of women of colour. Importantly, age of consent campaigns presumed a lack of sexual agency and created victims whom feminist reformers and progressives could save from white slavery.

Maternalist campaigns in this earlier time period bolstered race, gender, and sexual hierarchies on the basis of their middle class, Christian ideals that created pathological views of non-white mothers that led them to advocate for programs to save children, such as child removal and boarding schools (Jacobs). The virgin in need of rescue was the figure that underpinned many of these campaigns. These campaigns offered virgins as both a motivation and a prize to their rescuers. The rescue of the virgin is, then, an act that reinforces patriarchal sex/gender and racial hierarchies. In turn of the century maternalist narratives, virgins are described as remaining child-like so that they may be uplifted into proper domesticity (Jacobs).

In the later period, U.S. Progressive Reformers of the early twentieth century sought to enforce these sexual morality codes on white working-class females to prevent delinquency. Young women's delinquency was attributed to social and family environments, which in turn produced sexual delinquency. By moving away from a conceptualization of female passivity and victimization required in earlier age of consent campaigns, twentieth-century reformers' efforts focused on controlling young women and their environments through an elaborate construction of laws and institutions to correct female delinquency. In such a figuration, corrupt environments produce female sexual delinquency—working-class women are not inherently immoral but predisposed to delinquency due to corrupt environments. The role of maternal feminists is to save women from their future sexual delinquency by removing them from corrupt environments to preserve their innocence. The innocence of women, then, must be preserved in childhood before they take on their sexual agency. Virginity is essential in the spectacle of today's sex trafficking, moral panics in which child and woman become a singular category in need of mothering and protection by Western feminists. Similarly, only once anti-trafficking campaigns evacuate women of their sexual agency can adult women be construed as innocent—both in need of saving and deserving of uplift.

INVISIBLE CHAINS SERIES

"Hidden by thick brush, the so-called bedrooms are fashioned out of bent bamboo. These rooms of reeds are like catacombs. So small and coffin-like nearly impossible for an adult to stand up tall. The young girls are brought back here and forced to have sex on these dirt floors often servicing some 30 to 40 men a day," (*Invisible Chains*). The two-segment series aired on local CBS Miami channel 4 on April 29-30, 2004, and has been replayed in a number of venues. Gillen received awards and experienced significant professional success following this piece. The piece has been repurposed for *The Oprah Winfrey Show* and a conference (Gillen). Reporter Gillen is on a mission to tackle the "dark side of America"—human trafficking. In her investigative report, she quickly connects the U.S.-Mexico border to south Florida, where one woman, Ann, who is presumably trafficked, indicates she was transported by traffickers to pursue her "American dream." Gillen approaches women like Ann who are framed as incapable of speaking for themselves and in need of help while Gillen calls to her U.S. audience to "give voice to a suffering few have heard." Careful analysis of this segment, particularly Ann's story, highlights questions about the definitions of trafficking and the role of Western feminists like Gillen. Upon closer examination, Ann's situation appears more to be a case of domestic violence rather than trafficking.

The series tells the stories of three women. One nameless woman recounts that upon her arrival to the U.S., she was gang raped and held by a group of smugglers or "coyotes" celebrating a successful trip. Narrating her story, Gillen tells us that this woman was alone in the U.S. and turned to a man who held her in modern-day slavery with "invisible chains." The anonymous woman tells us in broken English marked by a Spanish accent, "I am so scared because I was illegal and no have rights." Explaining her experience in a dark room with barricaded windows, the woman describes severe physical and emotional abuse in addition to spending her nights being raped. Her only joy was her little dog, Chica. Finally, we see the woman behind a lace curtain being interviewed by reporter Gillen. Now, the woman, we infer, has left the house for freedom at an undisclosed location. Despite the fact that "they [sex trafficking victims] are being violated by their own people," the segment winds down with an emotional call for eradicating the problem of modern slavery on U.S. soil on the basis of human rights.

Throughout the segment, the reporter asserts her presence, silhouetted against a setting sun and walking holding the hands of another woman who we presume to be Ann. Ann has no agency and is infantilized by Gillen who must lead her away from the nightmare. Gillen's infantalization of Ann begins as the segment opens into her story. Driving away, there is a yellow school bus as the narrator excerpts an interview with a therapist of a non-profit who discusses her youngest case, an eleven-year-old girl. The bus, however, leads the viewer directly to an adult woman. This semiotic evacuation of her womanhood creates Ann as an eleven-year-old. Next, a shocking rhetorical flourish of Gillen's narration reveals the conflation of this woman with a child, and ultimately with her pet.

In a foreboding voice, reporter Gillen tells the viewers of the horror that ensued during Ann's imprisonment and translates her story for us. Gillen states, "Ann says that the catalyst for escape from her forced confinement at the hands of a man who threatened her life was trying to protect the life of her only comfort and companion." This is followed a long pause during which the viewer anticipates hearing about the woman's child. Gillen tells us that the catalyst is Chica. Then Gillen dramatically follows "her little dog." This narration is accompanied by translucent picture of a Yorkshire terrier flashing by on the screen as the reporter continues. The sequence evokes the familiar cultural narrative of motherhood—mothers assume agency in order to protect their children. In the voiceover the viewer anticipates that the woman's catalyst for leaving a brutal, domestic situation will be for the well-being of a child. The dog is a surprising substitution in this sequence. Even so, this is the first of two such pairings that cement the connection between "Chica," the dog, and *chica*, a girl.

After the doubling of dog and girl, the reporter shocks viewers with her next statement as she describes the rape of Chica. As a pet, Chica represents an innocent unable to offer sexual consent since she cannot, by definition, possess sexual or personal agency as a non-human. This act is constitutive in significant ways. Ann goes on to detail that day after day she could not leave despite the suffering *they* endure together. Viewers can visualize a recurring scene between Ann and Chica as she holds the tiny Yorkie to her face, promising that today they will leave. Through this sequence of promises, Chica and Ann are in it together as equals; the woman is constructed on the same level as her dog. This conflation created in the imagined promises between Ann and Chica is essential in vacating Ann of *adult agency*—as well as clearing her of any form of adult responsibility in the situation. Chica, Ann, and the imagined child are innocents without personal or sexual agency. The child can now hide. She and Chica disappear from the narrative at this point. Now, viewers can imagine Ann as an innocent victim in need of benevolent anti-trafficking efforts. In response, Gillen protects the unprotected through the slippages between pet, imagined child, and woman. The visual imagery pans to the reporter leading the woman through fields. Gillen embraces the power of maternalism to protect the unprotected and leads the woman-child away from such horrific conditions.

These semiotic shifts work to reinforce the hierarchy between Gillen, Ann, and the dog, who are up against the dog-rapist, Juan, the "Mexican Monster" (as discussed below). In doing so, Gillen reinforces a colonial mentality toward Ana who is reduced to an infantile-like state in the process of her rescue.

Gillen offers one example of the dynamics between Western feminists and "other women." These and other similar practices are characteristic of maternalists who speak for other women and, in doing so, reinscribe relations of colonial power between Western (usually white) feminists, working-class feminists, and feminists of colour around the world (Mohanty). These relations tend to foreclose the possibility of coalitions between groups, as many Western feminists, mainly white women, reproduce ethnocentric knowledge about "other women" while normalizing Western women as the invisible referent. In the sexual slavery discourses of the early millennium feminists have taken up a common colonial strategy that infantilizes women (Jacobs) while portraying "women as the degraded slaves of their cruel and lazy men" (112). White women mobilize maternalism as a kind of feminism to address the disadvantages experienced by non-white women and gain greater political authority to speak on public issues.

Importantly, once infantilized, colonized subjects are no longer able to speak for themselves. As Jacobs argues, white women then take up the role of spokespersons and scripted themselves as mothers charged with the care of "women they perceived as disadvantaged and in need of protection" (92). In the nineteenth century U.S., the field matron went to far-flung communities to reach the indigenous women who had strayed and offered them the opportunity to rebuild their lives (94). For this reason, this media analysis about the sex slave camp scandals examines the maternalism beneath the heroic efforts of many women involved in efforts to prevent anything they associate with sex trafficking. The border brothels and human trafficking discourses about Latinas recreate many of these same dynamics.[2] Fearless Western feminist reporters are the contemporary parallels of field matrons reaching the dark corners of America to help immigrant Latinas soiled by sex trafficking the opportunity to rebuild their lives.

IMMIGRATION

Through much of the rhetoric on trafficking, women are depicted as little girls without sexual agency or the ability to form consent. These contradictions of child, innocence, and agency are also easily uncovered when we probe at the large age range and variety of sexual experiences that could be contained within the age groups described in many media reports. For example, as an adult woman, Ann becomes an exceptional immigrant woman in that she is "innocent" and "undeserving" of such treatment. Certainly, the mistreatment she endured should be contextualized within the frame of migration, as she asserted that she was undocumented; this fact was a crucial element in creating the conditions she experienced. Immigration policy is one of the large and more pervasive "inhuman" social structures that treat immigrant women as disposable and contribute to creating the conditions of possibility for exploitation of migrants, including sexual and labour exploitation.

Many anti-trafficking and anti-prostitution activists use trickery narratives. In the debate on movement across borders, anti-trafficking the international laws assume that women cannot consent to being moved through underground networks. However, trickery is not always involved in international prostitution or sexual trafficking. Rather, adult women can be seen as informed victims, as part of such interaction (Claassen and Molina). Women from Colombia, Claassen and Molina assert, know what they are going to do, but they are often not aware of the conditions under which they must conduct their labour. Women have the agency and choose to cross borders (Agustín) to engage in sex work. They even choose prostitution if it will facilitate their transit in some cases. Their agency needs to be understood within these bounds, albeit sometimes narrow circumstances.

While kidnapping and forced detention do indeed occur, this is perhaps more an artifact of existing immigration policies rather than the sole creation of malicious traffickers. Interestingly, U.S. enforcement of this legislation has focused on prosecuting traffickers, offering few penalties to those who create the demand. By tightening immigration controls to restrict the movement of peoples and further criminalizing sex work, such laws only create conditions favourable for human trafficking (Sassen; Chuang). Trafficking has been leveraged in attempts to control undocumented immigration and organized crime (Kempadoo). This legal framework endorsed in 2003 offers some protections for the most egregious violations, but also fosters additional opportunities for exploitation by driving human trafficking further underground (Agustín). Ultimately, and ironically, this legal infrastructure provides a breeding ground for more sex trafficking scandals.

UNTANGLING DISCOURSES

What is the productive nature of such laws? By exceptionalizing sex slavery, we center a few innocent Latina immigrants against a backdrop of other foreboding, dark invaders. These rhetorics of innocence are notable in light of common depictions of Latinas. Commonly non-European (racialized) Latinas are represented as criminal and seductive. Instead of a half-breed harlot or homegirl—a contemporary version of the bandito (Ramirez Berg)—in this case Latinas have been sanitized of their sexual and personal agency by innocence. What is the agenda served in foregrounding these women as innocents instead of as a more common seductress?

Skepticism is warranted here, but there may be a special evil lurking. Benevolent human rights rhetorics are implicated in a racialized national project. The alleged poor treatment of brown women requires white saviours saving brown women from brown men. As Gayatri Chakravorty Spivak notes, central to these rhetorical moves are a racialized national and imperial project that constructs "uncivilized" men. The trafficking victims' protection act re-establishes narratives about those bad (brown) immigrants and creates a gendered distinction between a few innocent victims and the majority of guilty migrants (Chapkis). Border fear is invoked in news reports to remind viewers that it is "dirty Mexican men" who are perpetuating these sex crimes against innocent women and children. Where you have migrant workers you will have Juan the Mexican Monster (explained below) lurking around outdoor brothels filled with nine- and ten-year-olds. So, who will save them? The benevolent men and women in the form of law enforcement and anti-trafficking Western feminists are central to the plight of saving (sanitized) Latina women from these unimaginable, hyper-masculine creatures.

The field matrons of today, reporters, are our benevolent border heroes. The uncontrolled migrations and sexual excesses of Juan the Mexican Monster are crucial to the maintenance and recuperation of an imperialist project that is produced by and through border discourses and, importantly, bolstered by the discourses of motherhood. His monstrosity is productive and desirable. Without Juan, the masculinity embodied by the militarized U.S.-Mexico border would be excessive, and unnecessary. Like other sexual criminals (Chauncey), Juan's criminal sexual deviance is constructed as an essential aspect of Mexican masculinity that cannot be "cured." Juan's sexual deviance bolsters contemporary anti-immigrant sentiment (Chavez) and garners the energies of anti-trafficking activists, including many (white) feminists, further criminalizing migrant worker men as sexual deviants menacing the nation. In this way the border brothels serve as sites to bolster white masculinity against the shortcomings of monstrous Mexican masculinity that is inclined toward criminal sexual deviance such as bestiality and rape. To create domestic safety, Western feminists save a select few young Latinas from the menace and further secure the border from sexual predators.

As a site that threatens the inner most reaches of America, the border becomes a zone where men (and boys) prove their masculinity by preventing other men from penetrating the nation (Brady). Within the context of severe anti-immigrant sentiment in the U.S., portrayals of the pimps, traffickers, and johns invoked by these scandals support the further criminalization of Latino men as sexual predators. Reports ascribe Mexican men as part of the multitudes of workers/johns—the Juan. However, there is an animal-like sexual excess to depictions of Juan. These physical locations in the outdoors, where the brothels are supposedly located, are this creature's natural habitat, and the practice of brutal bestiality construct a monster. They are constructed as sexual monsters who have compulsive "unimaginable sex with little girls" (Carouse)—Juan the Mexican Monster. The U.S.-Mexico border is one marked by secrecy and clandestine activity. The desire to keep these monsters from invading a wide range of U.S. regions like suburban New Jersey or sunny Southern California becomes a project of racial conquest articulated through border discourses about trafficking and saving women.

Anti-trafficking feminist discourses on human rights offer an easy nexus for the convergence of these discourses. As protectionist discourses about race and state, border brothel media scandals constitute solvent cultural frames for validating white masculinity as bolstered by maternalist heroines. Through a discursive analysis of the coverage about the border and sex trafficking, this chapter highlights how Western feminist reporters embrace their gendered role, as mothers to Latina women. By conflating woman, child, and innocent, the anti-trafficking rhetoric at the border draw a wide-range coalition of supporters who can service a larger state agenda. As part of a racialized national project, these heroines work to ward off racial and sexual contamination by Juan. Importantly, a significant amount of human trafficking is also *forced* labour including debt bondage. As such, the desire to dominate and control migrants and their labour is obscured by constructing a sexual criminal who preys on innocent young Latinas. A sex work frame provokes us to make the distinctions between sexual labour, sexual exploitation, and slavery and shows these discourses as they bolster a racialized nationalist project. Such media discourses bolster anti-immigrant sentiments by criminalizing migrant men without interrogating the actual benefits of trafficking—the profits of labour exploitation. By prioritizing maternalist saviours, the media discourses of border brothels intensify the militarization of the border and migrant criminalization. Instead of saving women, such media discourses and the connected legislation exacerbate the conditions of sexual exploitation, work, and domestic violence that migrant women experience and speak to in their own voices.

[1]There is also a recent, eight-year history of numerous girls and women going missing, and others being found raped and murdered on the border in Juarez, Texas, that has been commonly featured in the media. Although the missing women are assumed to also be connected with illicit sex work, this is considered distinct from the sex trafficking scandals in that the women are generally disappeared or murdered—their murders are the focus of different rhetorics. For more information see (Nieves).

[2]Jacobs makes the case that indigenous women faced child removal as a result of these discourses, but that other women of colour deemed unfit did not have the same experiences during the late nineteenth and early twentieth century in the U.S. and Australia. This article does not examine the child welfare policies for Latina/o families, but the news reports of unaccompanied child migrants from 2014 indicate this area needs closer examination.

WORKS CITED

Agustín, Laura María. "Migrants in the Mistress's House: Other Voices in the 'Trafficking' Debate." *Social Politics: International Studies in Gender, State and Society* 12.1 (2005): 96-117. Print.

Alexander, Priscilla. "Prostitution: Still a Difficult Issue for Feminists." *Sex Work: Writings by Women in the Sex Industry*. Eds. Frédérique Delacoste and Priscilla Alexander. 2nd ed. San Francisco: Cleis Press, 1998. 184-230. Print.

Bernstein, Elizabeth. "Militarized Humanitarianism Meets Carceral Feminism: The Politics of Sex, Rights, and Freedom in Contemporary Antitrafficking Campaigns." *Signs* 36.1 (2010): 45-71. Print.

Brady, Mary Pat. *Extinct Lands, Temporal Geographies : Chicana Literature and the Urgency of Space*. Durham: Duke University Press, 2002. Print.

Bush, George W.*Statement by His Excellency Mr. George W. Bush.*

Perf. Bush, George W. *United Nations General Assembly.* Rec September 23, 2003, New York, New York, 2003.

Carouse, Janice. "The Sex Fields of San Diego." *Orthodoxy Today.* 2003. Web. 2014 November 20.

Chamber of Commerce, Oceanside. "Visit Oceanside." *Oceanside Chamber of Commerce.* 2014. Web. September 14 2014.

Chapkis, Wendy. "Trafficking, Migration, and the Law Protecting Innocents, Punishing Immigrants." *Gender and Society* 17.6 (2003): 923-37. Print.

Chauncey, George. "The Postwar Sex Crime Panic." *True Stories from the American Past.* Ed. William Graebner. New York, NY: McGraw Hill, 1993. 160-78. Print.

Chavez, Leo Ralph. *The Latino Threat : Constructing Immigrants, Citizens, and the Nation.* Stanford, Calif: Stanford Univ. Press, 2008. Print.

Chuang, Janie A. "Rescuing Trafficking from Ideological Capture: Prostitution Reform and Anti-Trafficking Law and Policy." *University of Pennsylvania Law Review* 158.6 (2010): 1655-728. Print.

Claassen, Sandra, and Fanny Polanía Molina. *Tráfico De Mujeres En Colombia: Diagnóstico, Análisis Y Propuestas.* Bogota, Colombia: Fundación Esperanza, 1998. Print.

Coyne Kelly, Kathleen. *Performing Virginity and Testing Chastity in the Middle Ages.* New York, NY: Routledge, 2000. Print.

Crouse, Janice. "Fields of Shame: Sex Slavery Exposed." *Antiochian Orthodox Archdiocese of America.* 2003. Web. September 14 2014.

Delacoste, Frédérique, and Priscilla Alexander. *Sex Work: Writings by Women in the Sex Industry.* 2nd ed. San Francisco: Cleis Press, 1998. Print.

District Attorney, San Diego County. "Human Trafficking." *San Diego County District Attorney's Office.* 2014. Web. October 6, 2014 2014.

Duguay, Christian. *Human Trafficking.* 2005. Television Broadcast, October 24, 2005.

Gillen, Michelle. "Invisible Chains: Human Trafficking." Invisible Chains: Breaking the Ties of Trafficking in Humans Conference. St. Thomas University Law School, Miami Gardens, Florida.

November, 12, 2004. Web.

HoSang, Daniel. *Racial Propositions Ballot Initiatives and the Making of Postwar California*. Berkeley: University of California Press, 2010. Print.

Invisible Chains: Human Trafficking Investigative Report Series. 2004. Television Broadcast. April 29, April 30, and November 11, 2004.

Jacobs, Margaret D. *White Mother to a Dark Race Settler Colonialism, Maternalism, and the Removal of Indigenous Children in the American West and Australia, 1880-1940*. Lincoln: University of Nebraska Press, 2009. Print.

Kara, Siddharth. *Sex Trafficking : Inside the Business of Modern Slavery*. New York: Columbia University Press, 2009. Print.

Kempadoo, Kamala. *Trafficking and Prostitution Reconsidered: New Perspectives on Migration, Sex Work, and Human Rights.* London: Paradigm, 2005. Print.

Kempadoo, Kamala, and Jo Doezema. *Global Sex Workers: Rights, Resistance, and Redefinition*. New York: Routledge, 1998. Print.

Mohanty, Chandra Talpade. *Feminism without Borders: Decolonizing Theory, Practicing Solidarity*. Durham, NC: Duke University Press, 2006. Print.

Nieves, Evelyn. "To Work and Die in Juarez." *Mother Jones* May/June 2002. Print.

Odem, Mary E. *Delinquent Daughters: Protecting and Policing Adolescent Female Sexuality in the United States, 1885-1920.* Chapel Hill, NC: University of North Carolina Press, 1995. Print.

Ong, Aihwa. "Neoliberalism as Exception Mutations in Citizenship and Sovereignty." Durham, NC: Duke University Press, 2006. Print.

Parrenas, Rhacel Salazar. *Illicit Flirtations: Labour, Migration and Sex Trafficking in Tokyo*. Palo Alto, CA: Stanford University Press, 2011. Print.

Pheterson, Gail. *The Prostitution Prism*. Amsterdam: Amsterdam University Press, 1996. Print.

Ramirez Berg, Charles. "Stereotyping in Films in General and of the Hispanic in Particular." *Latin Looks Images of Latinas and Latinos in the U.S. Media*. Ed. Clara E. Rodriguez. Boulder, CO: Westview Press, 1997. 104-20. Print.

Sassen, Saskia. "The Excesses of Globalisation and the Feminisation of Survival." *Parallax* 7.1 (2001): 100-10. Print.

Sb 473 Human Trafficking. California Legislature. 473 2014.

Sb 939 Criminal Jurisdiction. California Legislature. 473. August 22 2014.

Spivak, Gayatri. "Can the Subaltern Speak? Speculations on Widow and Sacrifice." *Wedge* 8.7 (1985):120-130. Print.

Walkowitz, Judith R. *City of Dreadful Delight : Narratives of Sexual Danger in Late-Victorian London*. Chicago: University of Chicago Press, 1992. Print.

U.S. Department of State. "Fact Sheet: Recent Developments in U.S. Government Efforts to End Trafficking in Persons." *United States Department of State*. March 18, 2004. Web. 28 May 2015.

U.S. Department of State "Fact Sheet: Trafficking in Persons Report." *United States Department of State*. June 14, 2004. Web. 28 May 2015.

Street Corner Moms

OGILVY & MATHER, BUENOS AIRES

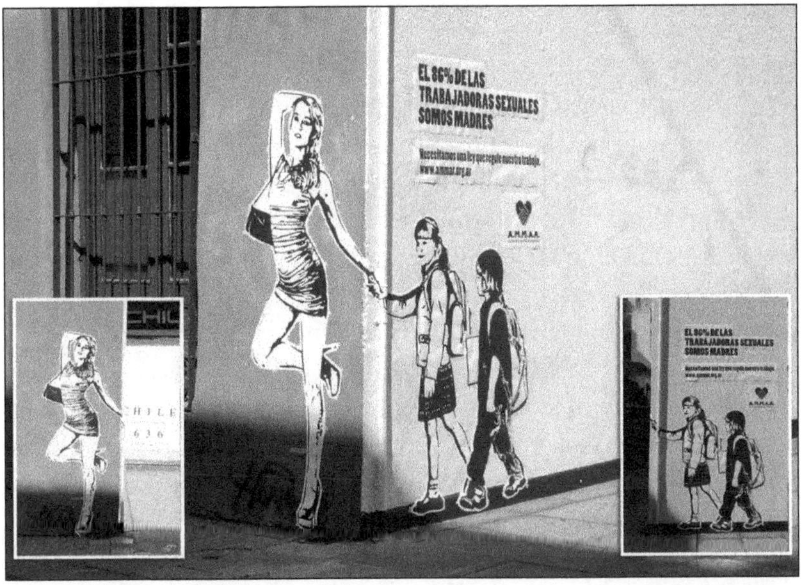

The Association of Women Prostitutes of Argentina (AMMAR) is an NGO that fights for the human and working rights of Argentine sex workers, 86 percent of whom are mothers. These mothers need a law protecting them from exploitation and police violence, but due to the controversial nature of this matter, their concerns and needs go unnoticed. Street corners are emblematic spots where sex workers offer their services, so AMMAR hired Ogilvy & Mather, Buenos Aires, to install urban art where pedestrians can see the full reality of sex workers once they notice the side oftentimes hidden by society: motherhood.

Mama Tiger Rising

ANONYMOUS

TOMORROW I HAVE A MEETING with social services, against my will. I will be forced to explain and justify my fitness for motherhood. To a lifetime of trauma, I now add the fear of someone taking my child from me. I feel powerless to protect her. I feel as if I am being raped by the state. I say raped because it is the same powerlessness, the same overpowering, the same domination that I have felt so many times before. Only before it was my body, and now it is much worse. Now it is my child who is threatened. I feel silenced, my objections disregarded, my will inconsequential. This is a familiar place to me, this panic, this fear, the terror, the unspeakable pain that leaves death as an only option.

My desire to die, this is why they are coming for me. A friend who knew I was suicidal called social services on me. Now all the concerned parties are using their bureaucratic might to look out for the "best interests" of my child. My child. Grown in my womb, birthed by my body, nursed on my breast, held in my arms, and now a case file in the Ministry of Children and Family Development.

Death is not new to me. I was a child when first I met death. When my body was first violated, when the first unspeakable shame and darkness came to drown me. Death was there when I was the daughter of a sexual perpetrator, death remained when I was molested by a stranger, death grew stronger each time I was beaten, each time I was degraded, each time I was raped. Death and I are old friends. Death is a foe really, I suppose, but I call him friend because he has been so faithfully present throughout my life. He calls me and begs me to come, promising an end to the abyss of pain in which I have always existed.

Death was the fly on the wall as I was thrown down a flight of stairs. Death laughed as a man tried to strangle the life out of me while he was raping me. Death haunted me with the threats of all my abusers whose voices and words constantly scream at me long after the men who spoke them are gone. Death cheered each time a beating left me breathless and gasping for air. And death also shed many tears each time the overdose didn't take, or when I took my neck out of the noose before it was too late, or when I was stumbling to my suicide and found just enough strength to hold on for one more day.

Death was there when I had been smoking pot for a few years to numb the pain and quiet the nightmares and flashbacks and aches in my body. There could never be enough pot, not one moment could be spent sober because each moment was a never-ending revival of every vile thing ever done to me. So I would smoke from dawn till dusk, and I could not stay in school or keep a job because there was an unending parade of men who wanted to show me how worthless I was. Only now do I understand I was yearning for their love, even if it came with violence.

So on that first day when I was starving, death was there. I had not eaten in days because any money I had went to pot. And then the older man down the street offered me food. Groceries for sex. So I lay with him as I had lain with many men, and then I had food to eat. And he was grotesquely older, but that also was not new for me because since I was a young teenage girl, old men took my body, and now I had food. And when the food ran out, I had more sex for more groceries, and when I would say no, he would rape me anyway. This was also not new, but it was at a time when I still tried to say no. Eventually, the objections no longer came, only silent submission to whatever wanted to be done to me. I was unable to speak because each new violent act just magnified the pain of all the other acts before it and left me unable to move, barely able to breathe.

Beatings. Rape. Repeat. And I stumbled around drunk on the desire to die. And I could not find the courage to throw myself in the path of a train, so instead I threw myself into the path of men and hoped that one of the beatings would finally be my last. That one of the times a man had his hands around my throat would finally end the life of sex and shame and pain that would not stop torturing me.

And I was transient, always looking for a place to stay. And when I had none, there were bushes behind a gas station where I could hide and feel safe. And sometimes when it was cold, I could find a man who would take me home, and I would have sex for a place to stay that night, and I would drink or smoke to be able to lie with men I did not know who wanted to do awful things to me. Violence and degradation were my most frequent lovers.

Then one fateful day on my fast dance toward death, I had sex with a man for $90 so I could keep myself stocked in pot. But this encounter was different than the others, a seed had been planted. Conception. And as this little baby started to grow inside me, she also breathed new life in me.

I had been suicidal each day for as long as I could remember, but suddenly taking my own life no longer seemed possible. All I could think was how it would stop this new life inside me. Already I wanted to protect her. I got sober and started to rebuild my life. I no longer had to live my awful life as a worthless whore. I could live for this new life. There would be a baby, and for the first time in forever, I saw some hope.

She grew and she grew and she grew and my body, which had been so desecrated for so long, was now a home for this sweet child. I rubbed my belly as my baby grew, and it was the first loving touch my body had seen in years. She was the angel who saved my life, and her first day on Earth was also my first. I was no longer all those awful names the men always called me. I had a new name I could call myself: Mother.

My daughter just had her fourth birthday. For four years I raised her as a single mom. The first years I could barely live on income assistance. The welfare check kept me below the poverty line, but at least we had a roof over our head. But it was not enough for food. And soon an old theme began to emerge: no money for groceries. I was no stranger to starvation, but it was suddenly unbearable on the day when my two-year-old daughter kept saying, "Mommy, I am hungry," and I had no food to give her.

But we survived, and I worked hard with the support and love of the community to give my daughter a good life. And as she came to the end of her third year, something else miraculous happened: I fell in love with an old friend. We got engaged, and my daughter and I were finally going to have the family we had always wanted.

This man, he loved me and cherished me and treated me well. Better than I have ever been treated before, and as the symphony of the past keeps reminding me, better than I deserve. And his touch is gentle, soft, and filled with love. Something that my skin and soul have not felt before. But even that most sacred touch awoke the monster of memories that are carved on every inch of my body. The flood of fear returns, the terrible times that I had learned to co-exist with are now holding me captive again. And the storm of past pain has been unyielding, and the desire for death quickened, and I struggled. And a friend called social services. And I now they judge my parenting, and I sit through interviews in which I have to explain myself, and they have no understanding of how the process is suffocating all my strength I had been saving for my daughter. And I am once again dominated.

But motherhood has also given me my voice. And I will no longer lie silent. The mama tiger, she fights. She is strong and brave, and she will let no one harm her daughter, not even the government with its child welfare policies, which often do more harm than good.

The men will come to the meeting tomorrow, and they will try to decide if I am fit enough to raise my daughter without interference. But motherhood has taught me something that I never knew as a girl or woman who was constantly pillaged. The love I have for my daughter is a love that can move mountains, it is a love that has been healing my heart, it is a love that would do anything to protect my daughter, and it is a love that will not let anyone, not even death, lay me down to die. So I will live, and I will fight, and I will raise my daughter according to my will because motherhood has given me the strength to say, "This is my body, this is my family, this is my daughter, and she is not yours to take."

Motherhood and Sex Work

A Negotiation of Identities

SATABDI SAMTANI AND ELIZABETH TREJOS-CASTILLO

MOTHERING IS OFTEN CHERISHED AS the most rewarding experience of a women's life. The societal expectations that we have of mothering as depicted in our everyday social life contradict the very reality in which we currently live, a world where a sizeable number of mothers are working moms. This chapter focuses on a specific category of working moms who are sex workers. The existence of sex work as a profession and its overlap with motherhood are indeed areas not well articulated in theory or research. The societal disapproval of sex work as a profession overshadows a mother's parental role, without actually giving a sex worker mom the fair chance to be evaluated on the merits of her motherhood. Every culture idealizes motherhood in certain ways; however, the dominant ideological discourse on being a good mother, especially in the U.S., does not seem to be in sync with reality but rather an idealized construction of motherhood. The standards of mothering that our society seems to idealize, which are a set of gold-standard parenting practices, are derived from middle-class white women who could afford to stay home (Johnston and Swanson). The social construction of the "good mother," therefore, leaves no room for discourses from lived experiences of women of colour, low-income women, women without a college degree, or women with other life experiences.

The social paradigm of a good mother and good worker seems to be a parallel discourse (Ridgeway and Corelle). Over the years, family researchers have often focused on the wage discrimination faced by female workers in comparison to their male counterparts. This difference perhaps often has an association to a female worker also fulfilling her obligations as a mother. Recent researchers have highlighted a wage gap between mothers and non-mothers, especially around age thirty-five. There is clear evidence to show that this wage difference is often larger than the wage difference between young women and men in the workplace. This leads us to understand that motherhood in general might be considered a status characteristic with significant negative perceptions when contrasted to workplace performance (Ridgeway and Corelle). It is notable that the function a mother performs is devalued as compared to recognized work done by women in the paid labour force. The wage gap thus affects the mother along with her children and is referred to as the "motherhood penalty" (Lips and Lawson 667). The motherhood penalty could be as steep as seven percent lower salaries per child on average when controlling for all other factors in young married women, and some studies show a steeper reduction for married mothers with a second child (Budwig and England).

Society, therefore, has built a social narrative for which a good mother and good worker are not complementary in characteristic but are rather supplementary. "Prostitution involved women rarely are recognized as mothers by society generally or academicians more specifically" (Dalla, "I Fell Off" 191). The hidden nature of sex work as a profession makes it very difficult to study patterns and trends found among people participating in it. The discourses of being a "good mother" and "good worker" are so mutually exclusive in our society that a profession as contested as sex work finds itself diametrically opposite to the value that is added to mothering in general. A sex worker who simultaneously also has to play the role of a mother faces a twin challenge of identities, and it is counterproductive as one role is inherently held at a better moral standard as compared to the other. The criminalization of sex work (except in a few countries or states where it is legal) along with societal disapproval of it makes it harder for sex workers who are mothers to fulfill their duties of mothering. They often find themselves at a crossroads between their profession, which denigrates them as human beings, and motherhood, which is held to societal standards of "good mothering," thereby putting them through an identity crisis of being unable to access social identification as "good or normal mothers" no matter what they do in caring for their children (Dodsworth 100).

Sex workers are not a homogenous group of people; some types of sex workers are unique to a culture and a specific country, while there are some commonly found types of sex workers across cultures. If we look at female sex workers, there are "call girls" and "escorts" working for affluent populations of the sex industry; "in-house" sex workers working in brothels that are situated in margins of the city or inner-city neighbourhoods; "street walkers" who exchange sex for money and are usually the most visible of sex workers, often found approaching their clients on sidewalks of cities; part-timers who complement their incomes with sex-for-money (we see a rise in college students in this particular group); and drug-involved, street-based sex workers who oscillate between exchanging sexual favours for money or drugs depending on their circumstances (Surratt et al.). It is important to add that less than twenty percent of sex work is street sex work according to most studies. All these women, some of whom are also mothers, have different social and environmental contexts as well as varying levels of vulnerabilities for their participation in sex work. We will try to capture the negotiation of identities made by the sex worker mother under different contexts, many of them participating in one or multiple types of sex work mentioned above. This chapter already has put forward the immense emphasis given to the construction of "motherhood" as a discourse, and now we focus on discussing how sex work as a profession and mothering stand juxtaposed.

THEORETICAL CONSIDERATIONS

The ideal mom is, therefore, the one who follows an intensive mothering routine also known as the "Intensive Mothering Expectations" (IME) (Johnston and Swanson 510). The IME is a dominant paradigm that both working and non-working mothers have embraced and have accepted as part of their motherhood goals. While intensive mothering has its benefits, like a substantial involvement in a child's life, working women build their identity of being an intensive mother along with being a good worker, which is a dual challenge that might lead to unintended, negative consequences. It is also possibly unrealistic that one could live up to both expectations with similar passion. It is, therefore, important for us to understand the interaction between the "sex worker moms" and "societal expectations of mothering" with the help of Symbolic Interactionism Theory, which studies proximal processes, gives meaning to micro-level interactions, and envisions how processes help in construction of the self at a later stage.

The theory of Symbolic Interactionism is guided by three basic principles. The first principle is process by which people ascribe meaning to things. Meanings arise from both verbal and non-verbal forms of communication. The second principle is that there exists an active social self that shapes one's behaviour; Kuhn advocated that the construction of self was derived from social roles. The third principle is that of context, of how society negotiates between a dialectic of freedom and constraint. In other words it is a contest between processes and structure. Society has a set of rules and wants individuals to act in particular ways; however, the self then, through social interaction, can influence and change society. Thus, a "sex worker mom" has to act in particular ways to fulfill her role as a mother and simultaneously navigate the societal rigidity on sex-work, which often compels her to distance herself from either one of her identities.

The literature surrounding sex work and mothering described in the works of Dodsworth typically revolves around three thematic experiences in identity negotiation: For some mothers it was a provision of financial security for themselves and their families and, therefore, a means to an end. These particular mothers also coped well with these situations and did not let any negative feelings from their profession get internalized. The other category of women struggled to make peace between their two identities, and they were usually victims of sexual abuse at a young age. Substance use was common among such women and often their participation in sex work became their sole identity, which influenced every other role they played. A third group of women, even though very small in number, actually saw motherhood as an incentive to exit sex work. The experiences of women, whose lives as sex workers determined their other identities, often had coping issues or felt they had a threatened sense of identity. Another common theme found in various studies conducted on sex workers who were mothers revealed that the presence of children in their household—as opposed to households in which the mother gave up her child to extended family members, fathers, or social services—made a difference in their role negotiations. Some women who gave up their children were extremely positive about their experiences, as they felt their children were safer with relatives, fathers, or adopted families, while others were traumatized by not being able to fulfill their roles as a mother (Dodsworth).

An interesting trend observed in developing nations was "sex worker moms" who used sex work to gain more economic stability and resources (Rivers-Moore). Sex worker moms had a clear set of ambitions in terms of balancing their profession and mothering. They did not think their profession contributed to their identity because their descriptions of lived experiences tilted toward their life as a single woman providing for their families. Similar findings are reported in a research study done by Basu and Dutta in 2011 on sex workers in India. In an interview conducted for the study, a sex worker mom reported, "We are called disreputable, but as mothers we are like any other mother in your culture" (115), indicating that they would do everything in the best interests of their child like any other mother. In developing countries like India, sex worker moms wanted to provide their children with resources like good education, good nutrition, and a healthy lifestyle to acquire the necessary skills for a better socioeconomic status. This idea of providing resources was very similar to middle-class parents' child-rearing practices, especially the investment of huge amounts of resources on education.

There was clarity on what sex workers thought were acceptable and unacceptable reasons for keeping their professions. The sex workers felt that providing for children and supporting their family was a legitimate reason to have entered and continued the profession; however, helping oneself get cosmetic surgeries or other levels of consumerism was regarded as an unacceptable reason for sex work (Rivers-Moore). Sex worker mothers in

Costa Rica were also very unsupportive of addiction issues when it came to unacceptable reasons for being involved in sex work (Rivers-Moore). Researchers have observed that the narrative of sex worker moms as a provider for children and families helps them negotiate their identity in more resilient ways than other sex worker mothers who interpret their work as a troubled profession.

The majority of sex worker moms defined motherhood as their primary identity outside their work life (Rivers-Moore). Some mothers identified themselves as an agency who felt empowered by managing their lives, surviving, and being an effective worker with a clear set of goals both as a sex worker and mother. Some mothers found their lives as sex workers bearable, as their focus was now on their children (Dutta and Basu). The narratives of sex worker moms do convey a robust sense of developing protective factors at the cost of moderate risks, a sense of choice and agency in the decisions they make (Dodsworth). Several mothers did not see sex work as the primary factor affecting their parenting responsibilities. However, the management of their profession along with secondary factors, such as dangers related to sex work, could cause harm to them and their families.

In a study completed by Dalla in 2004 ("I Fell Off") on forty-three street-based sex workers, it was found that sex worker moms were concerned about the intergenerational transmission of their work to their children, especially when they had daughters. Mothers often expressed anguish at how they did not want their children to ever participate in sex work. In the same study Dalla found that "cross generational themes, that is familial dynamics experiences by the participants in their families of origin and repeated in their families of procreation" (225). Among intergenerational themes, it was found that dysfunctional families had often influenced the sex worker to enter and stay in the profession, whereas the closeness of a parent-child relationship determined their personal relationship with their children (Dalla "I Fell Off"). The mothers themselves were also victims of high levels of domestic abuse, had experience with substance use, and had reported very few instances of parental mental illness. Often, the mothers themselves came from very unstable homes, and a large number of them were subjected to foster care, neglect, and low levels of support while growing, which resulted in them "running away from home" at young ages (Dalla, "You Can't Hustle" 195). These situations make them vulnerable, and they often fall prey to sexual abuse and participation in sex work. They also use sex work as a mechanism to cope, survive, and emotionally distance themselves from their trauma. In the study conducted by Dalla ("I Fell Off"), among sex worker mothers surveyed, some reported that they did not feel they were effective mothers as they were unavailable for their children, and they described their feelings by saying that they "fell off the mothering track" (190). It should be noted that in this particular study, nearly half of the participants had children before they entered sex work, and the rest of them had children while being a street sex worker.

Domestic violence among sex workers is a cause of concern to social workers in general. Sometimes the cycle of violence continues, as the sex worker mother could have been a victim to it as a child, and by participating in sex work, she could live in a fragile environment where her boyfriend or "the pimp" is violent to her. It is also often found that domestically violent homes are also the households with high levels of drug addiction and alcoholism (Dalla, "You Can't Hustle"). In Dalla's study, six children were removed from their moms because of domestic violence. Exposure to domestic violence is not just a public health concern for the sex worker mom and her children; it also poses greater risk to the child of long- and short-term psycho-social disorders. Sexual abuse is also common among sex worker mothers; about seventy-four percent of them in Dalla's study reported a history of sexual abuse in their own adolescent years. Some of the mothers in the interview said they were aware that one of their partners could have abused their children (Dalla, "You Can't Hustle"). In fragile families like these, there is frequently a vicious cycle of events that may lead to multiple generations participating in sex work with little or no incentive to break the cycle. Exceptionally, low social support from the community along with little or no support from state agencies makes sex worker moms vulnerable to deteriorated physical and mental health outcomes as compared to moms from any other profession.

VARIATION IN CULTURAL CONTEXT AMONG SEX WORKER MOTHERS

A characteristic of the sex work industry in developing countries is that girls as young as ten or eleven are often trafficked into paid or forced sexual labour. Trafficking of humans to service demand for paid sex is one of the fastest growing illegal trades in the world. Developed countries see this trend too but in disproportionately smaller pockets than developing countries; some of this could be attributed to lower levels of poverty, stronger laws, and heavy criminal penalties on human trafficking (Sabat, Rahman and Ahmed). In a study conducted in Israel on trafficked sex worker moms from the former Soviet Union, it was observed that escaping poverty was their biggest reason for being trafficked into sex work. Mothers who were separated from their children by the process of trafficking coped by knowing their children were better off financially and safe, while mothers who brought children with them to Israel coped by caring for their children, enhancing their perception of self-worth (Peled and Parker). Trafficked women who were not mothers faced similar problems as women who were mothers, and both the groups reported having post-traumatic stress disorder (PTSD) and depression (Cwikel et al.). Several factors of life history and vulnerability, such as exposure to childhood trauma, motherhood, and age at entry into sex work, acted as mediating factors in their decision to participate in sex work (Cwikel et al.). These mothers also had a constant fear of deportation, and this added to their existing stress from sex work (Cwikel et al.).

In another study on sex workers in rural areas of the U.S., it was found that due to the lack of economic opportunities accompanied by low-paying jobs, such as working on assembly lines, many women took up sex work as an adaptive strategy, as it had flexible hours and was economically more viable (Bletzer). A lot of women who participated in sex work in rural areas also had a history of running away or "aging out of" the foster care system, similar factors that were seen in urban populations of sex workers. There were also high rates of sexual abuse among rural sex workers and the cycle of abuse continued on to their children who had a similar pattern of alcohol use as their mothers (Bletzer). Mothers also felt ashamed and tried to keep their profession concealed or hidden from their children (Cox, Casablanca, and McAdams; Dalla, "You Can't Hustle").

In a study of sex workers from Nicaragua it was found that sex workers had considerably low subjective well-being and extremely low levels of life satisfaction (Cox, Casablanca and McAdams). Thc profession of sex work is in direct conflict with the notion of sexual purity, which renders workers unfit as mothers and wives. Also, a dominance of Catholicism in these countries further complicates and makes the life of a sex worker more prejudiced. In the study done by Cox colleagues, a sex worker described her guilt: "It is not the education that my mother gave me. Those are not the values she taught me during my childhood, and this is not life she expected from me" (Cox, Casablanca and McAdams 1470). In a study of Mexican sex workers in Tijuana it was found that female sex workers were often single mothers with low levels of information about contraception and therefore were more at risk of HIV/AIDS (Bucardo et al.). Female sex workers in Tijuana often had foreign clientele who would pay them more for not using condoms and low levels of knowledge on the benefits of condoms led to the workers not using them as a protective barrier for their own health (Bucardo et al.).

In a research study done for the LEADR project in Bangladesh, brothel-based sex worker mothers adopted three strategies about raising their children (Sabat, Rahman and Ahmed). In the first category, would-be mothers who raised their children in the brothels, thus children grew up to be aware of and knew the rules of the trade, and in all likelihood the daughters in these circumstances would eventually participate in sex work after reaching puberty. A second category of sex worker moms would send children away to live with a relative in another town or village, visit them occasionally, and help them financially sustain and achieve a better life than her own. In some cases, some of these sex workers would save enough to get their daughters married and provide a lot of expensive gifts. A third category of sex worker moms would raise their children away from the brothels only to bring their daughters back into their profession. This category of sex worker was often indebted to pimps or was "sex slaved," and as they aged, they were unable to repay their debt as they had a low levels of clientele visiting them. Their daughters were a source of economic sustenance as they were young and could bring in more money than their aging mothers.

In an ethnographic study done in a large British city in 2000-2001, it was found that the occupational hazards of sex workers are multiple, yet sex workers based out of brothels, saunas, and salons (in-house sex workers) are exposed to a continuum of risk in which they prioritize the risk outcomes of their profession (Sanders, "A Continuum of Risk"). Health-related risks are often a low priority for sex workers when considered against other forms of risk, like physical violence. The sociological concept of risk inherent in any profession has been described by scholars such as Douglas (cited in Sanders "A Continuum of Risk") as influenced by social and cultural environments; alternately, scholars like Rhodes understand risk behaviour to be an outcome of negotiated choices and not simply the outcome of individual choices (cited in Sanders "A Continuum of Risk"). One of the biggest risks that sex worker moms faced in this British study concerned their children knowing their profession: "I have got four teenagers. Can you imagine what they would think if they knew I worked here (sauna). I see their reactions to prostitution on TV, and if I told them they would be devastated. I'm their mum" (cited in Sanders, "A Continuum of Risk" 568).

POLICY IMPLICATIONS AND FUTURE RECOMMENDATIONS

Contradictory to widespread beliefs, sex workers indeed are an extremely heterogeneous group, and the incidence of risk varies depending on the style of sex work the individual chooses (Kurtz, et al.). Most countries lack policies required for addressing the needs of sex workers, which are often unique when compared to other similar vulnerable populations. There are also differences in legal frameworks. In some countries, such as Hong Kong, India, and Bangladesh, sex work in itself is not illegal; however, trafficking or soliciting for sex work is prosecutable. In other countries, such as China, the U.S. (except Nevada), and most Middle Eastern countries, prostitution in itself is illegal. In the U.S., Nevada is currently the only state to legalize sex work in eleven of its rural counties, which include thirty brothels (Weitzer). Sex workers in these counties are required to have registration and health checks. Rhode Island was the only other state in the U.S. to have some provisions for legalized, indoor sex-work, but the state legislature passed a law to criminalize it in 2009 (Weitzer). There are a few countries where prostitution is legal and government-regulated, such as the Netherlands, New Zealand, and Ecuador; in countries such as Bolivia and Colombia prostitution in itself is legal, but pimping for prostitution is considered illegal (Weitzer). In 2014, the Canadian Parliament passed a law stating that selling sex is not illegal, but buying sex is—and is a punishable offence (Chu, et al.). In the United Kingdom, prostitution is legal, but soliciting for sex work on the street is deemed illegal (Weitzer). Hence, most sex workers across nationalities have varying risks of prosecution depending upon the country in which they are located.

A common problem reported by most sex workers across different countries where prostitution or soliciting for prostitution is illegal was harassment in the hands of law enforcement (Bletzer). Repeated harassments often led to sex workers mistrusting government agencies, which would make them unlikely to seek help from such agencies in case of acute crisis because of the fear of prosecution (Dalla, "You Can't Hustle"). The children of such mothers are therefore invisible from the support system network that exists in some countries. The inherent distrust in government institutions often forces them to find care work or ask for financial help from people who could entrap them into a vicious cycle of debt or bonded labour, or eventually they could even become victims of human trafficking. Many social policy makers and law enforcement officials view both the sex worker moms and their clients as parallel evils in society. They often do not make the distinction that is required to create social policy changes that would help the sex worker mom.

U.S. policy interventions on sex workers still lack a child-centered approach (Bletzer). A study done by Dalla ("Et Tú Brutè?") in 2001 in the mid-west region of the U.S. and a similar one done by Weiner in 1996 in New York City both indicate that children are a huge source of support and a coping mechanism for sex worker moms, yet most of the mothers conceal their identities in order to refrain from losing their children to child-monitoring agencies (as cited by Bletzer). Dalla ("Et Tú Brutè?") reported that removal of children from sex worker moms voluntarily and involuntarily is perhaps not the best solution to deal with the risk associated with growing up in dysfunctional households. The focus of policy makers should be to intervene in the vicious cycle of poverty, family instability, and substance dependency observed among these families. A common theme across the studies from different countries was how participation in sex work was for economic need and sustenance. There is also a factor of globalization that has affected developing countries where there is an increasing trend among women participating in sex work, indicating a lack of employable skills among its most vulnerable populations.

The life course of a street sex worker is often self-perpetuating; many are physically or sexually abused as children, which leads to substance abuse and results in homelessness and their introduction to a sex work survival strategy. This often leads them to self-medicate in an attempt to escape the reality of events surrounding them, thus increasing their need for finances to afford more substances (Kurtz et al.). Sex work can have significant occupational hazards that could be categorized as health risks, risk of physical and sexual violence, and emotional risk (Sloss and Harper). The occupational hazards of sex work do not entirely hinge upon the fact that it involves rendering sexual favours for money; rather, sex work is complicated by the idea of what society defines as "moral behaviour" for an adult. Immoral behaviour, therefore, deserves no attention, much less the need for scarcely available resources to be diverted for their protection. Proper societal mechanisms of redress could reduce the dangers of sex work and in turn protect children of sex workers. There is also a need to recognize that sex work is not the only profession that has high levels of occupational hazards. The focus has been to address health-related risks, which have mostly been directed toward concern for sexual health among sex workers, especially in terms of using contraception to avoid HIV/AIDS. Therefore, advocates and activists who help sex workers are often left with the hard choice of determining if sex worker moms are able to surmount the hazards they face sufficiently well to care for their children.

In some research, street sex workers have sometimes been found to be more vulnerable to sexually transmitted diseases, as often they are coerced by their clients into having unprotected sex in exchange for some extra money (Kurtz et al.). Sex workers can face threats of physical and sexual violence when working, as multiple studies have reported physical assault, rape, abduction, and intimidation. Some sex workers, who have their own communities and have built some form of representation like an association, find it easier to navigate and refuse clients who have had a history of mistreating sex workers by having defined boundaries. Alternately, street sex workers who are more fluid and invisible as a population are more vulnerable to such offences. Emotional risk has been recognized in recent studies as a risk outcome for sex workers. There are no causal links between emotional distress and sex work, but there is definitely some evidence of psychological distress related to their profession (Sanders, "It's Just Acting"). Emotional and psychological distress is perhaps more often created in an environment of negligible social support, few family ties, and a constant struggle with the social perception of sex workers' profession. Also, in some cases of street sex work, women enter the profession as victims of child abuse or sex trafficking or have a history of substance abuse. It is difficult to ascertain through research if sex workers with such pre-existing, distressing situations continue to a further downward spiral of psychological and emotional distress. Some studies also have shown that motherhood could help inculcate resilience that might help sex workers function well in—and even improve—their situations, as they view their mothering responsibilities to be their primary objective.

Policy makers have an important task at hand: To shift the discourse from victimization of sex workers to recognizing them as productive citizens for an economy as well as recognizing sex workers who are mothers who often require the same basic service provisions as others in society (Dodsworth). Dalla's study ("I Fell Off") calls for a larger role of social institutions to provide for legal employment and skill-based education to sex worker moms. Child Protective Service workers sometimes can sympathize with a mother's situation but often feel a mother's profession puts her children at high risk, hence the request to remove children. A better intervention approach could be to observe a child's development and ensure that the child does not face basic resource scarcities.

Overall, sex workers report huge discrimination in both health and social service needs. Some basic social service needs relate to proper housing, employment, medical care, drug treatment, and mental health care requisites (Kurtz et al.). Sex workers report a huge barrier in terms of seeking help for health services because the structure of care systems, provider resistance, and priority of acute care over prevention care all affect access to basic health care provisions required by sex workers (Kurtz et al.). There is definitely a requisite to offer better public assistance and welfare support to sex worker moms, as their children are disproportionately affected by discriminations in institutional support, and thus the approach should be centered on children's well-being in society.

Mothering for sex workers runs contrary to the known societal narrative of the process of nurturing as a mother. Sex worker movements in parts of the developing world are helping to change the narrative, as most of them advocate for their work to be recognized as form of labour (Chowdhury). In countries like Bangladesh and India, sex workers have formed unions that are advocating for more social service provisions and more inclusive labour recognition laws for sex workers. The idea of intensive mothering is not consistent with values and beliefs of all mothers across cultures, and the measurement of a good mother as one who invests quality time, energy, and financial resources excludes mothers who are not privileged to have access to such resources (Peled and Rotbery). Research studies designed for interventions among sex workers clearly indicate that a community-mobilization approach as opposed to a sex worker-identity approach better facilitates the goal of bringing critical self-reflection and collective action to their lives, thus aiding their process for their social inclusion (Murray et al.). The legalization of sex work in some countries has definitely opened a dialogue on understanding the labour rights of sex workers as a community, but we urgently require a lot more attention in this area. Sex workers have been considered a population on the margins of urban spaces in society. However, social exclusion of sex workers has not helped us in overcoming our moral dilemma on the issue but has further complicated social systems by often making the population invisible from society's collective responsibility to assure well-being of one and all.

An interdisciplinary approach would be best suited to helping state officials better address the situations of sex worker mothers. Not only law enforcement and Child Protective Services officials but workers in several other agencies and institutions do work that affects sex worker mothers either directly or indirectly. Academicians would also have to make an effort to better research and understand sex worker mothers, as they face unique challenges. The state would need other social service agents, such as social workers, to reach out to these mothers without them fearing prosecution or the loss of their children. Addressing the discrimination against sex workers regarding housing, employment, and medical care would require stricter enforcement of existing discrimination laws. The current social and historical context has provided us an opportune moment to start opening the conversation for legalization of sex work in countries where sex work as a profession or prostitution in general is deemed illegal. In the coming decades, most mothers will have a career and a parental role as parallel life components that they will have to navigate in their personal work-life balance. In a life course, most human beings play multiple roles simultaneously and, therefore, enjoy various identities. The romanticism of the "ideal mother" phenomenon will have to fuse with what is realistically achievable by working mothers. Hence, constructing a set of virtues for being a "good mother" and offering a checklist for being a "good worker" are both fictitious and inconsequential to the larger agenda of balancing parental roles while working. Our resources and means should be directed to assisting the mother in her process of being both a parent and a worker simultaneously, and not on prioritizing one role over the other.

WORKS CITED

Basu, Ambar, and Mohan J. Dutta. "'We Are Mothers First': Localocentric Articulation of Sex Worker Identity as a Key in

HIV/AIDS Communication." *Women & Health* 51.2 (2011): 106-123. Print.

Bletzer, Keith V. "Sex Workers in Agricultural Areas: Their Drugs, Their Children." *Culture, Health & Sexuality* 7.6 (2005): 543-555. Web. 8 Sept. 2014.

Bucardo, Jesus, et al. "A Qualitative Exploration of Female Sex work in Tijuana, Mexico." *Archives of Sexual Behavior* 33.4 (2004): 343-351. Print.

Budwig, Michelle J. and Paula England. "The Wage Penalty for Motherhood." *American Sociological Review* (2001): 204-225. Print.

Chowdhury, Reshmi. "'Outsiders' and Identity Reconstruction in the Sex Workers' Movement In Bangladesh." *Sociological Spectrum* 26.3 (2006): 335-357. Print.

Chu, Sandra Ka, HIV Canadian, and AIDS Legal Network. "Brief to the House of Commons Standing Committee on Justice and Human Rights regarding its study of Bill C-36, the Protection of Communities and Exploited Persons Act." (2014). Print.

Cox, Keith S., Antonio Monte Casablanca, and Dan P. McAdams. "'There is Nothing Good About this Work:' Identity and Unhappiness among Nicaraguan Female Sex Workers." *Journal of Happiness Studies* 14.5 (2013): 1459-1478. Print.

Cwikel, J., et al. "Trafficked Female Sex Workers Awaiting Deportation: Comparison with Brothel Workers." *Archives of Women's Mental Health* 7.4 (2004): 243-249. Print.

Cwikel, J., et al. "'I Fell Off [the Mothering] Track': Barriers to 'Effective Mothering' Among Prostituted Women." *Family Relations* 53.2 (2004): 190-200. Print.

Dalla, Rochelle L. "When the Bough Breaks...: Examining Intergenerational Parent-Child Relational Patterns Among Street-Level Sex Workers and Their Parents and Children." *Applied Developmental Science* 7.4 (2003): 216-228. Print.

Dodsworth, Jane. "Sex Worker and Mother: Managing Dual and Threatened Identities." *Child & Family Social Work* 19.1 (2014): 99-108. Print.

Johnston, Deirdre D., and Debra H. Swanson. "Constructing the 'Good Mother': The Experience of Mothering Ideologies by Work Status." *Sex Roles* 54.7-8 (2006): 509-519. Print.

Kurtz, Steven P., et al. "Barriers to Health and Social Services for Street-based Sex Workers." *Journal of Health Care for the Poor and Underserved* 16.2 (2005): 345-361. Print.

Lips, Hilary, and Katie Lawson. "Work Values, Gender, and Expectations about Work Commitment and Pay: Laying the Groundwork for the 'Motherhood Penalty'?" *Sex Roles* 61.9/10 (2009): 667-676. Web. 14 Sept. 2014.

Murray, Laura R., et al. "'She's a Professional Like Anyone Wlse': Social Identity among Brazilian Sex Workers." *Culture, Health & Sexuality* 12.3 (2010): 293-306. Print.

Peled, Einat, and Tal Levin-Rotberg. "The Perceptions of Child Protection Officers toward Mothering in Prostitution." *Social Service Review* 87.1 (2013): 40-69. Print.

Peled, Einat, and Ayelet Parker. "The Mothering Experiences of Sex-Trafficked Women: Between Here and There." *American Journal of Orthopsychiatry* 83.4(2013): 576-587. Print.

Ridgeway, Cecilia L. and Shelley J. Correll. "Motherhood as a Status Characteristic." *Journal of Social Issues* 60.4 (2004): 683-700. Print.

Rivers-Moore, Megan. "But the Kids Are Okay: Motherhood, Consumption and Sex Work in Neo-Liberal Latin America." *The British Journal of Sociology* 61.4 (2010): 716-736. Print.

Sabat, D. M., T. Rahman, and S. Ahmad, eds. *Sex Workers and Their Children in Bangladesh: Addressing Risks and Vulnerabilities.* Dhaka: Center for Sustainable Development, University of Liberal Arts, Bangladesh, 2012. Print.

Sanders, Teela. "A Continuum of Risk? The Management of Health, Physical and Emotional Risks by Female Sex Workers." *Sociology of Health & Illness* 26.5 (2004): 557-574. Print.

Sanders, Teela. "'It's Just Acting': Sex Workers' Strategies for Capitalizing on Sexuality." *Gender, Work & Organization* 12.4 (2005): 319-342. Print.

Sloss, Christine M. and Gary W. Harper. "When Street Sex Workers Are Mothers." *Archives of Sexual Behavior* 33.4 (2004): 329-341. Print.

Surratt, Hilary L., et al. "The Connections of Mental Health Problems, Violent Life Experiences, and the Social Milieu of the 'Stroll' With the HIV Risk Behaviors of Female Street Sex

Workers." *Journal of Psychology & Human Sexuality* 17.1/2 (2005): 23-44. Web. 24 Sept. 2014.

Weitzer, Ronald. *Legalizing Prostitution: From Illicit Vice to Lawful Business*. New York: New York University Press, 2011. Web. 6 April 2015.